Conversations with Clarence Major

Literary Conversations Series

Peggy Whitman Prenshaw
General Editor

Photo credit: Lynda Koolish

Conversations
with Clarence Major

Edited by Nancy Bunge

University Press of Mississippi
Jackson

www.upress.state.ms.us

Copyright © 2002 by University Press of Mississippi
Manufactured in the United States of America

10   09   08   07   06   05   04   03   02   4   3   2   1
∞
Library of Congress Cataloging-in-Publication Data

Major, Clarence.
    Conversations with Clarence Major / edited [by] Nancy Bunge.
        p.   cm. — (Literary conversations series)
    Includes index.
    ISBN 1-57806-457-0 (alk. paper) — ISBN 1-57806-458-9 (paper : alk. paper)
    1. Major, Clarence—Interviews.   2. Authors, American—20th century—Interviews.
    3. Painters—United States—Interviews.   4. African American painters—Interviews.
    5. African American authors—Interviews.   6. African Americans in literature.   I. Bunge,
    Nancy L.   II. Title.   III. Series.

    PS3563.A39 Z464   2002
    818'.5409—dc21   2002022620

British Library Cataloging-in-Publication Data available

Books by Clarence Major

All-Night Visitors. New York: Olympia, 1969; New York: Olympia, 1970.
Unexpurgated edition, Boston: Northeastern University Press, 1998.

The New Black Poetry. Editor and author of introduction. New York: International, 1969; New
York: International, 1969.

Dictionary of Afro-American Slang. Editor and author of introduction. New York: International,
1970. Reprinted as *Black Slang: Dictionary of Afro-American Talk.* London: Routledge and
Kegan Paul, 1971.

Swallow the Lake. Middleton, Conn.: Wesleyan, 1970.

Private Line. Chapbook. London: Paul Breman, 1971.

Symptoms and Madness. New York: Corinth, 1971.

The Cotton Club. Chapbook. Detroit: Broadside, 1972.

NO. New York: Emerson Hall, 1973.

The Dark and Feeling: Black American Writers and Their Work. New York: Third Press, 1974.

The Syncopated Cakewalk. New York: Barlenmir House, 1974.

Reflex and Bone Structure. New York: Fiction Collective, 1975.

Emergency Exit. New York: Fiction Collective, 1979.

Inside Diameter: The France Poems. London: Permanent Press, 1985.

My Amputations. New York: Fiction Collective, 1986.

Such Was the Season. San Francisco: Mercury House, 1987.

Painted Turtle: Woman with Guitar. Los Angeles: Sun and Moon Press, 1988.

Surfaces and Masks: A Poem. Minneapolis: Coffee House Press, 1988.

Some Observations of a Stranger at Zuni in the Latter Part of the Century. New American
Poetry Series 2. Los Angeles: Sun and Moon Press, 1989.

Fun and Games: Short Fictions. Duluth: Holy Cow!, 1990.

Parking Lots. Mount Horeb, Wis.: Perishable, 1992.

Calling the Wind: Twentieth Century African-American Short Stories. Editor and author of
introduction. New York: HarperCollins, 1993; New York: HarperPerennial, 1993.

Juba to Jive: A Dictionary of African-American Slang. Editor and author of introduction. New
York: Viking, 1994.

Dirty Bird Blues. San Francisco: Mercury House, 1996; New York: Berkley Putnam, 1997.

The Garden Thrives: Twentieth Century African-American Poetry. Editor and author of
introduction. New York: HarperCollins, 1996.

Configurations: New and Selected Poems, 1958–1998. Port Townsend, Wash.: Copper Canyon,
1998.

Necessary Distance: Essays and Criticism. Minneapolis: Coffee House Press, 2001.

Contents

Introduction   ix

Chronology   xxi

Work with the Universe: An Interview with Clarence Major and
    Victor Hernandez Cruz   *Walt Shepperd*   3

Clarence Major   *John O'Brien*   10

Self-Interview: On Craft   *Clarence Major*   22

Reality, Fiction, and Criticism: An Interview/Essay
    Doug Bolling and Clarence Major   28

Clarence Major   *Nancy Bunge*   35

CU Professor Savors Literary Award   *Margaret Carlin*   48

Transition Is Tugging at a Local Avant-Garde Author   *Alan Katz*   51

Major's Passion for Life Transcends Life's Hazards   *Anonymous*   55

Clarence Major: Finding the Universal through the Specific
    Paul Kafka   58

Clarence Major   *Alice Scharper*   63

Beneath a Precipice: An Interview with Clarence Major
    Larry McCaffery and Jerzy Kutnik   70

Clarence Major   *Alexander Neubauer*   93

Define Guidance   *Fahizah Alim*   105

"What You Know Gets Expanded"   *Nancy Bunge*   109

An Interview with Clarence Major   *Rebecca Morrison*   123

An Interview with Clarence Major   *Charles H. Rowell*   128

Clarence Major on Poetry, Meaning, and Inspiration
    Barbara DeMarco Barrett   142

An Interview with Clarence Major
  Leigh Morgan and Wendy Sheanin   152

Imagining a Life   *Margaret Eldred*   158

The Vision of a Single Person: Clarence Major and His Art
  Mary Zeppa   172

Major's League   *Greg Tate*   184

Index   189

Introduction

Clarence Major carefully scheduled our interview for the Saturday after he would have finished grading final papers so he would not feel rushed. Then several of his students turned their papers in late, and I arrived early at the Davis train station. Although other people had transformed Clarence Major's Saturday from relaxed to hectic, one could not discern that from his easygoing demeanor. After greeting me, he announced, "Open trunk," pressed the remote for the car, and laughed when the back actually popped up. As we rode down Davis's quaint main street, he said, "As you can see, I've left the real world" and laughed again.

Major's love of books became obvious when we pulled into the garage attached to his house and found ourselves surrounded by boxes of them. Once inside, Pamela Major, who also teaches at the University of California at Davis, greeted us. While the interview took place in the living room, a repairman wandered in, climbed up a ladder, and fixed the ceiling, but Major's comments easily drowned out all distractions. When we'd finished, he walked me around their beautifully open house, showing me his paintings and a sculpture from a workshop he helped teach for children from troubled homes.

He drove past the motel where I'd made a reservation, taking me to one he suspected I'd prefer. After waiting to make sure I got a room, he started to carry my bag toward the door. A bellhop appeared and said, "Oh, you want to carry her suitcase." As he turned away, Major called out, "No, no, I don't." Then we shook hands, and he went off to finish grading. He undoubtedly treated his students' papers as patiently, thoughtfully, respectfully, and honestly as he did me.

Since Clarence Major has spent his life challenging stereotypes, it seems appropriate that he has produced over twenty-five books in multiple genres as well as hundreds of paintings while ambling through life with a welcoming and serene persona. It is no wonder that in her interview with him his former student Rebecca Morrison comments, "Someone told me you used to be a radical." Despite his amiability, Clarence Major nevertheless enjoys undermining spurious categories and judgments.

The "truism" Clarence Major has attacked most directly and persistently comes attached to the notion of the "black aesthetic": the idea that African Americans produce art in a particular way. Major repeatedly says that he has trouble understanding how race can dictate aesthetic principles. In the first interview included here, Major states his view starkly: "I don't see any objective way of dealing with the work an artist does, solely along racial lines." From the start of his career, he has also emphasized the positive corollary of this position: the most powerful art touches a shared humanity that runs deeper than cultural differences. He puts it this way in his 1978 exchange with Doug Bolling: "Great literature by definition transcends the social contexts in which it is produced."

Just as consistently, Major maintains that African Americans have produced a large body of art that has not received the appreciation it deserves. In interview after interview, he praises African American artists and writers. When talking to John O'Brien in 1973, he mentions Cecil Brown, Al Young, William Demby, Ron Fair, and Charles Wright. In a 2001 interview with Greg Tate, he mentions more than twenty writers, including Charles Chesnutt, Jean Toomer, James Baldwin, Thulani Davis, Danzy Senna, Colson Whitehead, Omar Tyree, and E. Lynn Harris. And in the interviews taking place between 1973 and 2001, he acknowledges the excellence and influence of many, many more African American artists and writers. Major has put together six books that document and celebrate the richness of African American culture: two dictionaries of slang, two anthologies of poetry, one anthology of short stories, and his early collection, *The Dark and Feeling: Black American Writers and Their Work.* So, Major has no difficulty acknowledging the significance of African American culture and its influence on his own work; but to embrace the notion that all African Americans will make art in one way denies them their individuality, their artistic freedom, and their participation in the human community. Major has steadfastly refused to endorse a point of view that places artists in an aesthetic ghetto no matter how popular or powerful this position becomes in the publishing world and in the university. While the labels swirl around him, Clarence Major never forgets that great art affirms people's shared humanity. In 1973, he writes in his self-interview that "it has always been the novel or poem that begins from and spreads all across the entire human experience that ends up liberating minds." In 2000, he explains to Mary Zeppa that writing "gives us a greater intellectual, artistic, and aesthetic sense of who we are as the human race." He also dismisses arguments that men, say, cannot understand or appreciate the perspective of women or that people from different cultures cannot understand and enjoy each other's points of view, arguing that a man can write well from the point of view of a woman and vice versa and a writer can render characters from another cultural group so convincingly that one cannot tell "an outsider" produced the work. Clarence Major supports this stance not only with examples, but also with action, producing *Such Was the Season,* a novel narrated by the very present voice of an older woman. He followed it with *Painted Turtle: Woman with Guitar,* a work featuring Zuni characters. Critics agreed that Major succeeded: *Such Was the Season* was a Literary Guild Selection in 1987 and was listed in the *New York Times Book Review*'s summer reading guide; the *New York Times Book Review* named *Painted Turtle* a notable book of the year.

Major knows he must resist politically and economically convenient viewpoints because one creates powerful art by telling the truth. The best work comes out of an honest connection to oneself: "Something that's coming out of a true place in yourself, then you have a fairly good chance to get something going and to feel excitement about writing it." But he confesses to Alexander Neubauer that this requires the artist to function with a level of integrity hard to sustain: "This . . . is the most difficult thing for a writer to achieve—to stay in touch with the truth of who you are. Because that truth is changing. . . . It's a big, big task to ask any human being to have that kind of sensitivity every day in the week, to have that kind of command of him or herself." Despite its problems, truth telling has brought Major enormous joy. When explaining why he finds making art so satisfying, Major often talks about learning, as in this comment to Margaret Eldred: "Despite the pleasure in the process, every time I attempt to write something, it's a struggle—a good struggle, though. . . . It feels so painful—yet fresh, like being just on the verge of some great breakthrough. I don't know why it's that way, but it keeps all kinds of possibilities alive."

From the beginning of his career, Major has understood that in order to preserve the integrity of his work, he has to rely on his own instincts to decide what to do next or whether to abandon or reframe what he has in motion. In the first talk included here, Major announces, "The only thing I trust now is my own intuition." The interviews reveal that he persists in trusting his inclinations, no matter how circuitous the route they recommend. As he tells Alice Scharper, he began writing *Painted Turtle: Woman with Guitar* from the point of view of its central character, a female Zuni musician; when the writing didn't go well, he made her boyfriend the narrator and the book proceeded smoothly. He can give Scharper little explanation for why this adjustment worked other than to allude vaguely to unknown emotional forces: "Maybe because I felt more comfortable with a male narrator at that time, I don't know." Major repeatedly underlines that in order to answer questions about his processes, he must make the unconscious conscious and so he cannot wholly trust his answers. Although he cannot always explain the logic of his choices, he persistently musters the self-trust crucial to artistic success.

The conversations show that he had self-confidence long before editors and critics praised his work. He tells Margaret Eldred that he felt angry when young because circumstances closed him in, but he maintained an optimistic faith that he would defeat them. In order to live his own life fully, Clarence Major had to achieve the improbable goal of becoming a painter and a writer, for he loved making melodies with words and painting pictures of the world around him from a very young age. He recalls that when he was four, his mother wrote him a poem that he had to recite before his church; that experience showed him that human beings could make literature and gave him a sense of language's musical potential. Major tells Mary Zeppa that before he attended grade school, he painted a picture of an apple that his mother proudly showed around, and with her encouragement he continued to paint. He also talks repeatedly of the Van Gogh exhibit at the Art Institute of Chicago moving him as a child. His stepfather reinforced the experience by buying Clarence Major an expensive catalogue for it. In retrospect, Major notes that Van Gogh also loved both pictures and words.

When he was young, painting came more easily to him than writing. Although he continued to paint in high school, studying at the art museum where he saw the Van Gogh Exhibit, he also bought a collection of poetry by the French Symbolists that became his "bible." As a soldier, he checked out books by authors like Melville, Hawthorne, and Conrad from the base library and fell in love with yet another kind of writing. Back in civilian life, he felt the need for feedback on his work, so he started a journal, *The Coercion Review,* and built his own literary community. And he read widely. In addition to the African American writers Major discusses, he acknowledges his debts to authors as diverse as Gertrude Stein, Peter Handke, Henry Miller, Genet, Russell Banks, Pinget, Mark Twain, Lawrence Sterne, Flannery O'Connor, and D. H. Lawrence. A variety of painters, too, receive acknowledgment as Major talks: Cézanne, all the other French Impressionists, Michelangelo, Rubens, Modigliani, Millet, and most persistently, Van Gogh.

The interviews collected here review the career that Clarence Major built on his fascination with words and pictures. The talks took place between

1968, the year before his first book, *All-Night Visitors,* appeared, and 2001; so they cover the span of his public life as an artist. Not surprisingly, since Major says he most values the learning that takes place as he creates, as he changes, so does his work and his understanding of it. In 1973, when he discusses his first two novels, *All-Night Visitors* and *NO,* with John O'Brien, Major sees both as attempts to come to terms with emotional realities important to him at the time. In *All-Night Visitors* he deals with the body by focusing on sex and death, while *NO* expresses "just how artificial and shifting the whole business of self becomes." By the time he answers Doug Bolling's questions in 1978, he now sees *NO* and *All-Night Visitors* as examples of "formal narration" compared to the two novels that followed them: *Reflex and Bone Structure* and *Emergency Exit.* These new books emphasize the profoundly subjective nature of that commonly called "reality" with nontraditional narrative structures that constantly remind the reader of the novels' artifice. Major tells Alan Katz that he didn't really commit himself to writing his next novel, *My Amputations,* until "walking up a mountain trail in Nice, he saw the book in his mind's eye in long Faulknerian blocks of prose," hardly a traditional narrative sequence. All these early novels deal with issues of identity and their aesthetics convey a sense of fragmentation.

Major confesses to Alan Katz in 1986 that he suspects his fiction will soon change, becoming "less ambiguous": "The complexity of my early poetry and fiction is a result of my own struggle mentally—my own inability to articulate a whole network of feelings." Major has come to some clarity about himself and predicts his new sense of personal coherence will manifest itself in his writing. Major implies that the change has already taken place when he describes *Painted Turtle: Woman with Guitar,* a linear novel, as "a personal breakthrough." A year later, Major tells Alice Scharper that by incorporating poetry into *Painted Turtle,* he has overcome the separation between poetry and fiction, a goal that tantalized him for much of his career: "It resolves any possible dormant conflict, for me, between prose and poetry. I can constantly work at both in a way that is unified." Major argues that through the music of its language, his novel *Such Was the Season* also overwhelms the distinction between prose and poetry. In *Dirty Bird Blues,* the music that constantly runs through Manfred Banks's head pervades the novel. Major reports to Leigh Morgan and Wendy Sheanin that he listened to the blues while writing the book.

During the past few years, interviewers' questions about the paintings Major has produced since childhood and their relationship to his writing have exposed yet another way that Major has brought together apparently distinct activities. He frequently describes himself as a "visual thinker" and talks about how he sees his work on the page. When he wrote *Reflex and Bone Structure,* he wanted every paragraph surrounded by substantial space; in *My Amputations,* he produced "verbal panels;" and in *Such Was the Season,* "I deliberately wrote with straight, traditional chapters because I didn't want the physical appearance of the page to attract attention to itself. I wanted the story to take over in the reader's mind." He tells Margaret Eldred that his painting and his writing complete each other: he paints things he can't write about and vice versa: "I can't paint a certain network of emotions as well as I can present that same network of emotions through the interactions of characters generated through prose and sometimes through poetry." Occasionally, writing moves him to paint. When working on *Dirty Bird Blues* he decided to attempt a painting that conveys a sense of blues; the result adorns the novel's dust jacket.

The interviews collectively reveal how Clarence Major's attention shifts outside himself as the disparate parts of his identity come together. His first writings focus on self-discovery, and he has never ceased making his own intuitions primary to both his writing and his painting. But he explains that, as his sense of himself became more secure and centered, not only did his novels become less fragmented; he became increasingly open to others' experiences. Major identifies his work on a book about Dorothy Dandridge, which he eventually abandoned, as the moment when he began to move outside the limits of his ego. He salvaged the best sections of the Dandridge book by using them in *Painted Turtle: Woman with Guitar.* Perhaps the crucial role that book played in his development explains why he, uncharacteristically, sometimes repeats himself when discussing the novel. He explains that the Zuni first interested him because a black man named Esteban played an important role in their culture, but as the novel progressed, this man became irrelevant while a Zuni woman assumed central stage. In order to portray her accurately, Major spent years studying Zuni culture, a "digression" he thoroughly enjoyed. And he thinks he has kept moving outside himself: "I was trying to get away from that self-centered approach, trying to move away from using myself as a model. And it took a long time to get it right. I think it worked with Annie Eliza, it worked with Painted Turtle, and I hope it's working with this blues novel."

His poetry also moves outward. His book-length poem about Venice, *Surfaces and Masks,* incorporates much historical information. He concludes

Configurations with "The Slave Trade: View from the Middle Passage," a poem written in the voice of an African who perished on a ship after being stolen from his home. The work includes so many rich references that the critic Linda Ferguson Selzer convincingly concludes, after a long analysis, that the poem presents Major's "own refiguration of literary and artistic history that ultimately locates the social function of art in the continuing battle of black artists to negotiate for themselves evolving and complex systems of cultural representation and production."

A number of Major's other recent books, like *Juba to Jive,* his dictionary of African American slang and his anthologies of African American poetry and short fiction, all seem disinterested attempts to draw attention to the liveliness of African American language and the excellence of African American artists. He describes completing the dictionary as "a killer," but when asked if putting together anthologies diverted him from his poetry and fiction writing, Major responds: "It was a pleasure because you have to take a break from your own writing and from yourself. It was energizing and very refreshing to read a lot of good work."

The latest interviews also reveal how engaging more of the world has enriched Major's perspective. When Charles Rowell asks him to discuss why he found painting easier than writing while young, Major first protests that he can say little on this topic: "Who knows why anyone is drawn to a particular thing?" But Rowell persists and Clarence Major takes off, drawing on the vast body of information and insight he has collected over the years to make a multitude of connections. He talks about writing being linear and painting spatial, about the way time and space need each other, about the Chinese and Japanese languages presenting images, about the history of painting, about the Egyptians struggling to get beyond representation, about the movement during the Renaissance towards representation, about Abstract Expressionism, and then he finally comes to rest in this statement: "I think since the mid 1950s, 1960s . . . we've had a much more democratic arena for both writing and painting, because you've got people doing everything you can imagine and using every conceivable approach you can imagine and much of it is good or at least interesting." He not only explores the links between a wide range of subjects and experiences, he starts from and returns to the impact of these ideas on people's lives, now.

Reading through all these conversations, one notes that as Major ages, his answers mellow. Flashes of anger surface in the first interview. He talks about an editor reluctant to publish some good poems because they did not persistently reveal the poet's African American background: "This is an editor, a person who can make decisions, sitting right there and saying that kind of shit!" In 1990, he tells Alice Scharper, "I've agonized over tags, and I think there's no way around them, so I don't fight them anymore." As a result, those asking him about the black aesthetic in later interviews will get not sharp replies but nuanced, complicated ones. The more recent the interview, the more fully Major responds. When Paul Kafka asks Major in 1989 whether "being a recognizably black writer" is a choice, Major responds: "A lot of what I write is a given, a cultural frame of reference. . . . What I try to do is make sure my work is not purely sociological, to make sure that I'm in touch with larger forces in life." When Jerzy Kutnik asks about the black aesthetic in 1992, Major puts it in the context of American history: "There has been a sequence or series of scenarios that can be defined as 'black aesthetic' corresponding roughly to historical periods." When talking to Charles Rowell in 1997, he internationalizes his answer, comparing the notion of a black aesthetic to Soviet art, to religious art during the Italian Renaissance, and specifically to Michelangelo.

Major's cultivation of change helps explain why, like all interview collections, this one has some repetition in it, but much of it comes from the interviewers. Clarence Major responds to an inquiry he has answered before as though hearing it for the first time, not out of politeness, but because its context has shifted and so, probably, has he. An honest reply will probably differ from that he offered last year, or even yesterday. By approaching his conversations this way, Major provides himself with the opportunity to learn from them. As he tells Barbara DeMarco Barrett, "Most of us want what we already know confirmed rather than wanting to open our minds and hearts and emotions—open ourselves to new experience or to new information." Major admits that he sometimes submits to this impulse himself, but "in my best moments, in anybody's best moments, we manage to put that tendency aside and be more open to fresh experience and new information." When someone asks him a question he has answered before, Clarence Major exploits the chance to reconsider the issues presented to him.

So, for instance, when one interviewer after another asks him to discuss the relationship between poetry and prose, he says different things. By the time Mary Zeppa poses this question to him in 2000, he could reply with a polished version of an answer he has used before. Instead, he protests that Mary Zeppa forces him to do something just too difficult: *"It's so hard."* He speaks the truth, for this question and others about his processes fascinate his questioners because answering them means explaining a largely unconscious and all but totally mysterious process. After this brief protest, Major tackles the difficult question of how the two principal genres he writes in differ from each other, once again. When he finishes, Mary Zeppa comments, appropriately, "I think you did very well articulating that," and they share a laugh.

And, indeed, his answers become fuller as he ages. For instance, he tells Zeppa, "In poetry, we try to say what cannot be said . . . something so innate we know it but we can't really say what it means." On the other hand, "fiction . . . represents, through the device of historical consensus, the truth of collective human experience." Twenty-seven years earlier, when John O'Brien asks him to distinguish between poetry and fiction, Major replies: "I am working very deliberately to break down what I think are the false distinctions between poetry and fiction." John O'Brien persists, "Is there an essential difference, though, that still exists?" And Major gives the correct answer for the moment: "No, I don't see the difference. But I am really in a state of transition with all of this. It is rather difficult for me to abstract theories about what this means and where I'm going with it." When he was younger, perhaps the possibility of confusing his own version of reality by indulging in theoretical explorations contrary to his point of view frightened him. But by the time Mary Zeppa speaks with him, Clarence Major not only believes one can fuse poetry and prose, he thinks he's done it! He can offer her a brandnew examination of the differences between poetry and prose because as his own identity has solidified, he relishes entertaining other perspectives. In 1999, he tells Margaret Eldred: "I believe it's healthy to look at a situation from a point of view that's not your own. I think that's really one of the most valuable imaginative activities we command. Usually it serves us well in dealing with other people."

Clarence Major brings this same respect for others' perspectives to his interactions with students, encouraging them to follow their own paths and discover their own voices. Exploring, understanding, and articulating his own perspective has brought him much joy, and he would like his students to experience it. As he puts it, "Most students in college today aren't going to have an opportunity to be in touch with who they are and where they come from in such an intense way ever again as they will in a workshop. They will go into different kinds of things: business, engineering, the sciences; but hopefully, they will remember how important it was to create a wedding of that voice that was theirs and that history that was theirs. . . . That's an entirely unique experience that there is no substitute for." One of Major's former students, Greg Tate, clearly came to share his enthusiasm for writing since he has made it his career. When he reestablishes contact with his former teacher, Tate recognizes and remembers the attentive gentleness that Major brings to his interactions with others: "He sounded as warm and encouraging as he had a quarter century ago when I attended his creative writing class at Howard University." Since Major helps his students become more fully themselves, as he has done, it is not surprising that he finds relief from the loneliness of the artistic life in the classroom.

Although Major always treats his questioners well, in the later interviews, his kindness becomes overt. In a talk with another former student, Rebecca Morrison, when she comments, "It seems like you work poetry into your fiction," he responds, "Well, you do that too." When a comment reveals that she knows his poetry, he acknowledges her effort: "You've been reading my work. I'm really flattered." When Mary Zeppa mentions that what one considers shortcomings can become transformed into strengths, he congratulates her: "Right, Right! *Exactly!* You said it very well. That's it." Major continues to celebrate her insight for a time, and ends the interview with an astonishingly modest comment for someone who has achieved what he has: "We have a history, a cultural history, that we are working out of and sometimes against. At best, what we do is add a little bit *to* that history before we go on." No wonder Barbara DeMarco Barrett, who interviews writers every week, concludes her conversation with Major by commenting, "For all your success, you're one of the most humble writers I know and that's a valuable commodity in this world of out-of-control egos."

Major's modesty has nurtured his mind, heart, and career. That he has all the answers is perhaps the only thing he has never imagined. Nor would he want them, for he understands well that joy comes from living, always, on a boundary and striving to push beyond it. When Clarence Major repeatedly claims in these interviews that truly great literature validates and touches our shared humanity, he articulates a democratic philosophy that shapes his encounters with other people as well as those with the easel and the page.

In accordance with the policy of the University Press of Mississippi for its interview series, the interviews collected here are reprinted in essentially the same form that they first appeared. Although typographical errors and errors of fact have been silently corrected, the interviews have not been edited in any substantial way.

I benefited hugely from Clarence Major's generosity when putting together this book, and I am grateful for his persistent, crucial, and kind support. I also owe much to the interviewers for their good will, their work, and their willingness to share it. The editors from the University Press of Mississippi have also been helpful and cheerful. I thank Seetha Srinivasan for her enduring interest in and useful suggestions for this volume; Anne Stascavage for getting me started and Walter Biggins for his prompt and kind assistance, especially as the deadline approached.

Chronology

1936	Born on December 31 in Atlanta, Georgia, to Clarence and Inez (Huff) Major.
1943	Mother and father separate; mother moves to Chicago.
1946	Moves to Chicago from Winder, Georgia.
1948	Begins to take art lessons with Gus Nall in Chicago.
1951–53	Attends Art Institute of Chicago on James Nelson Raymond fellowship for high school students.
1954	Prints *The Fires That Burn in Heaven.*
1955	Joins Air Force.
1956	Takes correspondence courses from Armed Forces Institute.
1957	Discharged from Air Force; paintings on display at Gayle's Gallery with Archibald Motley's, et al.
1957–58	Steelworker in Omaha, Nebraska, welding and crane operation.
1958	Marries Joyce Sparrow (divorced 1964).
1958–66	Edits *Coercion Review.*
1962	Moves to Omaha, Nebraska.
1963	Father dies in Atlanta.
1965	Publishes *Love Poems of a Black Man.*
1966	Publishes *Human Juices;* moves to New York from Omaha in December.
1967–68	Directs creative writing program at the New Lincoln School, New York City.
1967	Research analyst for Simulmatics Corporation; edits *Writers Workshop Anthology* for the Harlem Education Project at New Lincoln School.

1968   Teaches at Macomb Junior High School; edits *Man Is Like a Child: An Anthology of Creative Writing by Students;* newspaper reporter; visits Mexico for several weeks.

1968–69   Brooklyn College, SEEK program, lecturer.

1969   Publishes *All-Night Visitors* and *The New Black Poetry* (editor); writes television script, *Africa Speaks to New York.*

1970   Publishes *Swallow the Lake* and *Dictionary of Afro-American Slang;* wins National Council on the Arts Award.

1971   Publishes *Private Line* and *Symptoms and Madness;* visits France, Spain, and Italy.

1972   Attends New School for Social Research; publishes *The Cotton Club;* visits Canada.

1972–73   Lecturer at Queens College.

1973   Adjunct lecturer for New York Board of Education ACE Program; publishes *NO;* travels throughout Carribean keeping journal.

1973–75   Lecturer at Sarah Lawrence College.

1973–76   Columnist for *American Poetry Review.*

1974   Publishes *The Syncopated Cakewalk* and *The Dark and Feeling: Black American Writers and Their Work;* one person art show, Sarah Lawrence Library.

1974–76   Visiting lecturer at Howard University.

1975   Joins Fiction Collective; publishes *Reflex and Bone Structure;* attends International Poetry Festival, Struga, Yugoslavia.

1976   Pushcart Prize certificate for "Funeral" from *The Syncopated Cakewalk.*

1976–77   Assistant professor at the University of Washington.

1977   Receives Ph.D. from Union Graduate School; attends Poetry International, Rotterdam, Netherlands.

1977–81   Associate professor at the University of Colorado.

1978   Serves as associate editor of the *American Book Review.*

1979   Publishes *Emergency Exit.*

1980   Marries Pamela Jane Ritter on May 8.

1981–83   Fulbright-Hays Inter-University Exchange Award; visiting professor at the University of Nice.

1981–89   Professor at University of Colorado.

1982–83   Travels throughout Italy, Greece, France, England, and Germany.

1982   Visits Liberia, Ghana, and Ivory Coast; Prix Maurice Edgar Coincreau nomination for French version of *Reflex and Bone Structure.*

1984–85   Spends sabbatical in Venice and Paris; visits Poland and Algeria.

1985   Publishes *Inside Diameter: The France Poems.*

1986   Publishes *My Amputations;* Western States Award for fiction for *My Amputations;* one person art show, First National Bank Gallery, Boulder.

1986–   Fiction editor, *High Plains Literary Review.*

1987   Visiting assistant professor at University of Maryland and State University of New York at Binghamton; publishes *Such Was the Season.*

1988   Publishes *Painted Turtle: Woman with Guitar* and *Surfaces and Masks: A Poem; New York Times* names *Painted Turtle* notable book of the year.

1989–   Professor at the University of California at Davis.

1989   Publishes *Some Observations of a Stranger in the Latter Part of the Century;* Pushcart Prize for "My Mother and Mitch."

1990   Publishes *Fun & Games;* wins *Los Angeles Times* Book Critic Award nomination for *Fun & Games.*

1991–93   Director of Creative Writing Program at the University of California at Davis.

1992   Publishes *Parking Lots;* curator of "Spirit Made Visible," exhibition of paintings by African-American artists at Natsoulas Gallery, Davis, California: Robert Colescott, Raymond Saunders, Joe Overstreet, Mary L. O'Neal, et al.

1993   Publishes *Calling the Wind: Twentieth-Century African-American Short Stories.*

1994   Publishes *Juba to Jive: A Dictionary of African-American Slang.*

1996   Publishes *Dirty Bird Blues* and *The Garden Thrives: Twentieth-Century African-American Poetry.*

1998   Publishes *Configurations: New and Selected Poems, 1958–1998.*

1999   National Book Award finalist for *Configurations.*

2001   Publishes *Necessary Distance: Essays and Criticism;* induction into Literary Hall of Fame, Chicago State University; paintings exhibited at Kresge Art Museum (Michigan) and Porter-Troupe Gallery (San Diego, California).

Conversations with Clarence Major

Work with the Universe: An Interview with Clarence Major and Victor Hernandez Cruz

Walt Shepperd / 1969

From *The Dark and Feeling: Black American Writers and Their Work* (New York: The Third Press, 1974), 115–24. Reprinted with permission of Clarence Major. This interview originally appeared in *Nickel Review* (September 12, 1969).

Victor was upstairs in his smoking jacket, purple; it was summer and we were guests in a pleasant big house on a hill with a view of a lake through small trees. I called Victor down to meet Walt Shepperd, editor of the *Nickel Review*, and another guy whose name I forgot. Victor, a two-day guest, and I, a two-week guest, at Cazenovia College's Summer Institute on Black Literature, were *ready* to talk with somebody outside that circle. It was September, 1969, and my heart was broken but slowly mending.

Shepperd: Clarence, in your anthology, *The New Black Poetry,* are you giving us, by your selection of poets, standards for the definition of a black aesthetic?

Major: What I've had to come to realize is that the question of a black aesthetic is something that really comes down to an individual question. It seems to me that if there is a premise in an artist's work, be he black or white, that it comes out of his work, and therefore out of himself. Or herself. I think that it's also true with *form.* It has to be just that subjective. I don't see any objective way of dealing with the work an artist does, solely along racial lines. Black poets, for instance, are going in many different directions. There are so many forces at work.

Shepperd: If we could expand this question to include your book, Victor, *Snaps,* it seems, is poetry that the cat on the corner, particularly the young, can identify with easily. Do you see the emergence of an aesthetic of the streets, perhaps an aesthetic of the oppressed?

Cruz: The poems in *Snaps* were written in a period when that was more or less what I was coming out of. I used those experiences just like any poet

3

has done in the past. I don't like to say that my work is a part of a new thing that can be identified or pinpointed so that now I can have an umbrella over me or something because here I am in Cazenovia and I should be able to write poems about this. I feel that the writer—a black writer or a Puerto Rican writer—should have just as much right to talk about the universe and how it started as any other writer. I think that some of the people who are into this black writing thing really complicate it to the point where you've got to conform to it and if you don't you're supposed to be doing something unnatural. I think a writer should use his total spectrum and, no matter what the situation, he should be able to come out with his own thing. I'm Puerto Rican, but when I was on the airplane coming over here there was no Puerto Rican, there was just me up there in the air, and I could create out of that. I could create out of anything, and I think it's wrong to say that because you're black or Puerto Rican you can't use the whole universe as your field.

Major: That's something that I really began working on with these people in Cazenovia. They're at this conference to try to learn how to put together a Black Studies course, to go back to their black students and teach Black Lit. And like they're sitting there man, really expecting to learn how the black experience and therefore Black Lit is special and different.

They're expecting to be let into some kind of deep dark secret. Like, "tell us what it is . . . we have to know . . . what is this special thing, this experience of yours that we can't penetrate . . . what is it?" They really are so convinced that these problems are real; all this shit is in their minds. They can quote *Don Quixote* and get through it right away. They never lived in Spain and it would be a very strange place for any of them, and yet they can get through *Don Quixote* on a human level. And I think they could get through a lot of Black Lit if they didn't have these social hangups created by outside forces.

Shepperd: Let's talk about those forces for a minute. Victor mentioned black writers complicating their own scene. But you've both had experience with the big publishing houses; don't they have rubber stamps for the book jackets that say "bitter," "angry," "oppressed"? Don't the publishing companies really push you into that bag anyway, or at least try to?

Cruz: Well a woman in *Negro Digest* mentioned that she couldn't understand why my book was published by Random House. But I don't know, publishing seems better than it used to be. Most people who are in publishing seem eager to get black writers. I would have the same approach to the publishers no matter who they were. Today, especially in poetry, one of the most important things is to get it out there. And anybody into poetry knows how hard it is to get it out there.

Major: Along the same line, about the psychology of publishers. I had lunch with an editor not long ago and she's considering work by a young black poet, one of the poets in my anthology. He had submitted a manuscript of poems and she really dug them. She really thought they were great. But she couldn't possibly consider it or recommend them to her publisher *because* there's nothing there in the work to indicate that the poems were written by a *black* poet. And she says they can't possibly run on each page a photograph of the poet. And the assumption is, they would *have* to . . . if they published it. She said *that.* "We can't possibly run a photo of him on each page." This is an editor, a person who can make decisions, sitting right there and saying that kind of shit!

Cruz: This is the same kind of thing that happens with a black publishing company. They'll put you in a bag too. It will probably be quite some time before poets can stand on their own worth no matter what they're talking about. I think that Clarence's book, *All-Night Visitors,* is a milestone for a different thing in black writing. In the past some of the black writers have dealt with sex, for example, in a much different way.

Major: In other words, it is not a Christian book. That's why a lot of people won't be able to get through it.

Cruz: It's a *book,* man, it stands by itself, and you really couldn't go around trying to relate it to a course.

Major: The people at this conference are having a bitch of a time with it, by the way. It's required reading. But before I got there they were all like in the dorm whispering to each other about it. Probably reading the sexy parts. They were questioning my motives. Some thought the book was a put-on. A number of these people are over 60 years old. Two of them are nuns. Anyway, we finally got into a discussion of *All-Night Visitors.* I ran it down and gave them my impression of it and they were really *relieved!* Some of them said, like, "I'm really glad you told me what you were trying to *say* because it really puzzled me. I just would never leave this book lying around the house where my daughter could find it. And as a teacher I would *never* consider using it in a course!" So then I got into this business about the reason they couldn't get into the book. I told them, it's because of the whole thing of sex being dirty. Because of what St. Paul left to their culture, their western sensibility. And the only person there who came up to me later and said something positive about how I had explained it was a nun. She's not wearing her habit now. She said. "You know, you're right: we are too hungup."

Shepperd: Along the line of talking about leaving the books out for the daughters to see them, especially when these days the daughters have probably read them first. Victor's poetry seems to relate directly to what young people can see on the block. Are we reaching a point where we no longer need to append to a page of poetry that it written by a 14-year-old girl as a rationale for its not meeting certain aesthetic standards? Are we reaching a point where perhaps a 14-year-old girl in the ghetto can capture in her poetry the images that hit us in the gut perhaps even better than did Langston Hughes will all his aesthetic excellence?

Major: I think those standards should really be questioned. I'm doing it myself. I'm really questioning a lot of accepted standards.

Cruz: I think that a lot of what's happening in American Literature is that people kind of know what to expect. And if somebody from Harlem writes a book they are expected to be a manchild in the promised land. People only really like something when they know exactly what's coming. But I write what I really *want* to do. I'm dealing more with Puerto Rican music and Puerto Rican rhythm and I'm using a lot of chants. I'm relying a lot on religion, the spiritualism that has always been in Caribbean culture. And I'm dealing with the African gods and how people use them, the whole thing of being possessed by spirits. What I'm getting into is getting away from something you see in a lot of black poetry. The thing is, it's much more important to get involved in life and what people are experiencing, because that will be able to stand a lot longer time than an attack which may be over after awhile. Poetry should be creating life instead of using it as some kind of vehicle for some already known object.

Major: Ideally a writer might actually set as a goal the day when he can stop writing.

Shepperd: Getting back to what you said about being somewhat uncomfortable running down strictly criticism and interpretation, you mentioned that it was a more meaningful experience to read your work. But doesn't the writer run the risk of being put on the shelf as an entertainer?

Major: One person really got to that at the conference. Most of the participants call me Clarence, but she said, "Mr. Major, I sense in you an uneasiness like we're imposing on you and I don't want to bother you with a whole lot of stupid questions but I know that somehow all of us are missing the point."

And this is what she meant, "I don't want to force you to have to perform, to do something you don't want to do because what's going on in you in terms of yourself as a writer is a very private process." Then just for a moment we were quiet and I think we really communicated.

I read my work and that doesn't bother me, but it's afterwards, when people come up to ask dumb questions. Sometimes I can handle it but I don't like to be nasty. Like when I was at the University of Rhode Island. I read sections from *All-Night Visitors*. Afterward a teacher came up and said, "All those four-letter words! It's unbelievable in a school, classroom situation." But, she said, "After the shock wore off, it really became functional, and I saw what you were doing."

Cruz: The problem I find is that I go to read my poems and they want me to predict the future. Like what's going to happen this summer. And how should I know.

Major: What's happening there is that in this society if you've written a book it makes you an authority on everything.

Shepperd: Isn't this also a very subtle racism? People didn't go to Steinbeck and ask him what was going to happen in the ghetto. Isn't it because the ghetto is supposed to be full of illiterates, minority groups are supposed to be stupid and lazy, and here you both have conformed on the white standard of writing a book and getting it published by a major house. Therefore, you're made the spokesman, just like Richard Wright was made a spokesman, just like Baldwin was made a spokesman, just like Cleaver was made a spokesman.

Cruz: Right. One cat even asked me about Puerto Ricans in labor unions. They try to make you into something they can understand; then they can go home feeling OK. But with me, they went home without understanding me. And I don't understand myself; because I won't play their game.

Shepperd: This gets to a point raised in the conference about the balance in a Black Literature course between art and politics. In a time of social change everyone is pushing, and you as writers must get pushed pretty hard. What kind of relationship do you have to work out between art and politics?

Major: Well, obviously, art is always neglected. Look at a book like *Cane*, neglected all these years. Even now it's being brought back for the wrong reasons, political rather than aesthetic reasons.

Cruz: A good example of this is one time I read my poems and I said something about Puerto Rico's flag. Now the flag and all the symbols of the

Puerto Rican nationalists are very, very important to them. So afterward one of them came up and said, "Hey, what did you have to say that for?" You know, it shows that in a way all these revolutionary nationalist movements are really very conservative. LeRoi Jones said something about this. He said that the *true* revolutionary wants to change the culture.

Shepperd: In terms of changing the culture, Ishmael Reed seems to be telling us in his work, particularly in his use of Eastern and Egyptian symbolism, that we can participate in this kind of revolution if we change our cultural reference points. What he and Jones before him seem to be saying is that we need a new language. How do you come to grips with this in your work?

Major: I think that we're all suffering from cultural shock and there are a lot of things that won't be clear until we get beyond that. The only thing I trust now is my intuition. The American Communist Party has been telling us for generations that all we have to do to get things straight is to eliminate capitalism. But I think we're seeing that it goes way far beyond that . . .

Cruz: This is a racist culture and if you want to eliminate racism you have to eliminate the whole culture. Even in Cuba they're having problems because they're approaching problems from a European bag. Latin America shouldn't even be called Latin. It's really Indo-America.

Shepperd: Since the novel is a western invention, do we need a new form to express what the new culture will be?

Major: I don't know if the present forms of the novel are worth saving. The word "novel" itself is really totally inappropriate.

Cruz: I'm trying to work a thing into my readings with singing and Caribbean instruments, like the marracas, the cowbell, the cobassa. If you've ever heard Eddie Palmieri or Ray Barreto you know they have an *after* thing. After one sings, the others come in with something else. It backs you up. This is what I'm trying to do with some people from New York. This, after all, is what Caribbean music is: poetry. In Puerto Rico and Cuba they have street singers who walk the streets singing the blues or singing about happiness. Which in a lot of ways is like an Eastern thing. And this is what I want to get into because this is the way we can tell people to get up and dance. It's the same kind of thing being done by the Temptations. When you get people *into* the lyrics, not just listening to them. A big Latin dance in New York is something a very intellectual dude from Harvard can't understand because he can't catch the sensibility of it. Ray Barreto has a song called *Live and Mess*

Around. That's what I want to get to in my poetry. It's like a very rhythmic thing. It's like a tradition, like an ongoing thing.

Shepperd: Are these traditions that have been lost in our culture or have they been there all the time, in all sectors of American society?

Cruz: I don't know what the rest of America is doing but these are things that have been very much kept in black and Puerto Rican neighborhoods and in the mountains, too. It's a music, not a listening music; it's a dance music. If you talked to a group of Puerto Rican teenagers, they'd be talking about the dance steps and how to do them. And that's really where it's at. It's not something you can sit around and talk about. It's something you've got to get up and do: the invitation to the dance.

Shepperd: You've both rejected the role of prophets here, saying that you're forced into that role too often, but I'm going to ask you to prophesy just a little. What will we see in the literature of the 70s?

Cruz: I can only think in terms of what I'm going to be doing. I think that the whole presentation of the writer will change. Like the thing about having a book out. I could dig getting more into leaflets. The writer needs to get more into *his* world, what comes out of his head: feelings and emotions. Actually the only thing we should keep is words. Everything else should break down.

Major: I'd like to pick up on what Victor was saying, particularly about not generalizing. Yesterday Addison Gayle, a consultant to this program, asked me if it bothered me that James Baldwin sees the homosexual crisis as something intrinsic to the black experience. I told him that it didn't bother me at all because it wasn't—on a personal level—my problem. I mean to say with this example that somehow we're going to have to look at people on a one-at-a-time basis. We can't oversimplify when we're trying to be sincere, real.

Anyway, the future is another thing. I usually refuse to play the game of predicting the future but I can say this—I'd like to do something *new* with the novel. I'd like to do something new with the novel as form. And getting rid of that name would be the first step.

Clarence Major

John O'Brien / 1973

Clarence Major is the author of two novels, *All-Night Visitors* and *NO,* several books of poetry, and a soon-to-be-published collection of short stories and essays. His most remarkable accomplishments have been in fiction where he demonstrates a preoccupation with experimenting with the form of the novel. *All-Night Visitors* is both a daring innovation in form ("the universe is not *ordered,* therefore I am simply pricking the shape of a particular construct, a form, in it") and an experimental perspective on self-identity. Fragmented, disengaged, and terrified, Eli Bolton tries to reshape the chaos of his experience by affirming his body ("This thing that I am—it is me. *I* am it. I am not a concept in your mind, whoever you are!"). His immersion into sex, however, can lead him in two directions: it can bring him back into the "ancient depths of myself, back down to some lost meaning of the male," or it can lead to more depersonalization and separation. The novel, loose and episodic, catalogues the gestures of violence that occur without warning and threaten even the rudimentary pockets of meaning that Eli Bolton can discover. The novel ends uncertainly, as he makes his first real contact with people by inviting a mother and her dispossessed family into his apartment (*"Her* dispossession was my responsibility.").

Major's second novel *NO,* is even more radical in its experimentation than was the first. Whereas the first novel adhered to a chronology of events and rather well-defined characters, *NO* tries to destroy and at the same time gain a new perspective on language, time, and personality. As Major points out in the interview, he purposely mingled and confused the slang from various decades of the twentieth century in order to break down the limits imposed by realistic fiction. He also merged characters so that it is sometimes impossible to recognize whether it is the hero or his father. The purpose of all this is to help him in tracing an awakening mind as it moves through its earliest sensual awareness in childhood and finally blossoms into full consciousness at a bullfight, where the hero faces mutilation and death. And in following this mind, Major is not concerned with whether or not the "action" of the novel takes place in the imagination or in the real life of the character because, for Major, the two are inseparable.

Imaginative experiences have as much and perhaps more influence upon personality than do things in "actual" experience. It is of little importance whether the character at the end of the novel is confronting a charging bull, or whether he is sitting in a New York apartment imagining such an experience. The point is that the imagination can make it real.

Both novels are linked in their essential preoccupation with defining the "I," its elusiveness, its fragility, how it is threatened, how it comes to be. *NO* moves beyond the first novel in insisting that the self is a phenomenon of language and the imagination rather than of actual experience, time, and place. The self is created by and emerges as the product of an imagination that can give it meaning and direction through language. As with Stephen Dedalus, the first problem is being able to give names to things, which is the first step in gaining control over them and oneself. By placing his fear of death in a ritualistic story about a bullfight, the character transcends that fear. At this point art and life make contact; art becomes a vehicle through which life can be ordered and given significance. The artist does not reflect life but rather gives it meaning as he fictionalizes it. The "self" then becomes the artifact of whatever the imagination has been able to create and is limited only insofar as the imagination itself is limited.

At the time of the interview Major was living and teaching in New York. He has completed two other novels and is at work on more. In the interview Major was careful to note that his ideas about his work and the writing of fiction are tenuous and temporary; his ideas change as he writes more. He re-reads his own work very critically and is anxious to point out what he thinks are its weaknesses. The interview represents about four hours of telephone conversation that took place in early winter, 1973.

Interviewer: In Your essay, "A Black Criterion," you call for black writers to break away from Westernized literary strictures. Do you think of *All-Night Visitors* as being an example of a "non-Western" novel?

Major: I've changed since writing that essay in 1967. I now find repulsive the idea of calling for black writers to do anything other than what they each choose to do. A lot of blacks grew up in the United States and became writers. They are different because of the racial climate and because of this country's history, but they still are part of this common American experience.

They may speak black English and use Afro-American slang, and eat black-eyed peas and corn bread, yet they are not African. And certainly they are not Chinese. So what do we have? We are Americans. We work in English; it may be black English, but at its roots, it's English. This does not mean that there are not several very unique black writers. If you look at Cecil Brown, Al Young, William Demby, Ron Fair, and Charles Wright, you'll see how original the contemporary black fictionist really is. But as far as some kind of all-encompassing black aesthetic is concerned, I don't think black writers can be thrown together like that into some kind of formula. Black writers today should write whatever they want to write and in any way they choose to write it. No style or subject should be alien to them. We have to get away from this rigid notion that there are certain topics and methods reserved for black writers. I'm against all that. I'm against coercion from blacks and from whites.

Interviewer: Then you did not intend that your first novel be seen as working against a Western idea of what the novel should be?

Major: No. *All-Night Visitors* was not a non-Western novel. I was struggling against a lot of Western concepts when I wrote it, but it is still an *American* novel. I once said that it was not a Christian novel. Christianity is something with which I have been at war almost all my life. When I was a kid I believed the things I was told about God and the Devil. I think that in the West, Christianity's great attraction is that it offers life after death. It's something that people can lose themselves in because they can say that everything is going to be all right. Eastern religions don't have that built-in escape, nor do they have the tremendous self-hatred that's at the center of Christianity. These feelings about Christianity are in my work because I agonized with these things in my own experience of growing up, these problems of good and evil and sex. I think that's why there's so much sex in *All-Night Visitors*. Here was a man who could express himself only in this one natural way because he had absolutely nothing else. Christianity's view toward sex exists because of the great self-hatred that's so embedded in Christian teaching. Look at Saint Paul's doctrine of Original Sin. I can see it in everything around us: sex is something that's nasty and something to hide. *All-Night Visitors* was a novel I had to write in order to come to terms with my own body. I also wanted to deal with the other body functions. In *NO* I was trying to exploit all the most sacred taboos in this culture, not just sexual taboos, but those related to the private functions of the body, and that's where they all seem to center.

Interviewer: Sex in *All-Night Visitors* is used in many ways. As you say, it is the only means that Eli Bolton has of expressing himself, but it also reminds Eli of death and is sometimes quite violent and brutal. At the same time I don't think that sex is used in a metaphorical way to imply the changes Eli undergoes.

Major: Eli's attitudes about sex reflect the crisis of the 1960s. In speaking of the novel, John A. Williams said it is a sad book that gives off a kind of gentle helplessness and anger with no place to go and that it shows the discontent of the "death-wait" in our society. Now sex features very large in *All-Night Visitors,* and so does violence. I wanted it that way because this society is preoccupied with both. All kinds of negative stigmas concerning sex have been imposed on black men by both black and white people, and Eli doesn't escape this kind of psychological warfare. Some people feel that by showing Eli's sex life I'm playing right into the hands of white myths about black people. And white liberals have expressed pretty much the same sort of reaction to the novel. All I can say is that certain people have no interest in the human body and even hate it. These people seem to have no sex life.

Interviewer: Why does Eli see the relationship between sex and death?

Major: When you ask about sex and death in the same breath you really hit on something in the book, something most people concerned with the sexual aspect of the book never get to. And fiction that tries to deal with sex in an open and honest way and attempts to get beneath the purely physical is bound to come to terms with the link between sex and death. I don't mean that sex is here at the beginning and death there at the end. They are interchangeable. The expression of one can be found in the act of the other. I think that the French word for orgasm can be translated "little death." And I think that you are right when you observe that sex isn't meant to correspond with anything that Eli's going through. It is, rather, a kind of alternative to the brutality around him. That's one of the last natural things he has in a world where he cannot assert himself. It is a means of expression and, at times, a weapon.

Interviewer: Eli keeps complaining about how "unreal" the world about him has become. I wonder whether his search for some new reality, a search which begins with discarding old sexual myths, requires that he question all the "realities" that his culture lives by? Perhaps it also calls into question what the author's relationship with reality is. Does he reflect it, as the traditional realist supposedly does, or does he invent it, as the fantasy novel, begun by Sterne, does?

Major: I really don't like either idea. The novel is an invention in itself, which exists on its own terms. It has its own reality and I don't think it's designed to reflect reality in any kind of logical sense. It's not a way of showing reality and it's not really a fantasy. But then I'm simply talking about what the novel means to *me*. The kind of novel that I'm concerned with writing is one that takes on its own reality and is really independent of anything outside itself.

Interviewer: In some very real and practical sense, though, a writer is forced into relating himself to the outside world. He may choose to ignore it or try to see it in a new way in his fiction, but he must always be reacting to it in some way.

Major: But in a novel, the only thing you really have is words. You begin with words and you end with words. The content exists in our minds. I don't think that it has to be a reflection of anything. It is a reality that has been created inside of a book. It's put together and exists finally in your mind. I don't want to say that a novel is *totally* independent of the reality of things in everyday life, but it's not the same thing. It's certainly not the kind of reflection that's suggested by the metaphor of the mirror.

Interviewer: Well, I think then that you are ascribing to the tradition of the fantasy novel. Rather than life, it uses the imagination and the novel itself as its primary subject.

Major: Its subject-matter is the novel itself? Yes. I think that's closer to the truth. At the same time I know that my fiction has been directly influenced by other things. I regret, for instance, in my haphazard education my exposure to Freudian psychology because it has left its effect on my thinking. Since I finished *NO*, I found myself weeding out so much of it. I can't reject it all, because we live in a technological world where we have certain ways of dealing with reality. But that's one thing I regret about *NO*. I noticed the Freudian influence there and it's very disturbing. That whole sensibility is probably present in my earlier work too, and it's a sensibility that I want to forget. I don't want to get trapped in terminology. I worry that, despite the fact that *NO* came from the gut level, a large part of it seems to be caught in the sensibility of Freudian psychology.

Interviewer: One might also question what psychology's relation to reality is.

Major: I think that you should stop when you use the word "reality" because reality itself is very flexible and really has nothing to do with anything. I don't think reality is a fixed point around which theories adjust. Reality is anything *but* a fixed point. So it seems strange to me that a work of art could be an interpretation of *the* reality.

Interviewer: I agree with that, but we usually do not take that approach to a system like psychology which is really just as fictional as literature. Psychology is only an attempt to impose an artificial order on the chaos, but the chaos remains. In literature, we most often make a distinction between literature as an imaginative act and as a truthful picture of the way things are; but we don't make that distinction with philosophy, or with psychology, which really has no relation to anything except itself. I agree with you that reality is no fixed point, yet someone like Freud imposes his pattern and says, "Here it is. Here is the truth." Perhaps we should look at psychology as essentially an imaginative act.

Major: Yes, right. You're absolutely right. Freud was inventing. He was doing the same thing a novelist would do. He was creating his own reality. It was an invention just like Darwin's, despite the correspondences to what we call "facts." They are still inventions. That may have something to do with the nature of writing and thinking, thoughts relating to words.

Interviewer: I see so much of your fiction as an attempt to break away from the myths men have invented, which now tyrannize them. Sometimes those myths are Christian ones, sometimes psychological, and sometimes racial. I see very much the same thing going on in Ishmael Reed's fiction and Michael Harper's poetry.

Major: I see them in Ishmael's work. He was exposed to pretty much the same kind of background as I was. He handles this in a different way; we all do. And it isn't just Christianity in my work. There's the whole racial thing which I try to handle not as a psychologist or a sociologist, but as a writer who tries to integrate these things into a novel. This, by the way, is what I have against a lot of black fiction. So much seems designed to preach racial, or political, or sociological sermons.

Interviewer: At one point in *All-Night Visitors* Eli reflects that "I suppose we have all gotten used to it. Our dislocation is so complete." Do you think that the unifying theme of the novel is the various forms of dislocation Eli experiences?

Major: Yes, I'd agree with you that the dislocation can serve as a kind of unifying theme. I like the sense that you get from the novel. Not many people came away from it with the feeling that the story—if I can say story—is a nightmare in which a whole series of strange things happen. But that was the impression I wanted to create.

Interviewer: In the "Basement Rite" chapter you slip into a surrealistic style. It's interesting because the story up to this point has been very bizarre, but it isn't until this chapter that you break away from a naturalistic treatment of your materials. When it occurs, one hardly notices the shift in style because it seems like such a logical extension of what's been going on.

Major: Real and surreal are two tricky words, but I know what you mean. I can't think of a term at the moment that would be better. The entire novel is meant to have that surreal quality. Many people, unfortunately, missed this in the book because, I suppose, they were too concerned with the surface reality.

Interviewer: Why was the novel written in rather short episodic chapters? There's really little or no plot. Were you purposely breaking away from the traditional realistic narrative?

Major: I discovered early that what I was trying to do in *All-Night Visitors* could not be done in a smooth symphonic fashion. I needed short broken chapters, little twisted episodes. Omitting traditional plot and other kinds of traditional devices was dictated by the same need to capture all the elements of this "unreal world" into a form specifically designed for it.

Interviewer: What went into structuring these episodes?

Major: The arrangement of the chapters changed quite a bit in the several drafts preceding the final one. I followed my feelings with very little conscious planning. In other words, the writing itself was the discovery of what the novel was.

Interviewer: Unlike the rest of the novel, there's a lyrical spirit in the chapter "Week-End Away." It seems to clash with the tone of the novel and to suggest certain qualities about the character of Eli that are not present in the other chapters.

Major: What Eli feels and expresses in that chapter is very real. He would be a quiet peaceful person if his world permitted him to be. That chapter is one of my favorites in the book. I think it shows a side to Eli that one has to see in order to understand the other sides.

Interviewer: The novel ends with Eli helping a destitute Spanish family, and he feels that "I had become firmly a man." I am not sure how seriously to take all this, whether or not to believe that a change has taken place. All the evil that he has seen and felt does not seem to be balanced by this one moment of light.

Major: No one ever says, "Now I have become a man." That moment is never so clear. It happens slowly and in so many unseen ways that there isn't likely to be a moment as dramatic as the one Eli experiences. I had him stand in a doorway with rain falling, thinking this. It works all right in a novel, but I am not so sure that it works as well in what we call "reality." One person told me that she did not believe the ending. It was not credible that he could have given his apartment to a helpless woman and her children. Others have felt that the ending explained everything and gave the novel its point, if it has a point. Yet I wasn't trying to make any point when I wrote the novel. I was simply trying to describe Eli's life and what it was like for a black man in the 1960s. Ron Welburn in *The Nickle Review* said that the book had no overt message. That was the way I wanted it, because Eli's life really had no point.

Interviewer: One recurring concern in both novels is that of the "self." One way of looking at your characters is that they lack a sense of who they are and they must discover that. But seen in the way I think you intend it to be, the self is really a nonexistent thing, or something that is in a constant state of becoming. Moses in *NO,* for instance, *is* all the things that happen to him and all the ways that people look at him. In this sense, one cannot say that his problem is that he doesn't know who he is. The point is that he isn't one thing, but many. Is the self something that is created, rather than found, or uncovered?

Major: The notion of self in *NO* is dealt with in a superficial way. The narrator says at various times that he thinks the idea of a self is ridiculous. He's called by many names. This might be a clue to just how artificial or shifting this whole business of self becomes. (The search for freedom is another artificial thing in the novel. That's deliberately artificial. There's no such thing as freedom, in the sense in which it's used in that novel.) At one point he's called Nicodemus, which is something out of Negro folklore. And he's called C. C. Rider.

Interviewer: And at times "the Boy."

Major: Right. And Ladykiller, the Inspector, and June Bug. And there's a play on Nat Turner; the narrator is called Nat Turnips. And, of course, the name he usually goes by is Moses. Did you get the sense that there were two Moses?

Interviewer: Yes. One is the narrator and the other is the father figure.

Major: One is definitely the father image. And although it wouldn't be the wisest thing to do, you could substitute "God" for "father." It wouldn't be too far off either. . . . But to get back to your question about the notion of self. I was trying to show all the shifting elements of the so-called self. One way I did it was by giving the narrator all these names. The other Moses, of course, is not concerned with problems of who he is. He's a doer, he's a hard-hitting, physical type; the narrator is more reflective and spiritual. The father is really the "ladykiller."

Interviewer: Yes, literally.

Major: He's a sort of pimp, and he's a hustler. He's deadly and yet he's gentle. I tried to make his character difficult to penetrate.

Interviewer: I wanted to ask you about the bullfight scene at the end of the novel in relation to this question of the self. Does it suggest something along the lines of the Hemingway idea of the moment of truth?

Major: I hope that it's not that corny, but it may be.

Interviewer: What is that happens there? Must he have this encounter with death before he can be free of these terrible things in his past?

Major: He must come to terms with an ultimate act. He has to have that look into the endless horror of things in order to get beyond the whole petty business of worrying about it.

Interviewer: I wonder why you did not write *NO* as a naturalistic novel. In some ways it is merely a story of a boy growing up.

Major: Why do you think that he is young?

Interviewer: I assumed that he was now looking back on the things that happened to him as a boy.

Major: Right. That's what I was trying to do. I was trying not only to construct a chronological story but one that was psychologically unrestricted by time. You notice that there are elements from the 1920s, the 1930s, and the 1940s. And there are qualities out of the 1970s and the space age. I was trying to bring all of this together and blend it into a kind of consciousness that was not restricted. I wanted a landscape in language that would give me the freedom to do this. I felt that this freedom could not be achieved in a naturalistic novel.

Interviewer: Yes. You would not have had the range you needed. You move through all different states of mind and ages. The narrator not only sees the action and events of the story the way a child would, but also as a grown man reflecting on and shaping those experiences.

Major: You also probably noticed that I was grabbing at every useful reference that I could get my hands on: magic, mysticism, Judeo-Christian religion, philosophy, witchcraft, American superstition and folklore, black terminology, and black slang. But I didn't start out with any conscious notion of doing that; it just developed in a very organic way. It was only after I finished the first draft that I saw what I wanted to do. When I got that finished I started making out elaborate charts with the names of the characters, personality sketches, and their possible ages. I worked hard at inventing names that would really work with the characters, names like Grady Flower, Lucy Nasteylip, Grew . . . and B. B.—a name little black boys in the South are often given.

Interviewer: There are many Southern elements in the novel. At times I was reminded of Faulkner.

Major: It's very definitely a Southern novel. I tried to capture the flavor of the South as I remember it. There was also a subdued treatment of the relationship between the country and the city, but it wasn't fully developed in the novel. The paradox of the country and the city is very deep in me because I know both. I was born in the city, but shortly after that I lived in the country. It's been that way on and off ever since.

Interviewer: Was if difficult getting through the first draft of *NO?*

Major: What I am doing right now, very consciously, is to outline a novel and it's very difficult because I am watching what I am doing too closely. I didn't have that problem with *NO.* With *NO* I got teletype paper, put it on a spool, made a little platform with a stick, adjusted the typewriter, set the paper into the typewriter, and wrote it on this endless sheet of paper. It was a very spontaneous thing. I would write until I ran out of steam. It was very easy to do, because it was a story that I had been trying to write since I was twelve. It was the story I needed to write most. I wrote it in 1969, when my personal life was really tossed around in many ways. But I had finally reached the point where I felt that I could finally do it. Although it's not an autobiographical novel, its roots are very deep in my emotional life. So, though it's fictional in its design, the energy that holds it together is very real. This is true of any fiction.

Interviewer: You and I have talked before about the relationship between your poetry and fiction. What do you see as the relationship between the two?

Major: Much of my poetry is purely fictional. I sincerely believe good poetry should be fictional. I work hard to make all my poems work as fiction. My newest book of poems which hasn't been published yet, *The Syncopated Cakewalk,* is pure fiction. I think that it was Carson McCullers who said that poetry should be more like fiction and that fiction should be more like poetry. I am working very deliberately to break down what I think are the false distinctions between poetry and fiction.

Interviewer: Is there an essential difference, though, that still exists? Does it have to do with the use of language or with the fact that fiction is still narrative in nature?

Major: No, I don't see the difference. But I am really in a state of transition with all of this. It is rather difficult for me to abstract theories about what this means and where I'm going with it.

Interviewer: I know that you attended the Art Institute in Chicago for a while. Has painting affected your writing in any way?

Major: The Art Institute experience has often been misunderstood. It didn't involve any academic classes. I was there on a fellowship to sketch and paint. I learned a lot in those days, but mainly on my own, upstairs in the gallery and in the library. I was very serious about painting. I almost painted my mother out of house and home actually. We nearly ran out of space, but my mother always encouraged me to paint. She wanted me to become a painter. I think my experience with painting, the way that I learned to see the physical world of lines, color, and composition, definitely influenced my writing.

Interviewer: Can you describe your work habits?

Major: They change all the time because they depend on the thing I'm doing. If I'm writing a group of short stories, I might work exclusively on one each day. If I'm writing a series of poems I might do one or two a day.

Interviewer: How much revision do you do?

Major: I revise endlessly. Even after publication. I am not one of those writers who sees publication as a cut-off point.

Interviewer: Eli in *All-Night Visitors* says something very interesting and I wonder whether or not it describes your reasons for writing: "the universe is not *ordered,* therefore I am simply pricking the shape of a particular construct, a form, in it."

Major: I don't know. I suppose writing comes from the need to shape one's experience and ideas. Maybe it assures us a future and a past. We try to drive away our fears and uncertainties and explain the mystery of life and the world.

Self-Interview: On Craft

Clarence Major / 1973

From *The Dark and Feeling: Black Writers and Their Work* (New York: The Third Press, 1974), 125–32. Reprinted by permission of Clarence Major.

Q: Major, you write poems, novels, stories, essays and . . . what else? Tell me, *why* do you write?

A: I always feel silly trying to answer such questions. Everybody before me who ever tried to deal with this one I'm sure either felt the same way or, if the person attempted to answer, he or she was pretending to know something at a level no one can fully penetrate. I mean, we don't even know *why* we talk. We don't know why we write. All we know is how we do it and that we do have this urge to communicate. It all happens on a level we cannot explain. All we can do is guess and possibly create myths and religions about and around the mystery. I suspect the roots are at the level of being itself. But I can be fairly clear about the type of person I am and that, too, might lend a clue. If I had lived millions of years ago I'd probably be one of the ones drawing pictures on the walls of the cave.

Q: Drawing pictures, communicating, you mean, all the same as writing—any kind of communication?

A: Yes, but each form has its own material, you know.

Q: Speaking of material, what is the material you use for your work?

A: It depends on what you mean by material. Literary material in a sense has no real physical property. In one sense, it is only the arrangement of words that the writer can claim. No writer can claim each word or each letter. No manuscript in itself is the ultimate property. The characters in a story are not real people. They cannot be based on real people. They are words and not simply words on paper. What you end with, as a writer, is an investment in a network of ideas and impressions created by tools that belong to the community of man.

Q: I know I wasn't very explicit when I said material.

A: Well, I use the typewriter and pencils and pens. For longer works I use the typewriter. For poems, very often, I use pens then type the stuff later.

22

What you use and how you use it also determines the shape of what you make. The size of the page, you may be surprised, has a lot to do with the sense of size in the outcome of your poem.

Q: What about subject matter?

A: Subject matter is usually directly from my own experience. I try to wait until the experience is completely internalized before trying to handle it in terms of art. If I try to write about something that happened recently it usually turns out badly. I have to be emotionally removed to a degree. But, at the same time, if I am too far removed, emotionally, it won't work that way either. It becomes a question of balance—how I handle the interplay between what has gone into my unconscious and what remains controlled at a conscious level. And you might say the *ear* and eye participations, the senses, are the mediums through which I allow the plays to be made. By plays I mean the decisions, moment by moment. From letter to letter, and word to word. You see, I have to situate myself between those two poles, trusting them and what they do for and mean for each other. Yet I still have to be involved enough to care. I have to care about my words—the arrangements' effects. They have to mean a lot to me before they take on magical meaning for someone else.

Q: But do you write about your own experience directly as it happens?

A: No. Never. There is no such thing, really. Something that comes close to passing for that sort of work is journalism but journalism is as much a lie as fiction. All words are lies when they, in any arrangement, pretend to be other than the arrangement they make. On the other hand, what I try to do is achieve a clear and solid mass of arrangements, an entity, that passes for nothing—except flashes of scenes and impressions we all know—much outside the particular shape of its own "life." Again, the wedding of the conscious and unconscious. Anything I can use I use. Whether or not the material is directly mine from experience I use it if it has meaning for me. If I see a matchbox sitting on the kitchen table, while I'm typing, I might just stick it into the story I'm working on. See. Or, if I hear something on the radio, while I'm sitting at the typewriter typing a novel, I might just throw in a news report as I hear it, perhaps changing some of it to make it work into the novel. I do anything that works. I open my mind and make it completely— well, as completely as possible—accessible to everything and anything that comes into the circle of my senses or memory or personal space or all of these at the same time. Of course this does not mean that it is by any means possible to record everything. You snatch away from the whole mass of stuff only a tiny portion and it gives you the suggestion for some of the substance that goes into what you're doing, be it a novel or poem or whathaveyou. Direct or indirect it is all my experience. If I simply read a book it becomes *my* experience.

Q: Do you value *all* elements of your own experience—as material for fiction or poetry?

A: No, definitely not. I try to rely on a sort of unconscious screening device or selector. I try to let the feeling (somewhere behind the mind that guides the front part of the mind) determine everything. If I am lucky it happens successfully; if not, I have to try again.

Q: Then you write purely from feeling?

A: Not purely. It is thick with many other juices. It also has in it the substance of uncertainty and, on occasion, a touch of the ego. And selfishness at its worst. But no one can write purely from feeling; it has to be a mixture of many and different motives and means and ends. All of which calls into question who and what we are. Any one of us at any given moment.

Q: Do you ever find yourself unable to write?

A: Not really. Usually I *can* write *something*. I might not be able to write as well as I'd like to write all the time but just writing something, anything, is always easy. And it is not uncommon for the best poem or story to come out of a mood and state of mind that are cool and, perhaps, even a little turned off.

Q: What is the degree of your concern with artistic quality in your work?

A: It occupies a large part of my overall concern. Because I'd like to turn out top-rate stuff all the time. The thing I hate worse than anything else is to spend six months on a novel and have it turn out a turd. It can easily happen. But I can usually salvage most of my failures. But the artistic quality itself, for me, is the first consideration. It comes before shit like "message" and such jive. A lot of black writers tend to get hungup in militant rhetoric, thinking they can save their people. The deliberate effort, propaganda, has never helped anyone toward a larger sense of self. It has always been the novel or poem that begins from and spreads all across the entire human experience that ends up liberating minds. These militant fictionists, hungup in their slogans and dialect-writing, are simply competing with newspapers and the six o'clock news and house organs and cheap politicians. Apparently they never once stop to think about the artistic quality of their work, mainly, I guess, because white folks never told them it applied to them. And, by the way, I'm not talking about artistic standards based on European-American concepts of excellence. Rather, I'm referring to formative and functional standards that have their origins in African cultures. Aside from the most obvious uses of art, it is supposed to help deepen and widen one's sense and vision of life. Anyway, I don't want to get into all this too deeply . . . I've heard myself say it too many times.

Q: Tell me, Major, (that is, if I may ask) do you make a living from your writing?

A: Most of the time. When I don't, I teach writing or literature to supplement my income.

Q: Do you like teaching?

A: I don't particularly like teaching but I like working with students *if* they're interested in what is going on.

Q: I see. But let us get back to your own writing. Exactly how do you go about writing a novel? Do you use charts? Do you make a list of the characters first? Do you begin with an outline or . . .

A: It all depends on the novel. I wrote *All-Night Visitors* casually over a period of four years. I used bits and parts of other discarded works. Some parts of it were written many times over and other parts went in the final draft without any alterations from the original draft. It was originally a very ambitious book that got a lot of its life knocked out of it by its publisher, Maurice Girodias, who wanted it cut—and I cut it—to fit the format of hardcover books he was trying to publish at that time. Regarding how I worked on it, yes, I used charts and lists of names and everything I could get my hands on. I read a dictionary of the slang used by U.S. military men in Vietnam. I even worked some of my poems into the action.

Q: What about *NO?*

A: With *NO* the situation was altogether different. The first draft was done on teletype paper fed into the typewriter from a spool I made myself. I finished the first draft in, I think, about two months of very casual work. The second and final draft, done on regular typing paper, was done in about the same length of time. I finished *NO* in the fall of 1969.

Q: Do you want also to talk about *Reflex and Bone Structure?*
A: I certainly do not.

Q: Why not?
A: It is a question of time.

Q: All right, good enough. How about your poetry. How is it done? Can you talk about it?
A: Some of it is very personal and comes straight out of that kind of reference. Other poems are suggested by any number of things or situations. As I said earlier, I use anything I can lay my hands on. The only criterion is it *must* work. The impetus might even be something like the patterns in this rug here on the floor at this moment. They may suggest something, an idea that begins and expands, growing into a complex network of stuff. I like to think of the growth as organic—that is, in a sense, organic. Anything. The fish over there in the fishtank. Anything at all.

Q: Then, how do you know how to direct all of this once it begins?
A: It's simple. It builds itself, like a snowball. Or see it as crust, like the outside of cake.

Q: Crust?
A: Yes. In a sense, the stuff that is excess to the original idea . . . *Certainly you must know what I mean!* All of this seems, to me, so obvious!

Q: What about the creative process?
A: Well, what about it?

Q: Can you tell me something about it?
A: No, I doubt it.

Q: Your nonfiction. Does it differ in conception and process from your fiction and poetry?
A: Only on the surface, I think. With polemics, you know, there is the uppermost point of a *message.* It is the center of the universe of nonfiction. Whereas, on the other hand, in a novel or a poem, you may simply be concerned with producing a drama of an aspect of life or all of life. Personally,

I like fiction and poetry better. Nonfiction, due to the influence of the times I guess, I enjoy reading.

Q: Do you mean *The New York Times?*
A: That, my friend, was gutty!

Q: Gutty? Well, I won't worry about it. Can you answer a few more questions?
A: No more questions, my friend.

Q: Not even one?
A: Not one.

Reality, Fiction, and Criticism: An Interview/Essay

Doug Bolling and Clarence Major / 1978

From *par rapport* 2 (Winter 1979), 67–73. Reprinted by permission of Clarence Major.

Note: Doug Bolling sent me a list of questions. This was in September, 1978. The questions were generally aimed in the direction I wanted to follow yet I was not quite happy with them. I revised them and that was fine with Doug. This interview/essay evolved out of his original set of questions.

Doug Bolling: I wonder if you'd comment on your novels as a group. To what extent do you sense an evolutionary pattern at work?

Clarence Major: I see a movement from some restricting concerns for formal narration and from the trappings set up by the traditional assumption that experience itself to be—in literature—totalized. Added up to make some sort of systematic meaning out of it. Not true. I have come to the system of fragmentation the hard way, slowly. It's visible in *Reflex and Bone Structure* (1975) and in *Emergency Exit* (1979) but its beginnings are also visible in *All-Night Visitors* (1969) and in *NO* (1973). I've discovered that the work has to refer more insistently inwardly for its own validity. The digressive method works best for me. In this sense I am in the Melville tradition. The other main American tradition would be primarily sequential and its forerunners are writers like Hawthorne and Cooper. *All-Night Visitors* is certainly more formal in its structure than is *NO* and *Reflex and Bone Structure* represents an even greater departure from formal narration than does *NO*. Cora Hull (in *Reflex*) is right at the center of each moment in a network of events that are not in any sense chronological or linear. Recognizable events and believable characters are in both *Reflex* and *Exit* yet it is not these factors that justify their existence. This, I guess, is the main, big step I've taken slowly since about 1968.

DB: I see your novels as part of the postmodernist direction. If you agree with this would you care to speak about its aesthetics?

CM: There is a context or call it a category the four novels fit into but it's hard to define because you've got to let it stay loose. There is also a larger framework by which a certain type of fiction—not limited to any one culture or country—can be defined. There are aesthetic principles, too.

First, none of the terms used to define the fictions in the various categories in the larger framework are suitable: parafiction, metafiction, experimental fiction, postmodern fiction, contemporary fiction, surfiction, avant garde fiction, the new tradition, superfiction, on and on, none of them seem to work in a specific way and this is because the works they refer to so often defy neat, easy definitions. The category my own novels fall into is intensely American in its obsessions, especially in its insistence on defying academic principles and the linear and formal notions of realism traditionally practiced by Negro and Black American writers since William Wells Brown's novel, *Clotelle* (1857). Just as Ishmael Reed and George Schuyler have more in common with writers such as William Burroughs and Kurt Vonnegut than with realistic black writers such as Ernest J. Gaines and James Baldwin, my own efforts probably should be looked at alongside the works of George Chambers, Jonathan Baumbach and Russell Banks. To further illustrate the point: some other writers whose works fit the category are Ronald Sukenick, Steve Katz, Charles Wright, and Walter Abish. The thing these fictionists have in common is their tendency to minimize *representational effects* in their fictions. They abstract enough of the recognizable in the interest of putting together fictions that, in their various ways, take a unique place in the world as objects through which the reader can have an experience rather than an (ill-conceived) reflection of life. That's the category.

The larger framework would include not only these writers and many others but Gertrude Stein, Le Clezio, Pinget, Jean Toomer, Kenneth Patchen, Judith Johnson Sherwin, Anaïs Nin, John Barth, Donald Barthelme, Michael Stephens, Jerzy Kosinski, Richard Brautigan, Paul Metcalf, Ntozake Shange, Robert Coover, Raymond Federman, Rhoda Lerman, Douglas Wolf, Gil Orlovitz, Kurt Vonnegut and Rosellen Brown. And the obvious forerunners are Laurence Sterne, James Joyce, Samuel Beckett. And Italio Calvino, Borges, Carlos Fuentes, Gabriel García Márquez, Peter Handke. But Melville is still way back there as an ultimate forerunner. And so is Baudelaire. The larger framework begins to make itself manifest when one considers such writers together along with the various departures (their works represent) from the various established literary norms. The larger framework is necessarily loosely defined as something wherein a number of departures—both in form and content—take place but it is perhaps more precisely defined by several other factors: in the works *process* seems to have more importance than *conclusions, totalizations and resolutions.* Method is as important or more important than content; imaginative space commands more attention than story line, plot and character development; language itself is often the chief antagonist since many of these writers wish to renew it, reform it, make it work in a new, more effective manner in order to unearth stronger, richer, deeper impressions of and extensions of life itself. Of course these attempts do not always work. But, as Faulkner once said, the great failure is better than the safe, quiet thing done well.

The aesthetic principles are tricky to talk about because there's no suitable terminology. Roughly, the first principle is simple: there are no fixed principles except any that happens to be effective. Effectiveness is the key word. Any means of arriving at a workable effect is an ideal aesthetic principle of the so-called new fiction. The rules of totalization fiction are generally not considered effective aesthetic principles except in an historical context. I mean, *Invisible Man* is an historical example. It is a sequential novel and was never really meant to be in the digressive tradition of *Moby Dick*, for example. I make the comparison to stress the fact that most principles that are considered effective for contemporary fiction derive from the digressive tradition rather than the sequential one. And I don't think this is necessarily so because life itself happens to be more digressive than sequential in its nature. Fiction is and should always resist comparison with real life—that is the main way it manages to achieve its own life. But to get back to principles: any guiding sense of the requirements of a particular work is necessarily also individual and subject to change without prior notice—even right in the middle of any particular work—as long as the total effect is successful without making use of any antique system such as sequence-leading-to-resolution. I can't use my first two novels as successful examples of this theory. But *Reflex* and *Exit,* I think, are.

Each composition will have its own particular characteristics and these characteristics will emerge from the works themselves. Is the style the person? Hardly. But it's not far off. The tone? Is the tone the voice of the author? What about meaning? All of these aspects of fictional composition are generally considered in literature classes and I guess they are worthwhile things to talk about in relation to aesthetic principles, composition, point of view, narration and so on. They are signals and devices, they give the critic or the teacher a map that is helpful in finding the way into a chosen work of fiction . . .

DB: I'd appreciate your thoughts on this effort to get back to objectivity—the "natural," the "real" (or at least the phenomenal level) compared to the continuing explorations that allow fiction to be its own reality and a self-contained creation.

CM: Caught in the middle of this exchange and conflict between the realistic novel and the nonrepresentational novel is the question of the relation of so-called reality to the nature and purpose of a work of art, in this case, fiction. It is easy to assume that this question was resolved years ago but it wasn't. Since fiction obviously borrows facts and aspects from "real" life we tend to confuse its function and purpose with life itself. Some experts say life is one thing and fiction is another. Others tell us that fiction is an extension of experience. Still others say that it is meant to enhance our sense of experience—teach us a lesson. I guess on certain occasions it does, in varying degrees, a little bit of all of these things. But primarily fiction, at its best, is *not mainly a reflection of life* (since life *can't* be reflected). Fiction primarily offers a *text* that can be *read* in relation to real experience. It is legitimately a reading experience that allows the reader *to think* and *to imagine* certain possibilities or impossibilities. Even the worst fiction doesn't reproduce anything from real life. The realistic writer who imagines that he is really *reflecting* reality in his totalizing novel is a victim of self-deception. So is his reader who gets lost in the story. If it's not escape fiction it's illusionary fiction. Let it be said that I am renaming realism here.

Still this theory does not resolve the problem that arises when we try to understand what the straight (realistic) writer is doing in how the concepts and finished product relate to the concepts and finished product of the non-representational author (such as Gertrude Stein, for example).

The realistic writer, for a long time now, has operated from the assumption that reality, that is, day-to-day life, ups and downs, everything we do and say, all of our pain and love, all of our fears and joys, *can be reflected* in literature. The nonrepresentational writer, on the other hand, has never operated from that assumption. His or her assumption has been a little more complicated: from this writer's point of view it is possible for a man to wake up one morning transformed into a giant bug. This may be an extreme example but I think the point gets across better this way. Some of these nonrepresentational writers make their departures in terms of content, others make theirs in terms of technique or form. Ishmael Reed, for example, in his book *Mumbo Jumbo* decided to rewrite western history. Abstract painters will tell you that painting is not illustration. The progressive jazz musician will insist that the way he or she sounds does not have to represent, say, a sunset or serve as background stuff for a couple of lovers strolling along the walkway lining the bay.

And of course objectivity never existed anyway. There is nothing in literature that is natural: it's all made up. Myths as a basis for fiction are powerful but they are historical. Joyce finished myths. And like D. H. Lawrence said, Joyce was too mental.

What about criticism generally and black criticism in particular?

In its pure sense criticism is one of the best cultural tools we have. What do we need before we can approach literature? There are certain assumptions the writer makes about the reader. For one, the writer assumes that he/she is writing for someone who will be able to read the language the work is in. How much control does the writer have over the reader's response? The critic is a special sort of reader, one who is going to criticize or interpret the work. We can probably assume that the critic reads a work with the closeness not generally associated with the average reader. In other words the critic is a person who attempts to see the work on as many levels as possible. Concepts, meaning, purpose, and so on, are aspects of a work the critic will want to isolate and define. This mode of inquiry has been in a state of evolution, naturally, in its relation to literature but when it comes to the body of fiction I roughly outlined a moment ago, criticism has been either confused or tardy or both. There have been very few really excellent descriptions or explanations or analyses of works by American avant garde writers of the 1970's. I've been writing for over fifteen years and my books have been reviewed in the major newspapers for over ten years yet only recently has my fiction begun to receive serious consideration. And I don't believe this state existed because nobody thought my fiction serious enough to be analyzed. This situation can apply to almost any serious writer I can think of with a few exceptions such as Barthelme, Pynchon and Barth.

In a sense the critic is a teacher—a teacher of literature. Lionel Trilling once pointed out that literary criticism sort of relates to literature the way scientific investigation relates to nature. And it is at this point that Black Criticism or the Black Aesthetic becomes confusing at its very roots. The problem with the Black Aesthetic is that it sidesteps the serious proposition that a great or serious work of literature must refer inwardly for its own validity—in other words, it cannot be more dependent on external reality, every-day-reality for its validity than it would be on its own system. System is the key word. The reality of a work of art belongs to that work of art. You cannot legitimately claim that because somebody down the street is on welfare and somebody else is in prison because of racial and social injustice that it is the responsibility of a work of art to adjust itself to the issues stemming from such conditions. Those conditions may be used as a basis, thematically, for the making of art but once the system of that art has taken over, those issues are secondary. This is what the Black Aesthetic people have not understood. This is what Addison Gayle does not understand. And it is too bad that so many readers, black readers, white readers, all kinds of readers, assume that people like Addison Gayle know what they are talking about—on the basis of the fact that he is black.

Usually, for the average reader, it is not possible to obtain a deep, full, detailed understanding of a complex, great work of fiction on the first reading. Our minds simply cannot absorb multidimensional literary texts instantly and completely. This is why teachers and critics are allowed to help us. How we read a work is predetermined by a number of things: who we are, what we assume the work is about, the writer's outlook and so on. And since meaning is so often rendered through a critic's own set of values, expectations and ability to focus—with his own vocabulary—what he/she thinks a certain work is *about,* the innocent reader of criticism if forever running the risk of being misled and cheated. This is why it is always important for the reader to go *directly* to the work itself. White readers who assume that they cannot understand a work by a black writer because they have had little experience with black people—real black people—have been completely misled by critics like Gayle and white critics like Rosenblatt and Richard Gilman. Nowhere in the world is there any great literature that cannot be understood by anybody. Great literature by definition transcends the social contexts in which it is produced. Such critics as Rosenblatt and Gilman may, on the other hand, wish to claim that there is no great black literature. That is another matter. But they have not dismissed black literature on the basis of quality. Rather they have stood back—or focused on the basis of race. Like their black counterpart Addison Gayle they have allowed external factors and real cultural and real social issues to operate as guidelines for their examinations of black literature. I doubt that these same critics would treat any other body of literature in this strange manner.

The problem was always one of trying to get race to correlate in some significant, practical way to the principles of art. People, black and white, talked about it a lot in the late 60's, early 70's as though there were no problems—or for that matter, as though there were no questions stemming from this proposition. Dissertations and books and essays were written on the validity of Black Art. And I'm sure there are some aspects of the two experiences—that is, race and art—that can be related. But Jacob Lawrence once said to me that he had seen no evidence that Black American artists, for example, had developed a style that can be said to be racially distinct like, say, early Chinese Art or African Art. And, if we are not talking about content at all, this is very likely true. I think it is also true of writing. I'm now talking exclusively about form, style, and such. Ishmael Reed and Georgie Schuyler, both black novelists, are closer to, say, Vonnegut and Richard Brautigan than they are to most other Black novelists, who are, for the most part, realists and naturalists. I think we can go straight down the line proving this point on both sides of the racial thesis. Of course this will upset a lot of people who like to write about The Black Novel and The Black This or That. It's too bad. It's just one other category that, unfortunately, allows for a lot of subtle racism to pass for scholarship. I could name names but I won't.

Clarence Major

Nancy Bunge / 1981

From *Finding the Words: Conversations with Writers Who Teach* (Swallow Press/Ohio University Press, 1985), 53–67. Reprinted by permission of Nancy Bunge.

NB: You make a number of statements that seem to link finding yourself as a writer with finding yourself as a person. Do you believe that the two are connected?

CM: Yeah, I think the two processes are integral and interchangeable and inseparable—the continual redefinition of self and the process of learning how to write every day. I find that it's an endless lesson; you don't really carry that much information and skill from one piece to the next unless you're doing the same thing over and over. Each act of writing becomes a whole new experience which is why it's so difficult. It's not like a nine to five job where you know what you're supposed to do every day, so I think, yeah, I think the self is involved in that process. You're different every day and if you're trying to do something that's worthwhile, then you're going to have to rediscover yourself, and rediscover a new approach, a new technique, a new way of getting at the same old things about life.

NB: So every day when you sit down and write, you have to reconnect with yourself?

CM: Yeah, I think so. I think a lot of that happens automatically and unconsciously. I don't think we deliberately go about it in a programmed way; I think it's just there as an instinctive demand on the self.

NB: You wrote, "It was finally through the hard work I put into *All-Night Visitors* that I came (in Ralph Ellison's words) 'to possess and express' the spirit and understand *with feeling* the footnotes on who and what I was."

CM: Umm, yeah.

NB: Is there any connection between that discovery and the fact that you were able to write your next book, *NO,* so quickly?

CM: I really didn't know how to write a novel when I wrote *All-Night Visitors;* I took the best parts of three novels that didn't work and somehow pulled them together and created this novel called *All-Night Visitors.* But I never had any sense of direction while I was writing that book; I had to discover it as I worked on the book and finally I saw how I could pull it all together. That's when I sat down and wrote the book.

NB: Do you feel that once that focus was established, it carried over to your later work?

CM: Well, with *NO* it was different because I had a concept; I had a vision of that novel. I knew what I wanted it to be and it came pretty close to being what I wanted it to be. So I wrote it on an endless sheet of paper, which made it a lot easier. The things that I learned writing *All-Night Visitors* really didn't carry over to *NO.* And I wasn't able to use anything that I learned from writing *NO* in the process of writing *Reflex and Bone Structure.*

NB: So you go about writing each book differently? You wrote *NO* on that long sheet of paper . . .

CM: Yeah.

NB: And you never did that again?

CM: I never did that again. And also I never had a clear vision of a book like that. *Reflex and Bone Structure* was a mock detective story or a kind of murder mystery and that's all I had in my mind, that I was going to do this very, very strange murder mystery. But I never knew from day to day where it was going. I would just sit there and say, "OK, typewriter, here I am" and that's the way I took it from day to day. In the subsequent drafts [it] became a lot clearer to me what I could do with it, but the first draft was a learning process, unlike it was for *NO.*

And then the same is true all over again with *Emergency Exit.* It took seven, eight years to write that and during the first two years there were some very bleak moments when I did not know whether I'd be able to finish it. I had a vision of the whole thing as early as the second year, but I did not really know that I could pull it off. There were times when I didn't believe I could do it. And so even with the vision, I wasn't able to do it the way that I did *NO* which was easy and spontaneous. It was a struggle and I had to throw away a lot; I had to rewrite and revise and reshape and pull parts out and reshuffle parts and all those kinds of really frustrating and aggravating things. I'm not able to say I have now enough experience to go forward and write my books . . .

NB: Easily.

CM: Because I don't. I can't really use the experience. It's not like an automobile mechanic who works on Volkswagens and he knows Volkswagens, so he's able to really use that knowledge and it carries over from car to car.

NB: So it really is a matter of starting over every day.

CM: And starting over every day with complete innocence, with no tools. It involves discovering a new approach with each time, with each step. I could write to a formula, and write the same book over and over. Some writers do that and I'm sure it's a lot easier and less aggravating. Probably they make more money doing that; but in the long run, I don't think it would be very satisfying to do the same book over and over with different names. I really welcome the challenge. I'm not knocking it; I think it's vital and it's the only way to attempt to write anything that has any vitality.

NB: Do you think that writing clarifies your sense of yourself?

CM: I'm sure that's true, but I'm not sure that it happens in the same way all the time; what I think happens is that very often you'll look back at something you wrote, say, a year ago or two years ago or maybe ten years ago, and understand something about yourself that you didn't understand while you were making that piece of writing. Or you become very aware in the very process. So the learning process, for me, is never the same. I just finished a book about the late actress Dorothy Dandridge who committed suicide in 1965. It's a fictional treatment of her life, but I discovered while writing the book, a lot of things about my own outlook, about my own experiences, my own attitudes and prejudices, everything, through the process of trying to project myself into her, into her sensibility, into her mind, into her outlook.

NB: In a couple of things I read, you seem to condemn social realism.

CM: Oh, I still think that. I think that. I don't think that I've fallen into that trap in writing this Dorothy Dandridge book. In a way, I don't want to say this too often, I think that it's really a book as much about myself as it is about Dorothy Dandridge. The average commercial reader would not want to hear a statement like that. That's the kind of thing that if it's true, it should not be there as an interference for the average reader. Writers are usually writerly readers, so it's OK to know that sort of thing. Even if it is an interference, it's OK because you can read the writing or you can read the story or you can read both at the same time. I think it's possible to make the language have a life of its own. This is what I think does not happen in realistic fiction.

NB: Because they're interested in . . .

CM: They're interested in the story and they want the language to be transparent; the language is supposed to be some sort of window through which you see the experience. But I think that realistic fiction that pays attention to the life of the language itself and which allows the story to move is vital and has a chance of lasting. There are a lot of good examples of that kind of fiction around today and have been for the last thirty-forty years. Saul Bellow, for example, I think, writes very writerly fiction, and it's also readerly. There are so many others I could name.

NB: It's hard for me to read experimental fiction and that upsets me because your comments on the limits of realistic fiction make sense to me. Something you said about poetry and prose may explain my problem: "The distinction I had made all along between poetry and prose I gradually realized was and has been a serious trap. For me, at least, it was false and it had been hanging me up. I came to see what I had been trying to do in making a novel was the same thing I meant to do in producing a poem." I can read poetry that's not narrative, because I expect that; but when I pick up a novel, I think "This is supposed to go a certain way," so when it doesn't go that way . . .

CM: Right. I'm forever bewildered by that. People can read poetry and accept the most incredible leaps of the imagination and the most incredible experimental things and they can also watch surrealistic movies; even Buster Keaton and Charlie Chaplin were very radical in terms of the visual experience and the kinds of things that they did with so-called reality. You can see it especially in Chaplin, in things like *Modern Times;* the audience has no problem accepting *Modern Times* on the screen and yet they cannot sit down with a novel like Bathelme's *The Dead Father,* for example, and read that with as much interest because . . . I think it has to do with conditioning; it has to do with what we expect of language. The primary problem is that language is the thing we use to relate to each other and therefore, it's forever changing and losing its stance and losing its ability to hold still. For instance, paint or ink on paper will stay pretty much the way it was put on paper for a long time. But language changes and so a book that was written 100 years ago becomes not only a literary experience when you read it, it's also a historical experience because that language is not our language anymore; though that ink on paper 100 years ago is still ink on paper today, so the experience hasn't been subjected to such an incredible change in our perception of the materials. Literature is unlike any art form because it has the problem of language as its material, and also the problem of our perception which is always gauged out of this thing we call reality,

NB: You've said things that imply to me that you believe in order to write anything original or interesting, you have to get as close to your perception of things as you can.

CM: I don't remember saying that, but it sounds true. *(Laughter.)* I would say that it's very complex and difficult because this whole idea of getting into yourself constitutes a problem because if you're writing from an intensive, personal, subjective point of view, you're also facing the inevitable problem of near-sightedness. You're very likely to miss something. One example: I was living in New York. I was walking along the street and passing in front of the laundromat and a dog was tied to the parking meter. A little girl came out of the laundromat to pet the dog and the dog bit off her ear. Whack! Just like that. A lot of people gathered around and it was a very tragic moment. It was not the thing you would expect on a casual afternoon; people were feeling good in the city; it was one of the first warm days. I tried to write a poem about it. I wanted to say something about how it affected me and what the implications were: how unsafe I felt we all were, forever. To try to put that on paper proved to be extremely difficult and finally, impossible. I was just too close to it. I tried to do it that very day. What we very often need is some distance, not just from the experience, but from ourselves, in order to write anything worthwhile.

That distance is very necessary and can be achieved in different ways. I think it's possible to do a first draft, for example, and put it away. Usually that's my process. I'll do a first draft of something and won't know how I feel about it. I'll put it away and look at it six months later, three weeks later, sometimes two years later, and then I can start working at the thing in some sort of objective way, so that I can see what's there in a way that I wasn't able to see in the beginning. But that's my process. I tend to overwrite and have to cut a lot, so usually what I do is look for the essence of if and try to refocus the thing and glean out whatever vitality might be there.

NB: You write a lot about letting things happen when you're writing. Is that what you're saying now? You let it happen and then you sift it?

CM: First of all, I put it on the paper to try to see what it is, because I don't know, and then when I can see what it's trying to be, I go back and I try to reshape it and impose a kind of order upon it and focus and direction. But I don't necessarily encourage my students to write that way. We're all individuals and we're all different. There are many, many ways in which things can be accomplished. What I try to do is understand their processes and it's really interesting for me to see all those different ways that things can be made, watching the students work.

NB: So you try to understand how they go about it and then reinforce whatever . . .

CM: Yeah, right. And I don't ever impose a group assignment, but I make assignments optional so that they can pick and choose because they work in different ways and on a different basis and it would be unreasonable to try to make them all in my image.

NB: Or encourage them to do anything in a certain way.

CM: Right. Except their way.

NB: That must be exhausting.

CM: It is, it is. *(Laughter.)*

NB: Someone else I've spoken with said that his students think that all good writing makes an important point and so they spend all their energy trying to think up a significant thesis. Have you seen that problem in your students?

CM: Well, that's very true of my students, especially the fiction writers. They will have an argument that they need to give expression to and they will build the story around the argument. There are different ways I go at that. There is a student in one of my classes now who writes really excellent satirical pieces about political situations and you can see that the fiction is really there as a kind of conveyer for this argument. Well, then you think, that's what the history of satire has always been, really. You look back to Swift; you look back to Nathaniel West. I think it's OK and probably works pretty well, and it certainly has a substantial history and tradition. But the other kind is a lot more aggravating, where the students really have some sort of muddled notion of what the point of view should be and so on and really try to decorate that idea with a few pages of careless prose. That's a lot more disturbing from my point of view.

NB: What do you do?

CM: I do several things, depending on the situation. *(Laughter.)* I would try the positive approach and try to find ways to use these pieces in different ways to discuss writing problems. But I run into the problem of so many students being in workshop who are there for approval rather than tough, hard criticism and that's one of the more difficult things that I have to face in dealing with the kinds of manuscripts that are, quote—not worth talking about—unquote. These people are paying as much as anyone else, so they deserve their money's worth. I try to find whatever is useful in these things to serve as an example for the whole class without alienating the person, but there is always that problem.

A great example: I once worked with a woman and she was a very careless writer. She was a very frustrated housewife and full of anger and wanted to get out into the world and feel her presence, which was fine; but she came into the workshop with the wrong kind of attitude: she wanted a support group rather than criticism. She wanted encouragement and hopefully, I do give encouragement; but she wanted enthusiastic response and she certainly deserved it, but she probably should have gone to a support group. Her writing was just embarrassingly bad.

And then there are people who feel like they want to spend the rest of their lives writing and they shouldn't do that. What do you tell them? And so those are the difficult, sensitive moments; but those situations don't present themselves very often because usually the student serious about writing will have enough self-knowledge, self-confidence and talent to know whether or not he can expect recommendations, etc., encouragement . . .

I don't believe that I can always help anyone become a better writer, but I think I can always help them become better readers and then become more sensitive to the language and how it's put together. They take that writerly experience back to the reading process; I've seen it happen. They understand something of the process and therefore, they can read with greater sensitivity, and more pleasure too.

There are three or four, five perhaps, in each class that are really good. I've worked with students who have published books over the years and who are now beginning to make names for themselves. So that's very satisfying and I like to think that I had some small part, anyway, in their development. There is so much talent, it's just incredible. I'm sure most of it will just go down the drain and will never develop and I'm sure that happens with every generation.

NB: Why? Because they don't need to write?

CM: Because they don't need to write. Very often you get someone without any talent at all.

NB: Who needs to write?

CM: Who needs to write *(laughter)*—and that person will hit the top of the best-seller list in five or six years. It happens all the time. It's OK; it's the way it should be, I suppose. Well, it's not the way it should be.

NB: I gather from some of the things you've written that you're not very enthusiastic about people writing to make money.

CM: Well, I think that money from writing should be made accidentally; I don't think you should plan it. I don't think a writer should sit down and write a book for money; it's not a wholesome, healthy motivation for writing poetry or fiction because . . . We have a recent literary situation in this country and Europe as evidence of that. All the worst things that Fitzgerald did he wrote for money. All of his slap-dash stories for the *Saturday Review* aren't really taken that seriously; every once in a while, a critic will say, "Well, those stories are worth taking a look at again. They're not really so bad." But they really are bad because they were manufactured pretty much to a formula for money and compared to the kinds of things Hemingway did with the short story . . . If you compare the two, you can see how Hemingway allowed himself a greater sense of freedom and certainly he started with a healthier motivation.

The problem in writing for money is that, almost without exception, one allows one's knowledge of the market to dictate the form and direction of the work. And the market place and its notions of how things ought to be, is invariably wrong or shallow or mediocre; all those structures that have been tested, have proven to be sellable, are the kinds of structures that editors and publishers try to insist on.

NB: What about the view that writing programs are irresponsible because they are staffed with people like you who don't want to teach people how to make a lot of money writing, so you're taking money from these people and giving them nothing.

CM: I believe in making money and I believe in making money from writing. I know she's not a good example of a moneymaking writer, *(laughter)* but Gertrude Stein said something that is very, very fitting: she said that the writer should force the world to see things his way rather than adapting himself to the outlook of the world. I think you can address that statement to the conflict between the editor and the writer: the editor wants the writer to adapt himself to the formulas that have already proven successful, and she is saying, on the other hand, that the successful writer is a writer who invents a new way of seeing the world rather than simply imitating the old tested ways of seeing the world. I think it's possible to make money Gertrude Stein's way . . . Well, Hemingway certainly made a lot of money. I can think of a lot of excellent writers who made a lot of money; Dickens made a lot of money.

NB: In the introduction to your collection, *The New Black Poetry,* you said, "Unlike most contemporary white poets, we are profoundly conscious of forces that ironically protect us from the empty patterns of intellectual gentility and individualism and at the same time keep our approach fresh." It seems to me that the intellectual gentility doesn't produce that many writers; at least, I don't think many of the people I've spoken with would see themselves as products of the intellectual gentility, nor would they be seen that way by others.

CM: Well, it's probably true, for the most part, but it's also strange, isn't it, because writers always, until very recently, came from the upper classes. They were the only ones who had any time to write or even think about writing or doing any of the arts. There are few exceptions to that: Millet, for example, who was a peasant and on the doorstep of starvation half the time and I'm sure there are others; but, yeah, the social changes that have taken place since the French Revolution probably turned the whole world upside down. The kinds of suffering that people from the lower classes or lower-middle classes perceive, I think, really became more vital in terms of their implications in art than the kinds of perceptions that were coming from the upper classes.

My wife is working on her dissertation and she has done a lot of research on myth, ritual and metaphor, also on the early Spanish picaresque novel and by watching over her shoulder, I've learned that the early picaresque novel is almost without exception about the downtrodden, the vagabonds, or the outsiders. These books were written by people from the upper classes; even that early, the kinds of perceptions made from the lower depths, so to speak, about thieves and prostitutes and so on, were considered even then, four or five hundred years ago, as perhaps more vital or at least more interesting. That was certainly the forerunner, I think, of the modern novel.

NB: Someone I talked to suggested that in order to have anything to say, you have to put yourself in different social contexts; you have to put yourself in situations where you see things from a new angle.

CM: I think that's very true. I don't think you can feel safe and write any vital fiction. I think you have to place yourself in a position where a lot of forces are at work. As I say this, I'm also aware in the back of my head of all kinds of exceptions to this rule. I think about the fact that Rubens, the painter, was a comfortable middle-class man in politics and did some remarkable paintings. And William Carlos Williams was a baby doctor who never went without money. On the other hand, Modigliani was walking through alleys practically feeding himself out of garbage cans. So I think great art can come from any class, but I think it's a nice idea that one has to suffer in a garret somewhere in order to produce a great piece. It's probably true for a large number of people and it's certainly true for me. For many years I was living a dangerous kind of existence. I lived in New York for twelve years; I was not in the safe world of the university with a nice insurance policy and tenure and all those very nice things, so I was constantly working out from that place of insecurity. You can't argue with your own experience; it's there! But I don't think you can generalize.

NB: I have a couple of paragraphs of yours here that I didn't understand completely. The first one is: "See all this heavy disenchantment spreading through the early 1970s? It came from well-composed minds. People go mad only because they begin from something called logic. You have to be saved. And the way is through the lingo of magic understanding and a trust in the Dark and Feeling. They interchange."

CM: Wow! You want me to comment on that? Actually, what I was saying, I think, in simple language, is that one should trust one's instincts and if you're a writer, if you're trying to make a work of art out of prose or poetry, you have to go with your instincts. Follow them and you can use that knowledge that is there. It knows more than we know.

NB: And when people with well-composed minds order things, it twists everything?
CM: Yeah.

NB: Then the next paragraph says, "You can call it political action if you wanna but you get turned around, trapped in match and the spell of Rap. Dark and Feeling have moved nations since the beginning of man's reaction to woman's awesome ability to give birth to man *and* woman. It's how civilization began."

CM: Well, I got carried away. *(Laughter.)* But anyway, it's still about that trust of instinct, but I was getting at this whole thing about the woman being at the root of all . . . Nobody knows for sure, but it's one of my beliefs that there were, before recorded history, cultures in which women were either equal or leaders and I'd like to believe that those cultures were better than outs in some ways, that the people in those cultures were in touch with themselves in a way that we have not been because of our male-oriented cultures. If I had any religion, I don't have any religion, actively, but it's one of my pet peeves . . . The world probably would have been better off had women maintained their earlier stance. I think of it as a conspiracy, the whole arrival of civilization, as the act that put men in power, that made woman powerless.

NB: Why?

CM: Let me see if I can articulate it. I think that probably men set up systems in which they were able to gain some security at the expense of women. They had to establish their relationship with their god and in order to build that and to sustain that, they had to subject women to a kind of servitude; they had to create a distance between themselves and women in order to sustain their own identities and to create the false security that has always underscored their existence. And I think this happened because women were mysterious; they were associated with all these mysterious things like blood and birth . . .

NB: I think I read this in *Emergency Exit.*

CM: Oh, was this in *Emergency Exit?* Yeah, well I think that's where it all stemmed from; I think it all came out of that need to put that mystery at a distance and keep it under control. And in order to keep it under control, women had to be reduced socially.

Now how the conspiracy took place has been dealt with by several different kinds of researchers, anthropologists, historians, and so on. The act of conspiracy took place as a result of cultural factors like the mastery of writing, for example, or the making of picture language, which gave men—I don't know why men were the ones to create it, but they were—a kind of weapon for controlling and manipulating women. Levi-Strauss thinks language is the turning point, the invention of language. There are some researchers who believe that conspiracy evolved in the nature of language as a weapon rather than to be used in art, even the art of cave drawings of animals. All of that inspired language, too, in a sense. That's the kind of language I'm talking about. Earlier than that even, just magical utterings of some early tribal people. It's all also connected with metaphor and myth too; all of that is interwoven in the sense that the process of looking at an object and establishing a relationship between that object and a sound, for example, metaphor in that very primitive sense. Now why that should have been the property of men, I don't know. And I'm not altogether convinced that it was solely the property of men in those early tribal cultures except in the sense that it was used as conspiracy.

I remember one tribe that I read about had the practice of taking boys who were ready for the puberty rites . . . The men would take them out into the forest and would tell the women that they were going to take the boys to listen to God. And then they would tie a rock on a string and swing it around and the motion made a very loud, bizarre sound that the women could hear back in the village and they were told that that was the voice of God and that the boys were being introduced to God and therefore, they were privileged. That God is a metaphor and it's also language. So in that sense, that was the private property of men; women were not privileged to speak the language of God. And in early Christian cultures, man was made in God's image. I hadn't made those connections before his moment. Really, I'm not sure, but I think there might be something there.

NB: A large number of the people I've spoken with talk about the importance of having their students read aloud and listen to their writing. Is that . . .

CM: Yeah, I think so. Especially in poetry, but also in fiction. I will have certain kinds of prose read in class because they lend themselves to that kind of expression; it's not just a visual experience. I certainly learn a lot by reading my work in public; it's a way of educating myself in public, or not educating myself, but rewriting, which is an educational process. And a way of getting distance too, looking at my work from different angles. Very often right in front of an audience, I will make a mental note to change something I'm reading because I've suddenly had the experience of seeing what's wrong with it as I'm reading it. So I think it's important.

NB: One article I read suggested having the students talk into tape recorders and then write from that material. The author said he thought that would make what they wrote more honest because people tend to lie when they write.

CM: They only think of writing as an approximation of their speech and the extent of our normal experience with writing is to write a letter to someone and it's not really the same. It's always the same tired, worn-out expressions: "Dear Betty, I'm sorry that I didn't write earlier . . ." rather than doing it the way we would speak. We get into the habit of thinking that writing cannot be an instrument of the voice, but the most effective writing always has been an approximation of the voice. I'm always trying to get students to write in their own voices and also to write out of their experiences and to write about what they know about and part of that process involves using an approximation of their own speech, not the way Shakespeare wrote and talked.

NB: That sounds good. I had a student last year who used inflated language, because he was scared, I guess, and when he came to my office, I had him read his paper out loud. He knew right away what the problem was.

CM: I run into it all the time with students who will get fascinated with a certain writer and they'll be writing that writer's prose. That's fine as a learning process, but one should move beyond that and constantly think in terms of moving toward one's own voice and one's own speech and one's own rhythms. That idiom is a vital part of the experiences they should be writing about.

Most students in college today aren't going to have any opportunity to be in touch with who they are and where they come from in such an intense way ever again as they will in a workshop. They will go into different kinds of things: business, engineering, the sciences; but hopefully, they will remember how important it was to create a wedding of that voice that was theirs and that history that was theirs. No matter how much television one watches or how many movies one watches, the kinds of associations produced by those kinds of experiences remain marginal and accidental and incidental; they won't be like the experience of writing and discovering one's voice and creating that bridge to an audience. That's an entirely unique experience that there is no substitute for.

CU Professor Savors Literary Award

Margaret Carlin / 1986

From *Rocky Mountain News* (April 29, 1986), 35. Reprinted with permission of the Denver *Rocky Mountain News.*

As a skinny, scholarly 12-year-old growing up in a Chicago ghetto, Clarence Major knew he was different from the other kids.

"All I ever wanted to be was an artist and a writer," he says. "I think, looking back now, that I became entranced with poetry when I was about 4, and my mother made up a poem for me.

"That excited me, it gave me the notion that a person could do things with words—that poems didn't have to come out of big fancy books way up on shelves, they could come directly from somebody's heart."

Major, 49, is a professor of English at the University of Colorado at Boulder, an accomplished artist and much published poet and novelist.

Now he is savoring his most prestigious award to date—he has won the 1986 Western States Book Award for Fiction for *My Amputations* published by Fiction Collective, New York.

He will receive a $2,500 prize and his publisher receives $5,000. The award ceremony is May 23 at the annual convention of the American Booksellers Association in New Orleans.

Major says *My Amputations* is not autobiographical. "Any novelist uses his background and experiences in whatever he writes," he says. "A writer can only hope to work the truth of an experience into the story. No human can write purely from imagination.

"I've kept the idea for this book since 1971, when a strange thing happened. A man got into my publisher's offices in New York and insisted he was me—he wanted my royalty checks. He was convinced I was stealing his identity."

Major's novel recounts the picaresque adventures of Mason Ellis, a man in search of himself. Ellis is a black who grows up in the Chicago slums and dreams of becoming a writer. He winds up in prison, but he is convinced that he really is a major American novelist he sees on TV. Ellis' quest for his identity leads him across the United States, Europe and Africa, with many adventures, some hilarious and some hair-raising.

Like many young men, Major used the service as a springboard out of the ghetto. He joined the Air Force and spent most of his 4 years in Cheyenne and Atlanta.

"What did I learn?" he muses over the answer. "Well, the most important thing I learned to do was type. I also discovered the base libraries and read every book on the shelves. The Air Force is where I discovered Gertrude Stein, Nathaniel Hawthorne, Herman Melville, Joseph Conrad. I began to get an idea of the beauty and majesty of the English language. I teach Conrad today, especially *The Secret Sharer* and *The Heart of Darkness.*"

In fact, Major considers Conrad one of the "most profound voices in literature; his language is so raw and awkward, so truthful, like ordinary conversation, so wonderful, really."

After attending the Art Institute of Chicago and getting a degree from University of New York at Albany, Major earned a doctorate from Union Graduate School at Cincinnati. He is a specialist in contemporary American fiction and poetry and has lectured in Europe and Africa. He has written four other experimental novels and nine books of poetry.

As a boy, Major's dream was to live the romantic life of an expatriate in Paris, preferably on the legendary Left Bank. That dream never came true exactly, but Major has lived in France and Italy on various writing and teaching grants and has lectured in many countries.

He has been teaching on the college level for 20 years, and he finds that writing three days a week and teaching two days works best. "Writing is so lonely, and it helps me to get out among the students," he says.

His novel in progress involves a 68-year-old black woman in Atlanta and the political machinations of her powerful minister son and other members of her family. "It's all fiction," Major says, "but it's based on things I know quite a lot about. I have visited Atlanta and know members of the Martin Luther King family."

About his method of writing, Major says: "When I travel, I make lots of notes, because I know I might want to include a particular city or country as background in a novel some day. I get a great deal of enjoyment from observing people. When we lived in Nice (France), we always went to a few favorite cafes, we liked to watch the people come and go."

Although Major frequently is described as an "experimental" writer, he says he follows conventional rules—he uses outlines. "I make a broad outline first, and then fill in or change as I go, but I usually try to know where I am going."

Like many prolific writers, Major does not depend upon divine inspiration. He believes in sitting down at his computer and writing—on a daily scheduled basis.

But what he really is, he says, is disciplined. "Everyone, especially my wife, calls me a workaholic. I'm a Capricorn, the goat, always consistently climbing up the mountain, no matter what."

Major writes every morning. "Usually for three to four hours, intensely. After that, I kind of lose it, so then I read proof (of books) or do other things, gardening, cooking, that kind of stuff. It relaxes me."

Although Major was just coming into his own in the racially turbulent United States of the 1960s, militancy was never part of his baggage.

"Even from the first, I kept writing about the human condition, not necessarily the black condition," he says. "I do not write racial literature; I am a human being first, and then a black man. I write books about who are black, yes, but they are human beings first. Of course, I am a member of my family, my race, my culture, but I feel a kinship with people of good will and integrity, no matter their color or background."

Major does admire contemporary black literature, however, with the works of Charles Wright, Al Young, Ishmael Reed, James McPherson, John Wideman and Ntozake Shange high on his list.

He has been married for 7 years to the former Pamela Jane Ritter, who has a doctorate in literature from the University of Massachusetts and is his most valued critic. "She gives me really good feedback; she tells me if I'm getting way off the track."

The couple met at the home of mutual friends in Boulder. "We couldn't come from more different backgrounds," Major says. "She's sophisticated and has traveled a lot, surely that is true, but she did grow up protected in rural Iowa.

"I grew up in a Chicago ghetto and my parents were divorced. Our worlds were so different, but we get along fine. I guess you can call me a humanist; I believe in the goodness and worth of the human being first and foremost."

Transition Is Tugging at a Local Avant-Garde Author

Alan Katz / 1986

From *The Denver Post* (June 15, 1986), D1. Reprinted by permission of *The Denver Post.*

"Good writing is thinking clearly." That's what Roger Angell, fiction editor of the *New Yorker,* said in an interview last year in an interview with the *Denver Post.*

It's an opinion editors often express, but it poses a question. How can one write simply about something as complicated as, say, the identity of a black man growing up in America? Must "thinking clearly" translate into writing simply?

For avant-garde author Clarence Major, nothing about writing is simple. Critics have complained, perhaps a bit unfairly, that his work is dense, encoded, that it requires five or six readings. Even by his own admission, Major is a difficult author to read. His novel *My Amputations* which recently won the Western States Book Award for Fiction, is written in block style rather than paragraphs and is packed with obscure poetic imagery. Compounding the book's complexity is its narrator, who suffers from a dual identity.

During a recent interview in his study, a large remodeled tool shed adjoining his Boulder home, Major said that *My Amputations* arose from a real-life experience. He was living in New York in 1971 when a parolee from a prison hospital barged into his publisher's office, introduced himself as Clarence Major and demanded a royalty check.

When the secretary, who knew Major, refused to hand over the money, the ex-convict threatened her with a knife. Fortunately, he was dissuaded from using it.

"I was nervous about it for a week or two," Major said. "By and by, I moved to Connecticut to teach at Sarah Lawrence, and eventually I didn't think about it anymore. Many years later, when my wife and I went to France on a Fulbright, it occurred to me that that would be the basis for a novel."

Another novelist might have taken the same material and written a taut commercial detective story. Major decided his book would be about a young black man's struggle to establish an identity. But he couldn't begin writing it until one day, walking up a mountain trail in Nice, he saw the book in his mind's eye in long Faulknerian blocks of prose. He also wanted the narrator's voice to be intelligent, slangy and witty.

"I wanted to emphasize the important fact that a lower-class, disadvantaged character who spent time in prison could be brilliant, lyrical and sensitive," he said.

Experimental writers like Major usually toil in obscurity their entire lives, taking heart when the *New York Times* reviews their work or when graduate students analyze it in dissertations. Usually there is pressure, financial or otherwise, to re-evaluate one's own work and simplify it.

"I think I'm in a transition," the 49-year-old author said. "I'm in a stage where I want to try some experiments, perhaps be less ambiguous. It isn't just a calculated decision. It's really coming out of an understanding I've gravitated toward. The complexity of my early poetry and fiction is a result of my own struggle mentally—my own inability to articulate a whole network of feelings."

Major recently finished a linear novel about the Zuni Indians called *Painted Turtle.* He calls this book "a personal breakthrough." Now he's writing another novel, *June Boy,* about Atlanta politics and the relationship between government and church.

A professor in the University of Colorado's English department for nine years, Major grew up on Chicago's South Side and studied at the Art Institute of Chicago before attending State University of New York. His first ambition was to be a painter; today, he calls his writing style "painterly."

Among his other books is *Dictionary of Afro-American Slang,* derived partly from memory, partly from research, partly, he said, from a book Cab Calloway penned in the 1930s called *Hipster's Jive Talk.*

He has written four other novels—*All-Night Visitors, NO, Reflex and Bone Structure* and *Emergency Exit*—and six books of poetry. Occasionally he writes book reviews for newspapers and literary journals.

Critic George Davis in the *New York Times,* reviewing Major's 1973 novel *NO,* compared his writing to Ishmael Reed's calling them "the mavericks of the new black poetry."

But Major sees his major theme as the American identity. "I'm very much concerned," he said, "with the precise point that the ethnic identity and the

American identity meet. I'm convinced that a lot of people are more black than American. And a lot of people are more Jewish or Eastern European than American."

Black writers, he said, can be compared to Jewish writers. Saul Bellow and Bernard Malamud are concerned with ghetto-oriented characters who are more Jewish than American, while Phillip Roth's characters are more American than Jewish. "And then," he added, "you have the ones at the other extreme, like Norman Mailer, who doesn't write about Jews."

Completing the analogy, he spoke of Willard Motley, the black author of the 1950s who wrote *Knock on Any Door.*

"Motley was concerned with ethnic identity, and that point at which there is a struggle in one direction or another," Major said. "Charles Wright, a more contemporary writer who wrote *The Wig* and *The Messenger*—his characters are black, usually, but it isn't the totality of their identity. They're very American in their obsessions: They want to make it. They want money. They have all these American values. Or they're very jaded and dejected and isolated. In other words, blackness isn't necessarily the most important thing about them.

"Ishmael Reed is also one of those writers whose characters are as much American as they are black. I would include myself in that category," Major said.

"To other black writers like James Baldwin and Richard Wright, race is obviously a dominant factor. The relationship between ethnic identity and the American experience is more at war in Richard Wright's work than in Charles Wright's. But even Richard Wright is trying to resolve the crisis.

"I think that is the American theme, inescapably, for just about any writer true to his gut-level experience."

Asked if he's satisfied with the recognition he's received, the soft-spoken Major laughed and replied, "I don't think any writer ever gets enough. Recognition makes you feel like you're not in a vacuum, or in limbo, or talking to the wall. All art attempts to communicate. If you think you're communicating and no one gives a damn, then where are you?

"I agree that good writing has to be simple and well-focused, with a well-defined point of view," he added. "But I think what happens is, although one wishes to achieve that kind of simplicity, one is working with material that is enormously complex. The trick is to get it into a well-focused, direct, beautiful form.

"Let's take Hemingway, for example. He started off as an avant-garde writer in the truest sense of the word, along with Gertrude Stein and Ezra Pound. It was new and fresh and challenging—and nobody had ever seen that kind of simplicity.

"It challenged the tradition."

Major's Passion for Life Transcends Life's Hazards

Anonymous / 1988

From *Inside SUNY Binghamton* (April 7, 1988). Reprinted by permission of *Inside SUNY Binghamton.*

Clarence Major's "need to write was inseparable from the educational process. It began at the beginning and never ended." It was fed by everything he read, everything he learned, everything he witnessed, dreamed or imagined, Major said.

The author, the 1988 Visiting Professor of Creative Writing, discussed "Necessary Distance: Afterthoughts on Becoming a Writer," with a small group of faculty members and students on March 16. Major is author of *Such Was the Season,* a book that won critical acclaim in the *New York Times Book Review* and elsewhere, and recipient of a Pushcart Prize.

"Why did I become a writer? How did I become a writer? Every writer is asked those questions over and over," he began. Major first attempted to answer those questions as he tackled his autobiography.

His education began, he said, when he "shed his self-centered idea of self, when I saw myself mirrored in my mother's eyes. That's when the impulse to be a writer, to be a painter, began. Without my knowing it, my career had begun." A writer, he observed, must "learn to keep his ego, yet lose it at the same time, yet be an observer of himself and others in his social domain."

Born to a family too poor to afford luxuries, Major said he was driven to transform scraps into playtoys. "That showed me the possibilities. A poem is after all, like a machine. The connection between what I was creating at seven and what I later wrote is a given."

Major says he was a "guilty practitioner" of daydreaming and had an "almost mystical approach to nature. I could spend hours looking at a leaf, or on my knees watching ants or following the flight of birds with an almost spiritual devotion." Dreams also inspired him. "In dreams, I discovered a self going about its business with a mind of its own . . . engaging in one guilty pleasure after another. Those inventions became the rootbed of all I wanted to take charge of in harsh daylight. I tried to imitate those imaginative leaps . . . in my poems and fiction."

About the same time, he discovered "that writing had a life of its own," and sought books that "changed my perspective." Major was influenced by Hawthorne, Joseph Conrad, Baudelaire, and others, reading outside school while his classmates were reading O'Henry and Joyce Kilmer.

He gained much from his ponderings, dreams, and reading, but his parents saw those as "bad signs," he says, indications of laziness and values that belied their beliefs.

In fact, Major hit disapproval everywhere he turned while growing up in Chicago's south side. He often kept his passions both for writing and painting secret. "The goals of society were to make money, get an education and a job, go to church, marry and have a family, roughly in that order . . . I had to hide my plans to become a writer. Why wasn't I, after all, out there playing basketball?

"One didn't let down one's guard in the school. Anyone who demonstrated intelligence wasn't 'cool.' Smart boys were sissies who deserved to get their butts kicked."

In retrospect, he says "I must have been a difficult student for teachers to understand." As he hid his light under a bushel, or occasionally revealed it, one teacher thought him "sort of smart," another called him a genius, a third believed him retarded. He learned to survive with cunning rather than his fists on the playground and risked taunts of "sissy" for the poetry his wrote. His mother encouraged him "as much as her understanding permitted." So did an occasional teacher and a family friend. One teacher gave him a back-handed compliment. She told him that he couldn't have written what he submitted—it was too good.

For Major, painting went hand-in-hand with writing. As a boy, he took private art lessons, painted long before he mastered words, and drew inspiration from exhibits of Van Gogh and Cezanne. He painted all he saw—his mother sick in bed, scenes from his neighborhood, "anything that was compositionally viable. I was learning to see." The first poems he wrote were "strongly imagistic." He related painting to writing, drawing parallels, for instance, between perspective and point of view.

The author's family moved often, from Atlanta, to a rural setting, to Chicago. "My sense of place was always changing," he explained.

During his teen years, Major acquired the command of language to match his need to write, learned to live with rejection, to "detect my own failures and be the first to reject them," and solved the problem of publication. At 12, he wrote his first novel, all 20 pages of it, and sent it to Hollywood. "I got it back with a note of encouragement." At 14, he paid his uncle $10 to print his poetry in a pamphlet. "Then I realized that I didn't know three people who would be interested in it." He gave one to his mother, one to his teacher, and stored the rest. Years later, he destroyed them when he discovered "how bad the poetry was."

Then he started a literary magazine, "a substitute for an artistic community," through which he communicated with the other artists so lacking in his environment. Major subdued his desire to rush into print. "It taught me that I needed distance and to slow down, to see if a manuscript could stand up under subsequent editings. I became more selective in what I sent out."

"As I look back, I was always more fascinated by technique than the subject matter. The content was almost irrelevant. I was fascinated with how the painter, storyteller, poet seduced me into the picture, the story, the poem."

Major's quest "to gain insight in myself and into the nature of creativity itself," directed him to anthropology, sociology, religion, music, psychology, philosophy. "I kept searching for a better approach to human existence. But each quest left me with more questions than when I started."

"Was there a point at which I knew I wanted to be a writer? Probably, but it was irrelevant. I had been evolving toward that consciousness long before I was aware of what was going on."

"The long, unfinished process toward that goal" continues, Major concluded. "I'm still asking: Who am I? What am I?"

Clarence Major: Finding the
Universal through the Specific

Paul Kafka / 1989

From *The Sunday Camera Magazine, The Boulder Daily Camera* (June 4, 1989), 6–7. Reprinted courtesy of *The Boulder Daily Camera*.

Clarence Major, author of seven novels and eight books of poetry, is professor of literature and creative writing at the University of Colorado, Boulder. His work offers a unique contribution to American letters. Several of his novels establish him as one of the most important avant garde stylists working today. In his three most recent novels, *My Amputations* (Western States Book Award 1986); *Such Was the Season* (Literary Guild Selection 1987); and *Painted Turtle: Woman with Guitar* (*New York Times* notable book of the year, 1988), Major delights a wide audience with his gift for imaginative story-telling and poetic evocation.

Q: What are you working on these days?

CM: I'm working on a novel called *Faber Unauthorized*. I've discovered that it's about the same themes my books tend to grapple with. Alienation. The search for identity. Ways to connect with community, with family. Ways to mend the wounds of living.

I know in the back of my mind that I always write about these things. But I was struck this morning by just how much the new novel is continuous with my other work, and at the same time much more hopeful.

Q: What is the novel about?

CM: The narrator, Faber, is a black American writer who's born in 1915 and dies in 1976. He really gives me a chance to look at the first part of the 20th century. To see the enormous changes that occurred, and how they affected the life of a man who begins in a shack in the south and travels through the world to a position of relative fame and wealth. He lives in New York, in Paris, becomes a war correspondent for the Associated Negro Press. There was, of course, a black army and a white army in World War II.

The book is in part an epistolary novel—Faber writes letters to his wife, letters to his mistress, to friends, comrades, strangers. It's a patchwork. There are also journal entries, poems. What I'm hoping to create is a tapestry, a portrait of a life and time. He tries to heal himself and he succeeds in a way that none of my other characters have.

Q: Do you think that being a recognizably black writer is a choice for you?

CM: I think we only choose so much. A lot of what I write is a given, a cultural frame of reference. You come to terms with that and you do as much as you can to shape yourself in space and time. What I try to do is to make sure my work is not purely sociological, to make sure that I'm in touch with larger forces in life. You want to transcend your own boundaries through the particular, through the fiction in its strongest specificity. If I can find out what the particular nuances of my experience at one moment in history are, then I think I've reached the universal.

The danger that so many black writers face is that they can't escape their sociological trappings. It used to be called the "iron cage of protest writing." Those early writers were trapped. The real challenge is to be able to work with what you know, scene by scene, line by line and find what your true focus is. To know that you're not writing a political tract.

Q: In *Painted Turtle: Woman with Guitar,* you portray a woman musician who lifts herself out of the social and political jails into which she is born. Did you intend Painted Turtle (the character) to be emblematic of a kind of struggle?

CM: I wasn't so much concerned with making her representative of any one kind of struggle, although she is a woman and an artist. If she's a revolutionary, she's not a conscious one.

Q: In *Painted Turtle,* a man tells the story of a woman's life. Yet the novel never reduces Painted Turtle to the status of a lovely object for male contemplation and self-congratulation. How did you avoid this?

CM: I didn't know what I was setting out to do. Like so many of my books, *Painted Turtle* came out of a failure. It was supposed to be a novel about another woman—a black woman. Then I let Painted Turtle herself, a Zuni woman, tell her own story. That was also a failure. I discovered that I had to back off, to follow her story through male eyes.

I finally wrote a kind of love story about a woman who tries to find her way in a very hostile world. Her man, who is Navajo-Hopi, has faced similar difficulties in his home. I guess I wanted to portray two honest people.

Q: Was it liberating for you to get away in *Painted Turtle: Woman with Guitar* from the area of black and white relations?

CM: Yes. I knew I could depend on the essential human experiences of the characters. I knew I could trust that. I didn't feel that I was out of my terrain.

Certain writers get boxed into certain fictional agendas. I hope I've been successful in avoiding that.

Q: Your new book-length poem, *Surfaces and Masks,* is set in Venice. What draws you to that city?

CM: Well, first of all, I lived there. Venice seemed to me to be the crux of a lot of western experience. In Venice I could see Africa, I could see the formation of Europe. I could see the past and the present all brought together. I'm particularly interested in the ritual, the ceremonial nature of Venetian life. And the way it has always been a city of strangers. The alienated.

It's always been a place where exiles and outcasts have gone. I met the ex-Queen of an eastern European country in Venice. She would get her check from London and spend it on jewelry in three days. Then halfway through the month she wouldn't be able to pay her rent.

She's an example of the kind of person who ends up in Venice. It's a city open to individuals running from the past or in search of a new present or future. It's a city perfect for the themes I explore in my work.

Q: You have spoken of the artificial boundary between poetry and prose. Is there such a thing as a natural boundary between the two forms? If so, where would you locate this boundary?

CM: A useful distinction can be made, but it's also possible to erase it. James Joyce blurs the line between poetry and prose a large part of the time.

There is a technical distinction between poetry and prose, but it cannot and does not always apply.

Q: *My Amputations* presents an imposter, or a possible imposter, who makes his way through the world and through a number of American universities. Do you feel that the writer is always an imposter? Or is it more that the writer in the university setting must be a kind of chameleon, changing color and texture to blend in or stand out?

CM: I don't think the writer is an imposter. But I think a lot of phoniness is available on the literary scene. I think the task of the writer is to somehow get through it. To get in touch with what he or she knows to be worthwhile.

The university is no more of a stage for phoniness than any other environment where literary activities go on. We romanticize the past.

The coffee house scene in Europe, for example, was supposed to be a place for the foment of literary ideas. But there was as much phoniness there as in any academic department. And as much failure.

Q: Many see fiction in America as dominated by the minimalist aesthetic of the late Raymond Carver and other writers. Why do you think minimalist realism is so popular?

CM: It's easy to read. That particular kind of fiction is attractive to an age that is impatient with verbosity and ambiguity of any type. Minimalism in fiction correlates with movements in the other arts—painting, dance, video. Minimalist fiction is perfect for the commuter flight. You know, from Washington to New York, or wherever.

Q: *My Amputations, Emergency Exit, Reflex and Bone Structure* are stylistically acrobatic novels, while *Such Was the Season* and *Painted Turtle: Woman with Guitar* are, on the surface, beautifully simple in their construction. It's as if only the two extremes of the compositional spectrum interest you. Why is this?

CM: I try not to think about these things. I try to trust something that knows more than I do about what I'm writing. When I was living in France I was delighted to hear from people who had all kinds of theories about my work. It was very interesting to listen to. Literary criticism is a kind of construct that may or may not be as interesting as the literature itself. But I think once you have a critical work, a completed text, then that work probably has more to do with itself than it does with the literature it is supposed to be referring to.

Post-modern or reflexive writers are usually far more concerned with their process than I am. I still like the story. But I also like to be aware of the meatiness, the graininess of language.

Q: In an age when death squads seek one writer and hundreds of other writers live in exile, why is literature in this country considered a form of entertainment?

CM: Let me answer that in a roundabout way. When I was doing research on the Zunis, I discovered that in the old days they had such reverence for story telling that it had a legal role in their lives. If you were convicted of a crime, they would take you into the old mission, hang you upside down by your feet and flog you until you told them a really fascinating and convincing story. The key to your freedom was that the story had to be convincing and fascinating.

They had that much reverence for the imagination. It was trusted as a place of truth. I think we've lost reverence in our world for the truth of stories. Or at least our reverence is harder to locate.

But this is not to say that there's no place for novels, poems and short stories in our world. Literature is still very useful to us and we recognize that. The challenge now for us as writers is enormous. People have so little time. The reading of literature presents only one choice among a thousand activities in a day. The writer has to compete with aerobics, and shopping, and everything people choose and don't choose to do.

Clarence Major
Alice Scharper / 1990

Clarence Major has published seven novels and eight books of poetry. His most recent book, *Fun & Games* (Holy Cow! Press), is his first collection of short stories. He lives in Davis, California, where he teaches at the University of California.

Q: Your fiction and your poetry seem to be chronically referred to as "experimental" . . .

A: "Chronic" is a good word for it . . .

Q: . . . and that seems to be juxtaposed to the term "conventional," and these two terms keep cropping up. I'm interested in finding out what those terms mean to you, and why do you feel that "experimental" is used to describe your writing in general?

A: For me they're troublesome—very troublesome—but I think it's an effort on the part of people who need to define writing in terms of genres, in terms of categories, to do just that. It seems to be the convenient way of dealing with things that are in the marketplace. It's "black" or "experimental" or "feminist" or "historical romance" or whatever. Basically we live in a culture that requires these definitions. It's a kind of tag. I've agonized over tags, and I think there's no way around them, so I don't fight them anymore. Those are labels that are either useful or detracting at times, depending on where you are at the moment, or where the customer is at the moment, or where the researcher or book reviewer is at the moment.

Q: What's the connection to your writing? Why do you feel it's termed "experimental"?

A: Because, I guess, as the reviewer said in yesterday's *L.A. Times,* it's because there is a tradition of Afro-American fiction and poetry, and that tradition has been—in fiction, especially—realistic, or naturalistic. "Social realism" is what it's generally called. It means that Afro-American writers have traditionally made a sociological or psychological—and it's usually both—examination of the so-called black experience, which is another term that has no meaning whatsoever.

There is no single black experience. There are certain kinds of cultural aspects of the experience of black people generally that might be summed up in that way, but it seems to minimize the importance of diversity within the culture. That's just one of the troublesome things about labels. The minimization.

Q: Well, the terms are double-edged. Reviewers can employ them in an effort to valorize certain writers' work—experimental can be avant-garde and "fresh"—or they can marginalize writers through the same labels.

A: Yes, and this is exactly what happens, normally. Especially with Afro-American writers, or even any so-called subcategory of writers in this culture: women, Native American, Asian-American—whatever. It's generally considered "the other" division. There is a kind of crossover point, too, at times. It seems to me that the ethnic identity of a writer is not what causes that kind of definition to take place. We have examples of that—Frank Yerby, Willard Motley—just in looking at black writers. There's always been a concurrent tradition of black American writers who have not at all concentrated on the elements that cause Afro-American literature to be defined as a subcategory. Yerby, as you know, every book he wrote was a bestseller, but they were popular novels—romance novels, essentially.

I think the defining element takes place at one level of decision on the part of the writer—what an individual writer chooses to write.

It's also possible to write out of an ethnic experience and at the same time transcend those definitions, just as Ralph Ellison has done. Toni Morrison has done that. Also Alice Walker. That happens because the writer has tapped into some elements of the human experience that transcend the merely cultural. Now, when a writer does that, it doesn't necessarily follow that society is going to pick up on that and bring the writer into the mainstream; that doesn't necessarily happen. A writer such as Charles Chestnutt, for example, was never really brought into the mainstream as a celebrated American writer.

Q: You dedicated your novel *Emergency Exit,* published in 1979, "to the people whose stories do not hold together," from a quote from Hemingway in *The Sun Also Rises* in which he writes, "I mistrust all frank and simple people, especially when their stories hold together." What did that dedication mean for you in 1979, and further, what does it mean when a story doesn't hold together?

A: I was trying to justify the structure of that book, which was a system of fragmentation, but a system nonetheless. In other words, a fragmented form that was essentially a unified, coherent entity. I do believe art has to have form. As William Carlos Williams said, "There is no such thing as free verse." There is really no such thing as a free novel; it's not like life. Life is kind of formless and pointless at times, but a novel really can't be that way, just as a poem can't be that way.

Q: There's an organizing intelligence? A structuring . . .

A: Yes. It has a kind of internal integrity. It's like a leaf or a tree or a rock, or anything that can be seen to have its own intelligent system. In using that dedication I wanted to justify my form in that novel. I think it was probably the most radical novel I've written in terms of form, and therefore the least accessible, and commercially the least successful. But I don't know whether the novel itself is a success or a failure; I don't know that about any of my books. I haven't felt the need to write that kind of novel again. Once I've been down a river, I just like to travel another way.

Q: How do you make decisions about writing prose and writing poetry? How do you traffic between genres?

A: That's a good question. The biggest secret I have is that very often I will take about a dozen poems—or maybe two dozen poems—and work them into a novel in some way. Or vice versa. There are chapters sometimes that don't work in a novel and I'll throw them into a folder and a month or a year later and eventually get a poem out of a chapter that didn't work in a novel. There are some short stories that are more borderline than others, obviously. As in my latest book, *Fun & Games.* Some of the older things are certainly more borderline—bridging the two forms—than others.

Q: Does teaching nourish your writing?

A: I think so. In terms of my life, it gives me a way of getting out of the loneliness that surrounds writing as an activity. And I feel that it's a good balance, a good intellectual balance. It's a good way of going into the world and being involved in the world. It's constructive and educational. As long as I feel that I'm learning something, then it's useful; I have a kind of selfish motive to teaching: I love to learn. Teaching is important for me in that sense; I feel engaged.

Q: What do you actually teach when you teach creative writing?

A: Well, I'm not teaching writing, really. Usually when I'm teaching creative writing I'm trying to conduct—coordinate, really—a workshop in which there's an atmosphere generated, an atmosphere, when it's working, that should give the participants the opportunity to discover what they need to discover in order for their writing to go forward. When I'm dealing with people who have a lot of talent and a great need to write, then it's ideal, because that's when that method works best. When I'm dealing with people who will probably not become writers, then my goal is to try to create the same atmosphere and hope that they will come away from the workshop experience as better readers, at least, because they've learned how a text is put together, and how it's taken apart. That's all I expect from those who aren't specializing in creative writing. In all cases, it's a worthy goal.

Q: I want to shift gears and talk about some of your work more specifically. In your novel *Painted Turtle: Woman with Guitar,* published in 1988, the material is drawn from the life of a Zuni woman living on the fringes of her native culture. Where did the idea for the novel come from?

A: It came out of the failure of another novel I was writing at the time. That novel was about an Afro-American singer, and I realized that I needed some distance from it—some cultural distance—so I needed to be able to look at a culture the way you would look at a chessboard, maybe, or at a foreign language—let's put it that way—that has understandable, structural parts. So, there was my fascination with the Zunis.

I lived in Colorado for twelve years, teaching at the university, and I spent a lot of time in the Southwest and on the Navajo reservations. I became accustomed to the culture, and absorbed a great deal. Essentially, the novel came from another route. I had been fascinated with the Zunis for a long, long time because of their history. There's a mystery there. No one knows, for example, where their language comes from, for one thing. They may be the descendant of the Aztecs; that's one theory. But I was especially interested in their rebellious nature, and in their resiliency. Anyway, I had enough distance so that I could look at them as I would look at something under a microscope. There was a kind of structure, a kind of system, that was attractive to me. So I did the research, which took a couple of years, and I took my previous character and changed her a great deal. She evolved into Painted Turtle, but she became a very different kind of person, though she retained the sadness—but she also lost a lot of the despair; although Painted Turtle has some despair, she's triumphant. She transcends her condition, and she has much to deal with but she doesn't give up.

Q: What about the role of the male narrator, Baldwin Saiyataca?

A: That was a purely technical decision. The first time, I tried *Painted Turtle* in a first-person narrative, and it didn't work. I tried it that way and I could not make it work in her voice. Saiyataca was in the story, so I resolved the problem by rewriting it from his point of view. Maybe because I felt more comfortable with a male narrator at that time, I don't know. Anyway, he was a half-breed—half Navajo and half Hopi, and as such, he was in trouble. And Painted Turtle was in trouble, too. They were both in trouble; they couldn't find a place to be anywhere, and I think that's really one of the subtexts of the novel—it may not be a subtext, actually; it may be the main point. But they're looking for a place and a way to be.

Q: I noted, too, a recurring theme of shame in the novel, and this interests me a great deal. Was this theme a conscious construction, or did it evolve out of the characters themselves?

A: I think it evolved naturally out of the situation the characters were in. Shame is an essential element in all human experience, I think. I used to think of shame as a Judeo-Christian phenomenon, but as I learned more about different cultures I realized that it's universal, that shame and guilt seem to be motivating factors in the formation of a great many systems of thought, feeling, religious expression.

Q: I'm reminded of a poignant scene in the novel where Painted Turtle is riding the bus to Albuquerque and a young blond girl is sitting in the seat next to her. The girl turns to Painted Turtle and asks her, "Are you Indian?" and Painted Turtle says, "Yes." The little girl then asks her, "Do you live in a tepee? Do you wear moccasins? Do you dance?" The young girl has her particular set of assumptions about the world of the Indian, and Painted Turtle is sealed off from the world of the girl because of those assumptions. And Painted Turtle is shamed as a result of not being able to bridge that gulf between her culture and the girl's.

A: I think that's one of the unfortunate things that gets in the way of seeing how we are all essentially, at the deepest level, the same, except for our cultural differences. What happens is that the cultural differences become, somehow, more visible, rather than the equally significant universal elements.

Q: In your latest book, *Fun & Games,* from Holy Cow! Press, over what period of time were these stories, these fictions, being written and gathered?

A: Well, the oldest story in the collection is called "Old," and that was written when I was about twenty-five. It was never published before.

Q: That's the story of the elderly white man who has lived in the same neighborhood for thirty years and is distressed that it has "turned black."
A: Right. I would say the stories come from a period of twenty years. The most recent one was "My Mother and Mitch."

Q: When you mentioned earlier that some of the older stories in *Fun & Games* bordered on poetry, which ones in particular were you thinking of?
A: I was thinking of the middle stories—the ones about relationships—and those in the last section call "Triptych"; I think of those as prose poems. And "Fun & Games," "My Mother Visiting"—I think these are a little more playful. I felt a sense of freedom from conventional form, where I could create a more lyrical kind of system.

Q: How do you define prose poetry?
A: Prose poetry . . . I'm not sure. I would say that it seems to have about it a kind of self-consciousness; the language seems to be as important as anything else going on in it. In prose poetry, language seems to have the intensity of language in poetry, a concentrated quality. But this can be tricky, because if a person normally reads fiction and turns to this sort of writing it can become very disturbing, and they can be thrown off guard and confused.

I think it's very important, as a reader, to discover what a piece of work intends to be and to read it with a sense of respect for the writer's intentions. This doesn't happen often enough, I think. Not many readers have the kind of open-mindedness that's called for. We read for taste, mostly. If a piece of fiction isn't immediately captivating, on our own terms, we dismiss it. It's too much work. Very few of us come to a piece of writing with the intention of giving it a chance to talk to us; we would rather talk to *it*.

Q: We do this with people, too.
A: Yeah. You know, Flannery O'Connor said you can assume that nobody is going to give a damn about your work. In other words, no one is dying to read your work. From there, you work with the challenge that's set before you—which is to find a way to engage the reader—but I think those of us who are involved in writing and teaching writing work our way into being more diverse and generous, in terms of what we read. We're a little more willing to allow a piece of work to talk to us.

Q: What about the long poem, *Surfaces and Masks,* that Coffee House Press put out in book form. Is this the first long poem you've published?

A: Yeah, this is the first. I wrote it in Venice, and it was essentially a journal poem that I kept while living there. It turned out to be a record of what I was reading and living and thinking and feeling every day. That's where it came from. I just finished a big novel that grew out of that Venice experience. It's half poetry in a way—the protagonist is a poet—and a lot of his poetry is in the book, just as Painted Turtle's songs are in that book. It resolves any possible dormant conflict, for me, between prose and poetry. I can constantly work at both in a way that is unified.

Q: I want to end with a quick question about small-press publishing. You mentioned to me that you would much rather publish with smaller presses, and I was hoping you'd elaborate on this.

A: Well, it doesn't always happen, but when it does, the experience can be very satisfying in that there is one-to-one, personal, caring contact with the editor. With *Fun & Games,* the editor, Jim Perlman, was in touch with me nearly every day by phone. The chances of that happening with a large press are almost zero. With the larger presses, of course, you have advantages: distribution is better, the book *can* be found in bookstores—though not always. I mean, just because Random House publishes it doesn't mean it's going to appear in a bookstore. But in general, publishing with smaller presses is usually satisfying on the personal level.

Beneath a Precipice: An Interview with Clarence Major

Larry McCaffery and Jerzy Kutnik / 1992

From *Some Other Frequency* by Larry McCaffery. Copyright© 1996 by Larry McCaffery. Reprinted with permission of University of Pennsylvania Press.

Clarence Major first achieved literary recognition during the social and aesthetic turmoil of the late sixties. This recognition was initially due to Major's work as an editor, poet, and anthologist; later, the appearance in 1969 of his sexually charged, highly controversial first novel, *All-Night Visitors,* from Maurice Girodias's Olympia Press, began to establish him as one of postmodern fiction's most versatile and radical innovators. Major's first publication was a pamphlet of (mostly forgettable) poems entitled *The Fires that Burn in Heaven* (1954); following a stint in the Air Force, Major began editing *Coercion Review* (from 1958–61), which gradually brought him into contact with such leading poetry figures as William Carlos Williams, Robert Creeley, and Allen Ginsberg. Over the years, Major has continued to make editorial contributions to such journals as *Journal of Black Poetry, American Book Review,* and *American Poetry Review,* as well as publishing two anthologies of student work, which he edited, *Writers Workshop* (1967) and *Man Is a Child* (1969). He has also published a wide variety of reviews, manifestos, and critical essays (some collected in his 1974 critical study, *The Dark and Feeling: Black American Writers and Their Work*).

But Major first gained national attention with the publication of *The New Black Poetry* (1969), a controversial anthology of contemporary black poetry whose eclecticism drew criticism from both conservative and liberal factions of the black artistic community, who were both already heatedly discussing the implications of the "black aesthetic" being promoted by writers like Ishmael Reed, Ed Bullins, and Amiri Baraka. In terms of his own work, Major's first important poetry collection, *Swallow the Lake* (1970), explored some of the interests that would recur in his later fiction (music, alienation, and psychic dismemberment, male-female relationships, the relationship of art and reality, sex and death, and so on) in a wide variety of styles and voices; *Swallow* was rapidly followed by three more collections, *Private Line* (1971),

Symptoms and Madness (1971), and *The Cotton Club* (1972). Major's poetry is characterized by the same rich, unsettling mixture of humor and anger, passion and abstract intellectual interests, self-consciousness and let-it-all-hang-out energy, and formal daring found in his fiction.

Because Major has mainly avoided the social realist mode favored by most black American writers in favor of expressionistic, metafictional modes, his fiction has subsequently been analyzed primarily in terms of its "experimental" or "antirealist" features. Unfortunately this focus has tended to relegate Major to the "avant-garde ghetto" where his works have never attained the popularity or critical acclaim given his more publicly visible contemporaries like Alice Walker, Toni Morrison, and Ishmael Reed.

However, as with many other figures from postmodernism's first wave of literary innovators, what once seemed antirealistic to a generation raised on the illusionistic assumptions of traditional realism can be recognized today as simply new approaches to realism, either in the sense of describing a reality that seemed increasingly "unrealistic" by earlier norms or (as is more relevant for Major's work) of finding fresh methods to depict irrational, contradictory inner lives and selves that resist traditional formulations. Many of the features of Major's fiction are in fact designed to give voice to various irrational impulses and contradictory versions of self and personal identity that traditional realism could not express. Thus, Major's best fiction often presents a fiercely passionate vision of jagged, tortured beauty that is analogous to that found in Goya, Van Gogh, Hendrix, or Eric Dolphy. While such nonliterary analogies are always suspect, they are appropriate in this case due to Major's convictions concerning the inadequacies of verbal logic to convey the truth about experience.

The themes and forms of these books seem to trace a movement away from the radical sense of personal fragmentation and insecurity, graphic sexuality, and outrage found in the early works (*All-Night Visitors* and *NO* [1973], to a middle period where his interests in metafictional explorations of the fiction-making process, metafictional methods, and formal concerns find their most extreme expression in *Reflex and Bone Structure* (1975) and *Emergency Exit* (1979), to his recent explorations of more narrative styles and formal structures in works like *Such Was the Season* (1987). But as Major takes great pains to suggest in the following interview, such an evolution represents less a move "away from antirealism towards realism" than different stages in an ongoing effort to find a suitable means to give expression to his sense of himself.

As it happens, most of the early versions of "self" are prismatic, cubistic constructs reflecting not self but a shifting series of public, private, and imaginary selves. Most of Major's fiction unfolds as a bewildering array of discrete bits of visual images, fragments of contradictory plot elements, different voices, and reflexive ruminations about fiction. Major's novels nearly all focus on men whose lives are either coming apart or never had achieved any unity in the first place. Reading Major's important middle works like *Reflex and Bone Structure, My Amputations* (1986), and perhaps his most successful novel, *Emergency Exit,* you feel much as you did in reading Kerouac and Burroughs, Rimbaud and Artaud—figures who, like Major, felt the need to refashion an entire new language and set of narrative assumptions in order to conjure up "spaces" of the imagination and emotion never given voice to previously. Major thus developed a variety of discontinuous, collage-like structures to capture the movement of a mind which refuses to reduce his experiences to the sorts of unified narrative voices and causally related plot elements found in the realistic novel. As with other writers from this period who were exploring similar methods—for example, his fellow Fiction Collective writers Steve Katz, Ray Federman, and Ronald Sukenick—the result is akin to a jazz musician's improvisations, whose various tones, rhythms, motifs, and other sound patterns, expressed in different keys and tones, provide a means of access to the artist's inner self. The act of writing down the work we are reading thus should be seen as being not an effort to find a unified self, voice, or plot but an effort to provide a means to give expression to these multiple, contradictory aspects of himself. His novels, then, represent not the illusions of realism but the illusoriness of those illusions.

Although the influence of jazz, blues, and poetry on Major's fiction has been widely noted, his writing has probably been even more deeply influenced by the visual. Major began his artistic career as a painter (he attended the Chicago Art Institute briefly at age seventeen), and he has continued to produce paintings, which he has exhibited in galleries and exhibitions on numerous occasions. Major remarks in the following interview that he is "a visual thinker," and this quality is evident in the important role that visual descriptions and imagery have always played in his narratives. Although *Emergency Exit* is his only book in which Major has introduced reproductions of his paintings to reinforce or analogize the written materials, his use of visual images as a kind of objective correlative that reveals emotional resonances of the inner, literally unspeakable emotional lives of his narrators and characters has been a constant feature of his fiction.

The following interview took place at Clarence Major's home in Davis, California. Before the interview, the interviewers, along with McCaffery's wife, Sinda Gregory, and Major's wife, Pamela, had gone out for lunch in order to catch up on news and gossip. Back at Major's house, there was time before the interview to roam about examining the plants and small trees (whose presence indoors seemed not at all incongruous) and the many paintings by Major that hang on the walls. The conversation was friendly but serious, the atmosphere and mood combining with Major's reflective comments and soft voice to create an aura of quiet reflection.

Jerzy Kutnik: To what extent do you see yourself as consciously working in the "black aesthetic" or black narrative tradition?

Clarence Major: There is no single "black aesthetic." There has been a sequence or series of scenarios that can be defined as "black aesthetics" corresponding roughly to historical periods. So in the nineteenth century there were the black writers of the antebellum (1853–1865), the postbellum (1865–1902), the Old Guard (1902–1917), and Harlem Renaissance (1917–1929), and the period of social protest (1929–1959). They had their ideas about what a black writer in America should be doing, who a black writer should be addressing, and so on, that emerged out of specific literary and historical contexts. Despite all the different agendas throughout all the various periods, black writers were always working against a single dominant impulse in American culture: the use to which white America put blackness. Whiteness was about not being black. As such, black people were invested with all the negative crap against which white America defined itself. Black writers worked always to humanize black people and to overthrow the burden of this symbolism. To be human meant to be *whole*—good and bad, complex, and so on. At the same time, the Old Guard, for example, was resisting the young writers of the Harlem Renaissance, who were trying to assert a new kind of black presence and consciousness.

JK: And this presence wasn't likely to be accepted by whites?

CM: The point had less to do with white models or white acceptance and more about not feeling they had to be "proper." The accommodationists were about putting one's best foot forward for the white world, or for an equal reading public. In other words, you should never hang your dirty laundry out, never let the world know what's going on behind the scenes. If you have marital problems, family problems, drinking problems, all that should be kept quiet. Meanwhile you emphasize the positive, put your best face forward, that kind of thing. That was the black middle-class take on reality, and it should be the take presented in literature, which should be very uplifting. Then along comes Claude McKay with a book like *Home to Harlem,* which lets it all hang out, which shows the prostitutes and the pimps and the numbers runners and all the other good-time people—it was about people and situations that people like Weldon Johnson were calling the dirty laundry.

The point is that what people refer to as "black aesthetics" isn't some mysterious, inherent set of guidelines, but a set of historical motives. Aesthetics aren't a set of abstractions existing outside historical circumstances and daily reality; they're always grounded in the needs and aims of specific artists and audiences, influenced by the social setting and context. Richard Wright was concerned with the conditions of poverty, injustice, and so on that Sinclair or Wolfe and other white protest writers of the thirties were. Chester Himes wrote about those kinds of conditions too in books like *Cast the First Stone* and in some of his other forties novels. Later on in the sixties, you get this idea of the black aesthetic which comes out of Black Nationalism and operates as the cultural arm of that political movement. It's meant to be purely functional in relation to the political aim, but it seemed to me to be essentially replacing Eurocentric thinking with Afrocentric thinking.

Larry McCaffery: It's always struck me that there was a risk in this whole approach. Even if Afrocentric thinking seems somehow more "appropriate" to the experience of black people, the insistence on having black people adopt this mode of thinking winds up substituting one set of limitations, controls, norms, for another.

CM: That was essentially the problem I wound up having with this whole "black aesthetics" concept. The thrust of the movement wasn't so much an attempt to say Eurocentric thinking is limiting our attempts to function as artists and as individuals—I would have obviously supported anything concerned with opening up options, fresher or more liberating options for black people. Instead, you had this attempt to replace the Eurocentric with something that *closed down* the view of the writer and restricted it to the service of certain political ideologies that were as stifling as the ones they hoped to replace. That's why I instinctively opposed it, even before I could articulate the sources of my opposition. I knew there was something wrong. What I tried to propose even that early in the sixties (and what I still propose today) was something far more flexible, which is what I was trying to do with my anthology, *Calling the Wind: Twentieth Century African-American Short Stories*—namely, to find the terms on a more personal level, to get the best of all the different kinds of cultural influences feeding into my experience, and to come up with a personal aesthetic. It might at least be liberating for me.

LM: You can make the same argument about the great debate raging these days on college campuses about the canon.

CM: Exactly! We talk about opening up the canon so that we can bring the rest of the world into Western thinking, get outside of the restrictions we've traditionally imposed on our educational system, and somehow open up the whole process. Now of course I'm all in favor of the opening up of Western thought to other modes of thinking (who *couldn't* be?), but the minute you start talking about challenging the Western canon, the people who depend on it for their living get very terrified. It's not that anybody wants to derail Shakespeare—sure, everyone should have to study Shakespeare. But everyone should also have to study equally important writers and philosophies of other cultures. Why not?

LM: Since you started publishing fiction back in the late sixties, your work has consistently been discussed by critics like Jerry Klinkowitz and myself primarily in terms of its concern with its own processes and status as pure invention. Unfortunately, this emphasis on your works' alleged "nonreferential" or "nonrealistic" features ignored the possibility that these features might function in the service of a new kind of realism; it's also been used to relegate your work to the rarefied "art for art's sake" (or the "narcissistically self-indulgent") category and hence marginalize it. How would you yourself describe the role that formal innovation has played in your fiction? Is the common distinction between "realism" versus "experimentalism" valid?

CM: Absolutely not. Those distinctions have always seemed superficial. Since *Such Was the Season* looks very much like a piece of realism on the surface, some people claimed that I had jumped ship, betrayed my experimental goals. But that book is just as "experimental" as my other work in terms of realistic norms. For example, even though Juneboy appears in what *passes for* a realistic setting, he's also being presented through this folksy, down-to-earth woman's point of view, which filters everything through colloquial speech mannerisms and idioms in an utterly subjective manner.

LM: In the interview that appeared in *Finding the Words,* you described writing as a way of finding yourself both as a writer and as a person, adding, "I think the two processes are integral and interchangeable and inseparable— the continual redefinition of self and the process of learning how to write every day. I find that it's an endless lesson; you don't really carry that much information and skill from one piece to the next unless you're doing the same thing over and over. Each act of writing becomes a whole new experience, which is why it's so difficult" (Bunge, 53). You went on to say that your writing reflects the fact that you literally feel different every day. I mention this because subjective or not, Annie Eliza's perspective in *Such Was the Season* is undeniably more *stable* or consistent than what we find in your earlier work. Is this stability a reflection of your now feeling less fragmented personally, more certain of who and what you are?

CM: In terms of my own psychology, I do feel more secure—secure enough at least so I don't feel the need to ask the same questions that drove me to create characters like the ones you find over and over again in *All-Night Visitors* and *NO.* But what we're talking about here, both in terms of my writing and my life, is an evolution, not a sharp break. Exploring different personae in my earlier novels was something that grew out of my sense of personal fragmentation. Those feelings have changed somewhat as I've gotten older and had the opportunity to resolve some of those conflicts about myself and recognize integration rather than separation. When you're young, you haven't had the experiences that allow perspective on who you are or how to know what "you" consist of. From a personal standpoint, of course, this confusion can be very troubling, but an artist needs to take advantage of these things to produce anything worthwhile. Back when I was starting out to write, it felt perfectly natural to have my work reflect this sense that I was literally a different person every time I sat down to write. It was an interesting challenge to find narrative contexts for different parts of myself that needed voices to express themselves. So in something like *Reflex and Bone Structure* I consciously played with this whole concept of author-narrator identity, though in fact there were several personae there: the narrator, the protagonist, and the implied author. In *My Amputations* I had an implied author, the protagonist, and the narrator all working together in a concerted way. To write a novel in those days with stable characters or narrators would have basically falsified my own experience. Today the opposite would be equally false. All along it's seemed that to do anything *but* reflect my own self (or selves) wouldn't make sense. Why write out of some phony sense of narrative stability if that doesn't reflect how I feel about myself? There was a sense I didn't really *want* a stable identity, at least in terms of being an artist. There was something liberating about *not* knowing who I was going to be when I sat down to write. Projecting myself into these different personas let me discover things about these concrete presences which were outside of myself but also coming out of myself. In the process, I learned a lot about myself.

JK: In this regard, your presentation of Annie Eliza in *Such Was the Season* seemed a departure for you in that she somehow *didn't* seem to be someone based on yourself.

CM: There's been a steady movement in my writing toward diminishing that dependency on self. By the time I got to the creation of Annie Eliza, I had made an enormous breakthrough: this was my first novel where I was not the model for the main character. The Zuni novel, *Painted Turtle,* was a further leap in that direction, and now I'm writing a novel whose main character is not remotely like me.

LM: Readers of *Such Was the Season* may not be encouraged to identify you with the narrator—but what about Juneboy? Weren't there autobiographical impulses that started the book?

CM: I started *Such Was the Season* after I had taken a trip to Atlanta, and to some extent Juneboy is based on some of my experiences on that trip. But—and this is pretty true in terms of all the autobiographical material in my work—those correlations start to break down very quickly once narrative and aesthetic demands and all sorts of other things start to operate on these "facts." Like Juneboy, I hadn't been to Atlanta since I was eighteen, but I didn't stay a week like he did. And I didn't make a trip with my aunt to try to find my father's grave site either—or discover that it was under ten miles of concrete in, or rather under, a housing development. There was also no political scandal in the works like there was in the novel, although like Juneboy I did meet the mayor of Atlanta and Martin Luther King's wife, Coretta, at a dinner party at my cousin's house. But overall I'd say my own presence is so diminished in Juneboy's identity that he is at best a catalyst rather than a true persona. By the time you get to *Painted Turtle* "I" am not present at all, except in the design and creation of the book. These very general connections between autobiography and fiction are always present in my books, somewhere, though you may have to dig deeper in some works than others to recognize them. But as a novelist I've always felt that my obligation is to follow whatever ideas I'm trying to work through in a particular book, not to something which actually took place.

JK: Your *Contemporary Athors* autobiography essay mentions that you began *Painted Turtle* with a woman narrator but finally decided you couldn't write it effectively that way. Were you feeling that it was somehow inappropriate to write from a woman's perspective? What finally allowed you to maintain a female narrator's voice throughout *Such Was the Season?*

CM: I don't believe gender-specific arguments about the impossibility of men writing from women's perspectives (and vice versa), just as I don't believe that blacks can't write about whites, or whites can't write about blacks. If you can make it come alive, you can write *anything*. With *Painted Turtle,* what happened was that for various reasons I was unable to make that particular Zuni woman come alive. *Painted Turtle* taught me that if I was going to write in a woman's voice, it had to be a voice I felt comfortable with—one that would come naturally rather than something I'd have to completely invent. That was a big help when I started *Such Was the Season* a year later, but for reasons that are hard to explain, I found in *Painted Turtle* that I felt closer to the voice of the guy who falls in love with her. Strangely, a lot of people remember the book as being narrated by a woman. Maybe her voice is still present as a kind of subtext.

At any rate, from the outset I felt more secure with the woman's voice I was using in *Such Was the Season.* I didn't have to think about inventing that voice because I'd grown up hearing it, I knew its rhythms from the way my relatives in the South speak. It was already there, so all I had to do was just sit at the computer and correct the voice by ear, the way you would write music. If the rhythm was wrong or the pitch off, I knew it instinctively because I'd lived with that voice all my life.

JK: Do you recall what the origin of the Zuni novel was?

CM: It had to do with the fact that a black man—a huge African— apparently visited the Zunis in the sixteenth century with a group of Spanish explorers and then stayed on. He must have seemed extremely commanding to the Zuni because he became some kind of god for them—he had dozens of wives, and he appears in a lot of early Zuni legends and stories, and so on.

JK: I don't remember him appearing in the novel . . .

CM: He doesn't. It turned out he was irrelevant to contemporary Zuni culture, which is finally what I wound up wanting to explore. For whatever reason, this black man's presence is no longer found anywhere in recent Zuni culture. And since, in effect, he's been dead for them for a long time (since the nineteenth, or maybe even the eighteenth, century), I decided he wouldn't have any presence in my novel, either. Letting go of this story was disappointing—after all, he had triggered my interest in the Zunis in the first place, which had started me going down to New Mexico, visiting the reservation, and getting to know some people. But in the end his presence just didn't fit into my story.

LM: What sorts of research did you do for *Painted Turtle?*

CM: The trips I made to New Mexico (I was teaching at the University of Colorado at Boulder then) helped me get a sense of the Native American cultures in that part of the country; I also did a lot of research while I was teaching at UC-San Diego in 1984. To make that novel come alive, I had to learn a whole different culture. This took three years of research during which I absorbed tons and tons of stuff that was arriving from every conceivable discipline and in every conceivable way. I read the myths and anthropological transcripts, plus lots of sociology about the kinds of health conditions you find at Zuni, their education, really just about everything. I started writing the book right at the kitchen table in San Diego while still fascinated by the African man, so in early drafts he was present as a kind of mythic figure.

LM: Gerald Vizenor has recently argued that there are interesting analogies between Native American narrative traditions and those being described today in terms of "postmodernism." As you got to know Zuni storytelling modes better, what kinds of conclusions did you draw about their writing practices?

CM: Zuni storytelling is completely nonlinear. The traditional stories about Coyote never build towards a resolution the way Western narratives tend to do. Coyote wanders around involving himself in a complex network of activity that defies morality (and sometimes common sense logic). He gets involved in one thing after another, but these episodes aren't put together so in terms of progression, tension-and-resolution, and the other things we associate with the novel. It's the same with the various birds of the various festivals. They have their acts, their routines, but there's always an openendedness, a resistance to closure. Things don't have to turn out the same way at the end of the process.

LM: Did your own experiences as a black American make you feel a special sense of empathy with Zuni culture?

CM: I think so. Certainly in the sense of identifying my own experience with the Zunis as a subculture. Being a black man also probably allowed me to sense things that individual Zuni characters might feel in any given situation. I could immediately relate to what they would feel in social situations where they would feel uncomfortable, marginalized, that kind of thing. In fact, I found that Native Americans often suffer as much discrimination as black Americans, right in their own area, the minute they cross the line of the reservation. Indians can walk into just about any motel in New Mexico and find themselves being turned down for no good reason. That's just how it is. This might not happen as often to a black American in the West.

LM: One of the things about *Such Was the Season* that rang very true to me had to do with Annie Eliza being so wrapped up with the soap operas that they seemed every bit as real as anything else. Your early novels and poems also frequently examined technology's effect on people—usually from a negative perspective, it seems.

CM: Television *is* a very "real" part of life for a lot of people. It's an extension of what their daily lives are all about, not something removed from them. I've known any number of people who are basically housebound or who simply don't go out doing things in the world for whatever reasons. People like Annie Eliza become personally or even metaphysically wrapped up in the world of television so that its boundaries literally become the boundaries of their world.

LM: It's like what Baudrillard talks about regarding Disneyland—the illusion not only *seems* more real than the real world, it *is* more real.

CM: Right. Since Annie Eliza's television is never turned off, that world is always "on" for her; she goes to sleep with it on, and it's on when she wakes up—what could be more real than that? It's the way she lives. Besides, it's what she needs. When old people who have always had their family around them suddenly find themselves in a silent house, well, you can imagine how much they miss this bombardment of voices. Television fills the void, provides familiar voices, even if the voices are artificial. At least that space that's been vacated isn't empty.

LM: Since your generation of innovators emerged in the sixties, there's been an ever-increasing expansion of the so-called "media-culture"—this rapid expansion of images, advertising, information (the "dance of biz" as Bill Gibson refers to it)—into just about every conceivable aspect of our public and personal lives. This expansion may have especially dramatic, and potentially harmful, effects on black persons because the images, the people, and the situations they're encountering in the media are so predominantly white and middle-class—and as such they have the potential to distort people's perception of reality. But you seem to be looking at the positive role that, say, television plays in Annie Eliza's life rather than implying she's being manipulated or having her sense of racial norms or values impaired.

CM: That's because Eliza is looking at *human issues*—love, death, pain— that she's known all her life (and known completely) rather than racial issues. In her own life she has always identified with universals like raising children, deception, infidelity, seduction that having nothing to do with relative things like color or caste. Another important thing about her situation is that she's middle-class. She's owned her own house for thirty years and she identifies with the financial level of these people she's watching on the soaps. So on the social level their world is accessible to her. In my view, this is not such a huge leap either. Writers too can make this entry, imaginatively, into other cultures and genders, and make it viable and real in their works.

LM: In the interview you did with Jerry Klinkowitz in the seventies, you said: "All words are lies, in any arrangement, that pretend to be other than the arrangement that they make on the page." The idea that words and fiction are essentially formal aesthetic constructions rather than representations of something existing outside the page was, of course, very much in the air in the early days of postmodernism. Do you still agree with that? Or was this something that very much needed to be emphasized at a certain moment, but not at others?

CM: Using such an emotionally charged term as *lies* in that statement may have deflected readers away from the point I was making. What I meant to say—and this seems perfectly reasonable to me today as it did then—is that a word is just a sign, a symbol, and as such it can never really represent the thing it names. Words are entirely different from things, separate from their referents. They're autonomous entities, with their own linguistic realities, their own history, their own separate presences. Like other authors working against the grain of traditional realism, it seemed important for me back in the seventies to keep reminding readers that when writers start putting words on the page, they're not "representing" anything except the way their mind works. But once you say that, what does a writer *do* with it!? Having said this fifteen years ago, and then worked through all those reflexive concepts in my books, I simply don't need to do that again.

JK: And except in very broad ways, you don't repeat yourself very often, either thematically or in your formal concerns. With each new book, it's as if you've thrown yourself into a literary void—which is a risk for any artist. But in this sense, choosing to write *Such Was the Season* in a seemingly realistic mode was perfectly in keeping with what you'd been doing all along—that is, trying out new approaches.

CM: Like I said, writing *Such Was the Season* that way didn't mean I'd abandoned an interest in innovation. I was trying out all sorts of new things when I was writing *Such Was the Season,* even if these didn't have to do with my earlier compulsion to keep readers constantly focused on the page. The voice is what is innovative in that novel. I wanted to give that voice such a commanding presence that it would, in fact, become the main subject matter of the novel. I wanted to make it impossible for readers to stop thinking about the voice once they had started reading the book, to make that voice always uppermost, so that even though it was describing the things that were going on (the way voices do in traditional novels), they'd be constantly having to confront its own presence.

JK: Were there any models you had for the kind of thing you were after here with voice?

CM: *Huck Finn.* Before starting *Such Was the Season,* I had just reread *Huck* and once again, sentence after sentence, I found myself wondering, How did Twain make that voice come alive like that—make it so real? I may not have succeeded, but what I wanted to do in *Such Was the Season* was create a voice that would have the same kind of undeniable presence as the one Twain had created for Huck. I wanted to create a text in which the voice is literally the book's main subject matter—as I believe it to be in Twain's book.

LM: What you're saying would at first seem to contrast with the work you did for the *Dictionary of Afro-American Slang,* which distinguishes Afro-American idioms and voice from their English equivalent. I'm reminded of the remarks made by certain black writers to the effect that, "English is my enemy." Obviously having someone like Twain be such a strong influence indicates that you don't personally feel the sense that, as a black American author, you have to be constantly working "against" the English language— the language of oppression, and so on?

CM: My interest in this area doesn't really conflict with my appreciation of mainstream American idioms. What black people speak is actually very much in the mainstream of American speech. Not only is it not separate, it actually informs American speech in all sorts of ways. You can even argue that it's the nucleus of American speech, one of its roots. Black speech, as a matter of fact, influences Huck Finn's voice, as well. The history of the American language can't be separated from black speech. It's just *been there* all along, so intrinsic to American speech that there's no conflict whatsoever.

JK: Has black slang changed much in the last fifteen years?

CM: Absolutely, especially with all the new slang that's been emerging out of these new subcultures—hip-hop, rap, and so on. I've compiled thousands of words and phrases that have been coined or just surfaced in the last ten years. I find them in different places and not necessarily print sources—magazines, journals, and novels, but also rock videos, songs, films, street talk.

LM: In the courses I teach in rock music I use rap as a way of talking about the role that language has played in black communities and the admiration for the person that can speak well. This whole tradition of "rapping" and "dissing"—improvised contests to see who can use language most skillfully—has always been there in black culture.

CM: The saying always was, "He's well spoken. He's got a preacher's voice. That boy's gonna grow up to be a preacher, he's so well spoken." [laughs]

LM: You were immersed in blues and jazz, growing up. You lived in Chicago in the late fifties and early sixties, when the music scene there was really happening. Muddy Waters, and so on. That scene obviously had a strong impact on your work, just as it did for so many others, white guys like Kerouac, Coover, Sukenick, and Federman, as well as black writers. Is rap going to have a similarly liberating effect or influence on young black writers today?

CM: It's already happening. I can see the evidence of rap running through a lot of the works of the younger writers I included in *Calling the Wind: Twentieth Century African-American Short Stories.*

LM: Jazz, blues, and rap are distinctly black art forms that use black vernacular, the idioms you hear out on the streets, in the ghetto, and so on, as well as having formal roots in earlier folk arts. But at least in this century, you've also got all these white musicians just waiting to "borrow" features of these forms and turn them into something more "refined" that white audi-

ences will relate to (and purchase). You've also got brilliant, formally innovative black artists like Charlie Parker, Ornette Coleman, Jimi Hendrix, Prince,
who keep pushing things to the next level, practically reinventing the forms,
maybe to stay ahead of the white guys.

CM: Yes, although I personally have trouble with the concept of artistic
"refinement" whenever this winds up moving so far in certain directions that
it becomes inaccessible to people. You can see this in the social history of
jazz in particular—the way it's become institutionalized and removed from
our lives. Jazz has its roots in the folk tradition—in blues and even going
back beyond blues. When you follow its evolution, you see a progression of
refinement that removes it from everyday accessibility. After a while, it
becomes an acquired taste; in order to really hear what's going on, you have
to be educated in classical music, and it becomes something you have to learn
to appreciate. Pretty soon you find yourself putting on a tux when you want
to go listen to it, rather than having it as part of your daily life, the way it
should be, even if it is high-falutin music.

LM: You began your career apparently thinking you were going to be a
painter—you were at the Chicago Art Institute for a while, and so on. Did
this background in the visual arts have any lasting impact on your literary
sensibility?

CM: No question about it. I was drawn to painting in the first place
because I'm a visual thinker, which isn't something that's going to disappear
later on when you're writing.

JK: Who were some of the writers and other artists who had a significant
impact on your literary sensibility early on?

CM: Van Gogh and Cézanne among the painters. Gertrude Stein, Jean
Toomer, Rimbaud, Henry Miller, D. H. Lawrence, Richard Wright, Radiguet,
and Genet among fiction writers. Bud Powell has to be mentioned here somewhere as well.

JK: What do you mean when you say you're a "visual thinker"?

CM: I remember things better visually than verbally. I make connections
between things more on the basis of visual associations than verbal or logical
ones. If you tell me your name, I may not hear it as well as I can see it.

JK: How does your being a visual thinker relate to writing fiction versus
poetry? Most people would say that in poetry you think more in terms of
images, visual things.

CM: That's true, creating poetry is more directly involved with images. But this isn't an either/or thing. I often try to get those same kinds of images in my writing of fiction.

JK: Do you find any differences in the creative process involved in writing poetry versus fiction?

CM: There are, of course. When you're writing a poem you're concentrating on pushing language in certain directions that you don't ordinarily travel in when you're writing fiction. I try to use the language of poetry when I'm writing a novel, but only up to a certain point. You don't want to push things so far that your material becomes inaccessible as a story.

LM: What "poetic qualities" are you looking for in your fiction writing?

CM: Mostly a certain lyrical quality. Tone, pace, cadence, the music of speech. This isn't true in every case—there are things I attempt in fiction that don't lend themselves too well to a lyrical treatment. That's okay. I don't need to do the same thing over and over. But overall when my fiction is at its best, it usually has a kind of lyrical quality. I think Annie Eliza's voice, for example, has a kind of lyrical quality. Even though her voice seemed familiar to me, it wasn't something I thought of as being my private voice, which meant that the lyrical, poetic quality was something I had to consciously think of while writing.

LM: You've said that you think of some of your recent stories as being prose poems really; you've also said that sometimes some of your poems wind up being stories. When you start out writing something, how clear is it that something is going to be a story or a poem? What's the basis of this judgment?

CM: I don't always immediately know. *Usually* I do, because there's a different engagement involved in writing poems versus fiction. This gets even more complicated when you factor in other kinds of writing I do. For example, *Surfaces and Masks* started off as a journal I was keeping when we were living in Venice. Somehow these entries kept resisting being turned into prose, so after a very short time I let them come out in terms of lines. I realized that something about the material needed to be rendered in terms of measure, meter, and stanza breaks rather than in journal entry form.

LM: Is there any actual difference between the narrative voice you create in your fiction versus the one in your poetry?

CM: Formally, yes, and in the classroom I try to make those distinctions because I don't want to confuse students. But for all practical purposes, I don't separate things out like that. In fact, I'm usually trying to *bridge the two* by informing the narrative possibility with a lyrical quality.

LM: When an interviewer once said that audiences tended to have difficulty with even relatively mild disjunctures in fiction that they would readily accept in poetry, you made an interesting point about audience acceptance of truly radical narrative structures in film. Can't fiction writers take more chances today precisely because readers are now used to dealing with film and TV shows based on the principle of juxtaposition and montage?

CM: The problem is that audiences today tolerate a lot less disjuncture in fiction than they do with other art forms. People were much more willing to accept innovations in film even as early as the twenties. Audiences had no trouble with any of the stylistic innovations introduced by Chaplin or Buster Keaton. Jump cuts, leaps, animation, and all that camera technology stuff— they all made perfect sense to audiences. Whereas when you try out something analogous in a novel, you're somehow put aside as unreadable, inaccessible. Narrative or fictive conventions have had a longer time to rigidify, so readers have more difficulty when somebody is doing something different with narrative material; whereas with film or rock videos or whatever, the medium is so new that its audience just accepts the idea that its conventions are more fluid.

JK: Why didn't the radical experimentation of work written by your generation of postmodernist fiction writers help break down these readerly expectations?

CM: What happened is that the spirit of radical experimentalism and innovation gradually mellowed out during the seventies and eighties and are now finding their way into the mainstream of American writing. That's true of a lot of other things about the sixties that have filtered into our daily lives without our being aware of it. Certainly that's true of fiction. The radical fiction that writers like Barthelme, for example, were doing in the sixties was so radical in nature that it had to affect later writers. Subliminally their influences are there throughout just about the whole spectrum of American fiction today—so much so that we don't notice that they're present in a more diffuse way in the culture and in American fiction writing. This summer I read two hundred novels for the National Book Award and I can see the innovation there. It's more muted today than it was back when I was starting out as a writer, but it's there nevertheless. I remember a story about a couple of guys who are waiting down beneath a precipice to shoot a lion. A couple of lions are up above them, not knowing the men are down there, and the guys can't move, of course, because the lions might come down on them. What does the writer do with this situation? At the end of the story he says: "Well, I've given you this dramatic situation, and I hope that's enough. I mean, what more do I need to do? This is it, this is life!"

LM: I agree that the sixties brand of radical experimentalism has had a pervasive effect on recent writing, but there are also some crucial differences. Part of this just has to do with changes in the world today, especially the expansion of the media culture, the greater bombardment that everyone today is subjected to, the greater facility with which everything can be reproduced, reified, commodified. This changes the whole function of innovation: "the new" becomes merely another commodified style rather than having any social or aesthetic impact.

CM: Part of what's new is the constantly changing technical means by which literature is being made and consumed. I'm thinking of computer network fiction. Hypertexts. The speed with which new technologies erode is equally staggering. The minute I upgrade my computer it's already obsolete. So, what's new? "New" in the Ezra Pound sense no longer stands still, even for a moment. And at the same time—even with all our questing for the self-directed technologies—the younger generation of writers seem to be desperately reaching back for the homespun, the tried and tested formulas of the past, despite the innovations they've absorbed. And I see all of this as exciting and very promising.

LM: In the interview that appeared in *Finding the Words,* you argued that trying to create the distinction between poetry and prose turns out to be a trap and that "a book that was written a hundred years ago becomes not only a literary experience when you read it, it's like a historical experience because the language is not our language anymore . . . literature is unlike any other art form because it has the problem of language as its material, and also the problem of our perception which is always gauged out of this thing we call reality" (Bunge, 57). You seem to be making a distinction between perception and language, and then locating literature's uniqueness as having to do with the fact that since its "materials"—language—change over time, it necessarily always has this "problem of language." But isn't this true of other art forms as well? For instance, in painting don't you find changes in perception also affecting the "materials" it's created out of it? If you look at

impressionist paintings (which I know you love), you can see artists register-
ing these sorts of changes. In other words, is literature really so unique in its
ongoing concern with the elements that produce meaning in it?

CM: Literature is unlike the other arts. If we're talking about oral storytelling—the essence of literature—we're talking about pure language. Naturally
it's going to be limited to those who can speak and understand it. And it's
also always evolving in ways that lines and colors (in painting) and stone (in
sculpture) are not. Those materials evolve in their own very different ways
and aren't subject to the constant practical communication uses language is
subject to. A word's purity can be destroyed in a way that the color yellow,
theoretically, cannot.

JK: Do you see any connection between your painting and your writing,
beyond your having such a visual imagination? Are there any formal issues
or problems that you found yourself being drawn to early on in your painting
that you took up in your fiction as well? It would seem that painters have to
be reflexively concerned with the materials they're using in a way that's
analogous to the reflexive concerns you were dealing with so much in your
early novels.

CM: The reflexive "problem" all writers have to face is that the materials
fiction is created out of—that is, *words,* language—"mean something" in the
sense of making references to the outside world. That's why I feel these
materials are so different from those used for painting and sculpture. Colors
and textures and shapes in these other forms don't "refer" to anything. The
same is true for dance, of course, which has no "material" except the body—
and the body isn't really operating in the same way as paint, texture, and
color do in painting, or the way language does for literature. With dance you
have space defined by the presence of the body.

LM: I was really struck with a passage in *My Amputations* where your
narrator says: "He came to realize he wanted it all flat, or upright and permanent like Cubism. Like things, surfaces." Did that express what you're aim-
ing for when you're writing? Why did he want it this way?

CM: He wants it flat like cubism because in art you control, define, and
assign meaning to things otherwise swept along in the tide of time and space.
In cubism, he would be able to use all sides of the experience, stop, weigh it.
Think about it. Reflect on it. Cubism is just a term to refer to an attempt to
gain control of the shape of his life and to give it meaning.

JK: An unusual formal feature of *My Amputations* is the way prose is presented almost as physical objects—"blocks" of materials that aren't related the way that paragraphs or other organizing principles are in linear narratives. This seems like it might be related to the visual orientation of your imagination.

CM: That's because I literally tend to "see" my books this way. In the case of *My Amputations,* I remember the very day the book came to me. Pamela and I were walking up a hill to the Jewish cemetery in Nice, and I said, "I'm going to write a book in blocks of prose. Just panels. Not paragraphs." The only thing I needed to know at that point was that this book had to be a book composed in blocks or in panels.

JK: "Such Was the Season" is from Jean Toomer. What's involved for you in selecting titles for your works?

CM: Sleeping on it seems to work best for me. I let it be the last thought before I fall off to sleep, and by the time I wake up the title will have taken care of itself. I always have a title when I'm working on something, although I don't always end up using it. I grabbed "My Amputations," for example, somewhere along the way in the middle of the book. The same was true with "Such Was the Season," which was called "Juneboy" for a while; then I realized that wasn't a good title since it's not Juneboy's story at all, which made me start shopping around for another title until I was eventually led to "Such Was the Season."

LM: Your early novels, *All-Night Visitors* and *NO,* dealt obsessively and relentlessly with sex (which maybe isn't a strange preoccupation for a young writer) but also with *death,* both individually and the way it connects with sexuality. How do you explain that fascination?

CM: Thank you for bringing that up. When people talk about those two books they always mention the sex but they forget the death. [Laughter.] But is there anything particularly unusual about my preoccupation with death? In fact, this preoccupation with sex and death is probably more of a young man's thought or activity, than it is for an older person who's had a chance to adjust after the initial shock. If they're alert at all to what's up, young men are inevitably very interested in sex. That typically comes first, followed a bit later when they're around twenty-one by the shocking news that they're going to pass on. It may take five or six years for the shock to wear off. Death really is one of the biggest discoveries you ever make in your life: "My God,

I'm going to die!" That news can kick your ass for quite a while until you get used to it.

LM: Were there any more abstract sources for your interest in the relationship of sex and death—had you been reading Freud early on, for example?

CM: Yes, I had read widely in psychology when I was young. There's no escaping Freudian thought for any of us in the twentieth century, certainly not for our generation. I was definitely aware of that as a young man but I was also interested in trying to define another kind of self outside those kinds of definitions. But all that sex-death material was gut-level stuff that came not from anything I had read but out of my own personal reaction to getting the news. I honestly wasn't consciously putting much of *anything* into those early books. Beyond wanting to keep the energy level up, I was just including whatever bebopped into my head and hoping for the best.

LM: I gather, though, that you find yourself incorporating intellectual interests into your works more than earlier. Does this interfere with keeping your creative energy level up?

CM: Maintaining that early energy level is just as hard to sustain as the creative recklessness we just talked about. And, yeah, I'm reluctant to try and write out of areas that don't have any experiential, gut-level basis to them. So I consciously try to keep my intellectual interests out of my writing. I've found that those things interfere with my writing rather than help.

LM: Tell us a bit about the circumstances surrounding the publication of *All-Night Visitors*. The story goes that Girodias forced you to edit (or hatchet) the book, the result being that all the sex was left in but much of the background materials were jettisoned. Being edited that way certainly made your book have a very peculiar feel to it. You must have been disappointed in the way your book was cut, but weren't there some benefits that came of this? The cuts probably made it look more radically experimental than it would have if the full version had been published.

CM: Well, it's important to note that since I did all the revisions myself, I had some control over the end result. This wasn't a matter of having somebody else go through my book and having no input on what happened. I thought about it and decided I wanted the book published enough so that I was willing to do what they were asking, and then I tried to edit the book in such a way so that it would still be something I could live with.

LM: You mentioned earlier that your early works seemed to feed off your own personal sense of fragmentation. I'm wondering about the "creative problems" that being in a more secure personal position pose. Many of the writers I've interviewed admit that they were rather displaced people when they were younger—and that this in a sense helped them gather material for their works, the incoherence of their daily lives and the kind of experiences that they were having fed into their work. But what happens when you find yourself a more stable person? Can *that* fuel your imagination as much as the earlier situation? Or can you simply "recall" this earlier point in your life and feed off of that?

CM: You're describing something that most writers don't want to admit (or talk about at all!) but that affects almost any artist who does a significant amount of early work living on the margins, somehow, of success. In my own case, becoming a university professor, having a stable relationship with Pamela and a more secure sense of myself—these things have placed me in a radically different life-style and personal situation than what I was in when I started out writing. Of course, these changes have been enormously beneficial to me from a purely personal standpoint, but almost inevitably they are also going to present creative challenges. What happens is that you sacrifice some things—certain "negative" emotional energies that you can sometimes channel into your work, maybe a kind of direct empathy and contact with situations and people you don't encounter later on, or a kind of attitude like, "Since I'm out there on the margins, I'm going to do this really wild stuff that seems right to me, and fuck the establishment!" In other words, there's frequently all sorts of frustrations, financial and personal difficulties going on in the lives of many artists that can produce a positive, exciting sense of creative recklessness and originality in their work (though it's only fair to add here that probably *most of the time* these circumstances wind up just destroying the artist). If you do manage to make worthwhile art out of this situation and gain some recognition, that youthful sense of recklessness and energy will almost inevitably be sacrificed; but hopefully those sacrifices are offset by the other things you've gained—financial security, medical care, that whole range of middle-class comforts. Sometimes I don't think people are really fair about this with artists. You wind up being put on the defensive when "The Good Life" finally appears one day, miraculously it seems after everything that's come before. It's as if the audience is pissed off because now they're not going to be given their vicarious share of pain and anger and humiliation any more.

Still, there's no question that lessening your anxieties and gaining these middle-class comforts do wind up having an impact on your work. I know

I'm not as adventurous as I used to be—or let's say that being adventurous doesn't come as "naturally" as it did when I started out. I have to work harder to find innovations. I have to struggle against being content with what's familiar or the experimental approaches I've already used. Having a lot more experience in doing innovative work limits your options. I do know that I have to work harder to achieve the kind of genuine recklessness that came as second nature to me when I was younger. I remember sitting at my desk when I was twenty-five, banging the typewriter, throwing the carriage bar, radio going on this side, the window open, the neighbor beating their children. I was *in that world,* watching and listening and writing and getting the sounds of that world into my work. Not thinking about it, just letting whatever was in my soul come pouring out on the page. Well, I can't do that anymore. What I can do, though, is still try to be daring. I still find myself sitting down to write something (now at the computer terminal rather than the manual typewriter I used to peck away on) and feel myself pushing for some of that sense of recklessness I used to inhabit, come on, come on, push for it! Devil may care, get it in there!

In terms of creativity the good side to all this is that I don't think you ever completely lose touch with whatever it was that drove you to do what you did earlier on. Or at least if you want to keep it bad enough, you don't have to lose it. For instance, I think this six-hundred-page novel I've been recently working on has some of that craziness. It's just that now you've got to want it, whereas earlier it was just in the air, all around you, something you didn't have to grab because it was the air you were breathing.

Clarence Major

Alexander Neubauer / 1993

From *Conversations on Writing Fiction* (New York: Harper Perennial, 1994), 177–92. Reprinted by permission of Alexander Neubauer.

Born in Atlanta in 1936, Clarence Major grew up in Chicago. He graduated from the State University of New York, Albany, and received his doctorate from the Union Institute in Ohio. Among nine books of poetry and seven novels, he is the author of *My Amputations* (which won the Western States Book Award, 1986), *Such Was the Season* (a Literary Guild Selection, 1987), and *Painted Turtle: Woman with Guitar* (which was a *New York Times* notable book of the year, 1988). He has received wide recognition for his experimentation with and across fictional forms, including the novel, fable, and poem.

Clarence Major has taught both literature and creative writing at colleges and universities since 1968, among them Brooklyn College, Sarah Lawrence College, Howard University, the University of Washington, Seattle, and the University of Colorado, Boulder, where he taught for twelve years. He is currently director of the graduate program in creative writing at the University of California, Davis. In these pages he speaks of a consistently open approach to teaching writing, with no rigid style imposed on his students. In this regard, the importance of remaining open to influence is made clear: "Once you write a book, the experience of writing it will not in any way prepare you for the next one. It's always new, always fresh, always dangerous, always a struggle, word by word, step by step." He also speaks eloquently here of the great challenge for writers of all backgrounds to reach beneath a surface of culture, its "trappings and decorations, [in order to] tap into levels of human experience" to which all people respond.

Most recently, Clarence Major served as editor of the anthology *Calling the Wind: Twentieth-Century African-American Short Stories* (1993).

The University of California, Davis, offers a B.A. in English with writing emphasis and a one-year minimum (normally two-year) M.A. in Creative Writing.

Q: In your introduction to *Calling the Wind,* you write that you tell your classes, first thing, "I think we can begin from the assumption that storytell-

ing is vital to human health. It gives us workable metaphors for our lives."
What do you mean by that, and what are some of those metaphors storytelling
offers?

A: Any good piece of fiction seems to me to come out of a place in the
writer that is true—to put it very simply—a place that is true to who he or
she is in terms of just basic human experience, the whole inner landscape of
a human being. And at the same time, as I hear myself say this, I am thinking
that this in itself is the most difficult thing for a writer to achieve—to stay in
touch with the truth of who you are. Because the truth is always changing.
The challenge for the writer, it seems to me, is to keep up with that changing
truth, and to know how to identify it. It's a big, big task to ask any human
being to have that kind of sensitivity every day in the week, to have that kind
of command of him or herself.

Q: For young writers, would-be writers, I would think it would be especially difficult.

A: Absolutely. This is what I'm always trying to get my writing students
to understand, because, although we all want to stretch out and try things
slightly beyond our experience, to break new ground and reach into other
territory in terms of the kind of subject matters we choose, it's a tricky business. It can be done, but it has to be done while at the same time staying in
touch with all the really nebulous business going on inside that has a life of
its own, that really knows more than the writer knows about what people are
going to respond to.

Which is a long way of coming around to responding to your question.
What people are going to respond to *is* that human element, and the writer
has to stay in touch with that and it has to be true. The reader can tell instantly
when it's not true.

Q: When the writer drifts too far from his inner truth, you mean.

A: Even if it's not the *reader's* truth. Or let me put it another way: Even if
it doesn't have the same cultural definition as the reader's definition, the
reader will still recognize the essential human truth of it.

Q: To what extent, then, should the writer be active in trying to create
those metaphors, those truths, for someone other than himself? Or should he
not try at all? In what sense should he be actively reaching outside himself?

A: That's a good question. I think it's a tricky business to make any conscious effort in that direction. Because very often you step onto your own

feet, you get in your own way. To make a conscious effort, I think, is very often problematic.

You manage to do your best work, I believe, when you let it happen. When you find a way to listen to yourself, to let that true self give expression to itself. But let me just footnote that. You *do* have to make an early conscious effort at the same time in order to get to that truth. There is *always* the engagement of consciousness. It's just like dancing or skating or riding a bicycle. You learn how to ride a bicycle, to keep the two wheels going—but then you need to let it happen in a natural way. That may not be the best metaphor I can come up with, but I think it pretty much says what the creative process needs. It needs spontaneity and naturalness. If you're dancing, for example, and you're self-conscious and looking at your feet, you're going to lose your rhythm and get out of step.

Q: You've spoken of how much students from all backgrounds responded to the short stories by African-American writers that you've read to your classes, even though they previously hadn't heard of anyone aside from Richard Wright, James Baldwin, and Alice Walker. Why haven't those stories been used more?

A: Well, of course, we know why. We know of the whole pervasive existence of institutionalized racism, certainly in the curriculum, and the curriculum reflects the society. I think that probably explains a great deal of it. There have been efforts on the part of individual teachers to correct this and turn it around. I think it's very refreshing to watch my students discover characters who happen to be African-American and be able to identify with them. It creates an enormous amount of excitement in these kids to be able to see their own parents and themselves in these characters.

Q: You even mentioned it transcended ethnic boundaries.

A: It's just amazing. You see the papers they write. They get really turned on by that human element and identify totally. They also realize that, once they get through the cultural trappings, human beings are all pretty much alike and have the same kinds of aspirations and fears. It really makes a difference.

Q: This goes back to what you were saying in the beginning. In what sense should a writer who is trying to express a background, a culture, an upbringing, bring that background to the fore, and in what sense actively aim beyond it to universal concerns? It must be an extremely difficult balance.

A: And I'll tell you why. The necessary thing for any fiction writer is to reach down deep enough in him or herself to connect with this magic that will make the writing talk to readers. It's never a matter of getting *beyond* the ethnicity. I think it's a matter of reaching deep enough into it, below it. In other words, I like to think in vertical rather than horizontal terms— reaching down to a subtextual level, below the purely social level of experience and staying in touch with that as one creates a piece of fiction. I don't think it's any more difficult for the ethnic writer, black or Chinese-American or whatever, because that task alone is a very difficult thing for any writer to do. The tendency, no matter how smart or sensitive you are, is simply to reach for the easy identifying marks on the surface.

What you do, when you create a piece of fiction, is present a terrain that is essentially a surface. What makes it valuable to a reader, what makes it last as art, is the fact that a lot is going on beneath it, through implication. Teachers call it subtextual. All of it is implied. Hemingway had a term for it, the iceberg, the iceberg effect, where you show the tip and imply the rest. There's this huge, enormous amount below. The surface has to shimmer or vibrate in such a way as to radiate all of that other stuff beneath.

And it's pretty much the same for any writer. Life itself is enormously complex for anybody, and the business of trying to render it is always very tricky. I don't think any writer, no matter how intelligent, has any guarantee of being able to do this each time. I think you might succeed this year and then have a hell of time to repeat the performance. And you wouldn't even want to repeat it. To succeed you need it to be different.

Q: Those you've spoken of in the past who succeed at both levels, the surface experience and what's below—Ralph Ellison, Toni Morrison—do it so easily, effortlessly.

A: That's the magic of it. They've worked so hard it seems easy.

Q: But for a young student the stumbling blocks must be many in that regard.

A: The younger the writer, the more likely it is that he or she will not have had the experience to write about. There is also the possible problem of not being fully in command of the craft. Even if they feel things deeply, and many of them do—after age eighteen most people have enough experience to write a novel—the problem is to have distance as well as the technical ability to realize it.

Q: This might bring up the question of how one measures success in the classroom, both yours as a teacher and theirs as students. How would you define it?

A: Well, there are different kinds of success. In an undergraduate class, what I try to do is work with students on an individual level as much as possible, trying to create a context or atmosphere in which each student can discover what he or she needs to improve. Now, some people will come into an undergraduate workshop with more talent, some with less, and some will never be writers. No one is working at exactly the same level. In those cases where I know the student will never be a writer, I try to encourage that student to understand what makes the writing good, and through that help make them better readers. That's something that may stay with them the rest of their lives. With the others who are committed to writing and have talent, the only thing you can really do is be there for them and help them straighten out a few technical things, keep them on the right track. And that's what I do.

Now, in the graduate fiction workshop, it's much more likely that the participants will all be on a fairly advanced level. So you're talking to a different crowd. What I try to do there is treat them with respect, respect their talent, and talk with them pretty much as an editor would to a writer, to put it one way. To show them how to improve their work on technical terms and help them if there is some sort of conceptual problem.

Q: Are you trying to discover what they are trying to do and help them with that?

A: Yes, exactly, that's the main thing. And on the individual level, I tell my students all the time: Listen, you'll hear a lot of things in the workshop that are not going to be useful, and what I would advise you to do is be patient, sit through it, until you do hear something that is going to click with you. You are the only person who ultimately knows. You may not know it consciously yet, but eventually you will know what you need to do to make this thing work. Occasionally someone will say, "Well, how will I *know* when I hear what's right for me?" Well, you may not know what's right for you at the particular moment. I mean, that's one of the other things, at the risk of sounding immodest, that the instructor is there for, to sort of nudge the writers along in the right direction. Not to say, "Listen to this; don't listen to that," but to say, "Try this and see if it works." I try to be as diplomatic as I possibly can. I've discovered that a lot of good writers can be bad critics.

But I don't want to alienate anyone. I'm not a rude person anyway. It's really a difficult tightrope to walk, to keep everybody on the positive side and also direct them where I think they're going to benefit from what they're exposed to.

Q: Even though you don't try to impose your own style, can it ever be a completely communal experience? You are the teacher, and maybe there are some implicit psychological effects of your presence there as one who simply *knows*.

A: Yes, that's very true. When I don't know, I'm very honest about it, but most of the time I think I do know. I've been doing this for twenty-five years, I've read enough, I regularly review books for newspapers, and I'm always thinking about books and stories in critical terms, so I think I have some kind of expertise and some kind of right to say something about these matters.

But as much as I know, I don't know everything, and I don't think I'm always right. I also believe that there is no single correct way of reading a story or correcting a story. There are several possible ways to go. I've discovered that when there are problems in a piece of fiction there are several possible ways to fix those problems. Assuming that one individual has the answer creates the danger of falling into a very narrow path.

Q: From what you've said elsewhere about the process of your own writing, it sounds as if you allow the experience you want to write about to bubble up in its own time—two months, six months, a year—and the form you choose to write in will find itself also, poetry or prose. Is that right?

A: Yes, but the later truth is that a novel is a whole other ball-game. I can feel a novel, a *true* novel, that is—not a novel that didn't get written, and there are a lot of those, too!—but a true novel I can feel coming on like a storm. You can feel the atmospheric pressure like the weather, the whole shift in climate—I can feel it gestating. It's different with poetry. Poetry tends to come in shorter, quicker, faster doses, in shots, but then of course it may take a long time to work out.

Q: Can you, in so many words, tell your students, "Look, whatever confinements you find here, be sure to ignore them later on, because you have to find your own rhythm and pace?"

A: Absolutely. I believe that. When they sit down to the blank page, that's a whole different experience. Nothing I or anyone else has said is going to really save them or help them that much—unless they've already absorbed it and forgotten it. You know what I mean? If they've absorbed the best of what's said, put it in a useful place, and understood it at a gut level, then they don't need to think about it anymore. Again, it's just like riding that bicycle; you don't think about what makes you stay up on two wheels. Well, when you sit down to that blank page it's really the way it has to be. If you sit there with lots of critical information in the fore part of your mind, you couldn't get anything written. You can't remember anything that Professor Major said, or anybody said, that's going to help you.

Q: I'm curious about the twelve years you spent teaching at the University of Colorado in Boulder. While you were there you spent time on a Zuni reservation, didn't you?

A: I did a lot of research for a novel on Zuni. I used to go down to New Mexico and Arizona a lot, to the Navaho and Zuni reservations. Initially, I got interested in the Zunis because they were visited—I guess it was in the 1580s but I can't remember precisely—by a giant African. They had never seen anyone like that and they immediately made him into a god. And he stayed there and lived among the Zunis for many years. Well, as it turned out, by the time I got around to writing a novel about the Zunis, which is called *Painted Turtle,* he was left out entirely. He doesn't appear at all, not even mentioned. Once I learned about modern-day Zunis—met some of them, got invited to some of the ceremonies, and so on—I got more interested in writing about contemporary culture. The novel is set in the 1960s and deals with a young Zuni woman who is raped. She gives birth to twins, which is a very magical but also a very troublesome and problematic thing for the Zunis, as it is for most tribal people. No one seems to know what to do about twins. It's some kind of blessing and curse at the same time. I included a lot of the ritual and ceremony and songs. She's a folk-song writer and guitar player who makes the circuit around to these cantinas, playing music. It's one of the books I'm proudest of. I feel close to that book. And though it's set in another culture, a culture I had to acquire, I felt that every moment of it came from the truest place in myself that I could conjure up. Which is another way of saying that, no matter what the cultural trappings are, or what the window dressing might be, or what the cultural decorations consist of, it's still necessary to tap into that level of human experience people will respond to.

Q: How limiting is it that students in a graduate writing workshop don't have the luxury of that kind of research and the time to throw out a character and pick one up?

A: Well, actually, that's not always true. One of my students last year, for example, a woman of Anglo-Saxon heritage, actually finished a novel about a young black girl based on her experience in Philadelphia. She became so involved with this girl's life she actually identified enough with her to be able to write a novel. It was a most convincing thing. You wouldn't believe as you picked it up that someone who wasn't black wrote it. That happens all the time and we don't notice it.

Richard Price, for example, did it just last year with *Clockers* about a young drug dealer. And it's a genuine thing, a piece of art. He managed to get down to that genuine level that counts, rendering this drug deal in the most human, believable terms imaginable. So I take the position that the cultural stuff is fairly superficial; all you can do is understand what it means. The stuff that truly counts is beneath it. I could think of dozens of examples of that happening. For instance, James Baldwin writing *Giovani's Room* with depth and sensitivity, which has no black characters in it whatsoever. And Richard Wright's *Savage Holiday,* with no black characters, and it's a truly felt, deeply rendered story. There are dozens and dozens of examples, and not just across racial lines but in many, many different cultures.

Q: James Joyce writing as Molly Bloom at the end of *Ulysses?*

A: That's another example. The whole false argument that you can't write as the other gender. It's ridiculous, and we have some of the best examples in the world to prove it. An equally good one is [Defoe's] *Moll Flanders* in the voice of a woman, one of the most believable female characters I've encountered, written by a man.

Q: Does this relate to what you have said about there being no single "black experience"—that it's rather many different individual experiences and thus available to a variety of people.

A: This is something Ralph Ellison wrote about in the introduction to the new edition of *Invisible Man.* He talks about how his experience growing up in the Southwest was a black experience but a particular kind of black experience that was very different from the particular black experience Richard Wright had in the Southeast. Both experiences might be culturally defined as "black," as African-American, but they're different. They're shaped by different geographical and historical forces, and these two men coming in contact with each other would have had some communication problems.

Q: So if Richard Price is successful, then, he is not trying to represent an ethnic experience as a whole but rather one individual character within that experience.

A: And that character has larger implications for a whole part of the culture, but can't be said to speak for the whole culture—just as we wouldn't expect Richard Nixon to represent all of Anglo-American culture.

Q: Let me just ask you: "A shimmer of verbal energy made visible" is your wonderful phrase about good language in fiction. How important do you find language for your students today; are they experimenting with it or is it incidental to the content they're looking for?

A: Most of my graduate writing students are operating on different levels. Some are more sensitive to language and care about the quality more than others, so it's difficult to generalize. I try constantly to talk about how important it is to have that sensitivity, not just to get a handle on the language but to get in touch with a kind of lyrical intensity that's necessary to make the reading experience truly vibrate, truly resonate, to give the reader the fullest advantage. Now, as I say that, I am also thinking that a lot of it simply has to do with talent, some innate individual talent.

Q: And you either have it or don't.

A: Yeah, I didn't want to say that, but that's what I was thinking.

Q: Is a talent for language, actually, the same as saying that someone understands the human voice, its tone and rhythm?

A: I think so. That's what I mean. And some people have a sense of the voice, know how to listen and render that voice, just as some have a talent for music. Some have a good ear.

Q: I also wanted to ask you about the notion of a writing career. Rosellen Brown thought she remembered a quote from Toni Morrison to the effect that there was no such thing as a career in writing, that it really was just word after word, each individual effort one at a time. And then I ran across an article by James Fenton quoting Byron. Byron said that poetry is an expression of an excited passion, and that "there is no such thing as a life of passion any more than a continuous earthquake." And no such thing, therefore, as a life of poetry. Maybe that's what Toni Morrison was saying, too. What do you think?

A: I think they are both getting at the fact that it's never easy, that once you write a book, the experience of writing it will not in any way prepare you for the next one. It's always new, always fresh, always dangerous, always a struggle, word by word, step by step. And there are no guarantees. Unless of course you're writing formula fiction, where all twelve novels have this particular plot.

Q: Do you think students going into a program expect of that career a series of successful novels? Or do they see it as the struggle you described?

A: It looks very glamorous to them early on, a very glamorous way to live, to create these beautiful things called novels or poetry. I think at some point, if they're lucky, if they're smart enough, they realize it's a lot of hard work with uncertain benefits, a very risky business, and certainly not anything to go into expecting to make a lot of money. I think the ones who *have* to write will pretty much hang in there, because they're driven to do it.

Now, the tricky thing is that some people are driven to write even if they have no talent for writing. That's true. The two things have nothing or little to do with each other. Some people are driven to write who also have enormous amounts of talent and that's pretty lucky for them. But it still doesn't guarantee anything.

Q: And American writing programs, in that sense, are no different than anything else in life, I suppose. No guarantees. Although you've heard the criticism of them.

A: In twenty years we've seen our best writers come out of programs. I would say most of the best writers we have on the scene today—writers under forty—have come out of creative writing programs and have not been hurt by them—and some have even gained quite a bit.

The criticism that they all write alike is absurd; it's a prejudice with no truth whatsoever. It's a charge that's constantly made in print—I see it all the time—and it's absurd. We could create a list if we had the time of at least a dozen writers under forty who have come out of one program or another, and we could see just how different they are.

Q: Where did *you* learn to write, and from whom?

A: I never took any creative writing classes. I wish I had. I probably would have moved along faster than I did. It took a long time to evolve to a place where I could do good work. Had workshops been common, which they weren't. . . . Of course, in the context in which I grew up I can't say I regret that; they just weren't available. Very few people of my generation actually had workshop experiences. There were a few places I could have gone. Iowa was there, and Wallace Stegner was doing something at Stanford. But I can't think of other places actually involved in the teaching of creative writing in the sixties.

Q: But here you are, writing, teaching. . . . So how much would you say it hurt you that you didn't take these classes?

A: I think that had I the opportunity of insistent and continuous critical feedback, I would have benefited greatly. I didn't have people around me who could read my work and give me some smart criticism. I only had honest friends whose judgment I trusted. That was the way it was done.

Q: Do you feel you missed having role models in the classroom?

A: My role models were writers, I read their books, and I very often learned a lot from just the examples of the books. I can think of being absolutely swept away by one writer after another from the age of fifteen through twenty-one, being passionately devoted to them for that period of time. I think I learned a lot that way. I outgrew some of these obsessions, but I went through them and they were good for me. I was imitating these writers and that's a way of learning. It was a kind of apprenticeship for me. So I found my way by reading and imitating.

Q: What about incorporating outside reading into your workshops?

A: At the graduate level I don't use any texts, but at the undergraduate level I've used books and collections of stories. I think that's a good thing for writers beginning to get their feet wet, beginning to understand how to put words on the page that create a world we call fiction. I think it's really good at that level.

Q: Are your students clearly taken with certain fiction writers as models?

A: Oh yeah, absolutely. Not just [Raymond] Carver, but I have a student who is passionately devoted to a particular writer, and you can see it reflected in the work. There's nothing you can do about that but watch the student and help him or her in the technical things. In other words, when the echoes are strong, you know that it's just a phase and it's going to pass as the young writer gravitates to his or her own voice. And when they get through it they will retain some useful part of that experience, carrying it over into a fuller sense of self that has to be in place, out of which they write the real stuff.

Q: "Very few of us," you've written, "come to a piece of writing with the intention of giving it a chance to talk to us; we would rather talk to it." Do you feel even today, as an accomplished writer, that you should keep open to another book's influence?

A: Far less today for me. Although I will admit that there is that possibility.

The tendency is still there—I won't deny it—that if you read something you really like, you can actually absorb something and find yourself echoing it.

Yes, the tendency is there and we're open to it. That's why we read, isn't it? If not to have our lives changed, certainly to enlarge and deepen our sense of what our experience is all about.

Define Guidance

Fahizah Alim / 1994

From *The Sacramento Bee* (March 10, 1994), D1, D5. Reprinted by permission of *The Sacramento Bee.*

History often weaves a pitiable story of millions of African slaves looking at each other in helpless confusion, unable to communicate because they came from various tribes that spoke different languages.

Not so, says Clarence Major, author and English professor at the University of California, Davis.

"In Africa, there was a Bantu language that consisted of some 500 generic words that were common to 15 to 20 different African languages," says Major.

Slaves communicated with those words, many of which remain in some form in African American slang today. And some have even made it into American English, says Major.

"It's amazing how few people really realize the impact of Bantu on the American language," says Major. "The words 'funk,' 'juba,' 'rap' and 'hip' are straight out of Bantu, and there are many more."

Major, 57, has compiled these words of African derivation and thousands of other African American slang words created over the years, producing the most comprehensive publication to date: *Juba to Jive: A Dictionary of African-American Slang.*

"Slang is a private language with its own center of gravity, integrity and shape," Major says in a recent interview in his office at UC Davis. "African American slang itself is the classic example of a secret tongue. Since the days of slavery, this secrecy has served as a form of cultural self-defense against exploitation and oppression.

"Slang is integral to mainstream American language," he says. "African American language is the legacy of African culture and African words— specific words and grammar that came down from Bantu, that were still left in the pidgin language that the slave owners, slavers and drivers were speaking. It was a broken pidgin language that got all mixed up and everybody was speaking a mixture of everything.

"I don't buy this theory that Southern speech comes from Elizabethan

English, which is what a lot of linguists try to sell us. It comes primarily out of that hodgepodge (of English, Spanish, Dutch etc.) which includes Bantu. A large part of Southern speech is influenced by African grammar and African vocabulary."

Major refers to two recent publications that support his argument on the subject: *The African Heritage of American English,* by Joseph Holloway and *Black Legacy: America's Hidden Heritage* by William Piersen.

"Both of those books, published last year, deal with the influence of African culture and language on American culture generally," Major says. "The first one deals more specifically with the language. These are very exciting books. They kind of pull together research that has been going on for more than 75 to 80 years into the African American influence on American culture.

"If language didn't change, it would die," Major says. "It has to constantly change and evolve even if we're speaking at a small, secret level. It has to grow. Words are like organic things, they don't just go on. Some are reborn in different form."

Like the word "dope."

Did you ever think that getting the "dope" can be a good thing? According to Major's book, "dope" is also slang for information. And youth began using it as an adjective meaning good or outstanding. And fat with a "p" as in "pfat" is even better than being dope. Because "pfat" means superb.

How about a strong dosage of "Hoopdie Swoop"? (that's African American for a quick romantic pickup) at the "crib" (an old one for home or room).

Indicating today's fast pace, many African American youngsters have shortened the phrase, "all the time" to simply "24-7"—24 hours a day, seven days a week. Like: "Feels like I work 24-7."

There are many slang words that most people are familiar with, like "cool" or "right on", but then there is the slang that is peculiar to people of a particular region or those who work in certain professions.

"Broom to the slammer that fronts the drape crib"—meaning "Walk to the clothes closet." It's a phrase Major insists was popular in Harlem during the '30s and '40s and still is alive today. Or "Frisking the whiskers," which is the warm-up that musicians do before swinging into a full jam session.

For each entry, Major has given an etymology that gives the approximate date of the arrival into the language, geographical/group origin, examples of word or phrase in context and citations from primary printed sources or field resource.

Juba to Jive has slang from the 1720s to the 1990s, representing four main categories of African American slang: the early Southern rural born out of slavery; the slang of the sinner-man/black musician of the period between 1900 and 1960; street culture slang out of which rap and hip-hop evolved; and working-class slang.

"The point is," Major says, "that not all black speech is street speech. But a surprisingly large number of Americans believe this to be so." It's hard to imagine English professor Clarence Major using the language of a "sinner-man." Smiling-eyed and soft-spoken, his genteel countenance is more befitting the reputation he is gaining in this country's literary circles as a major talent possessing great versatility.

The author of seven books, 57-year-old Major is a poet, critic, novelist, essayist, editor and teacher. His vita is nine pages long with an exhaustive listing of his published work.

His fifth novel, *My Amputations,* won first place in the Western States Book Award contest in 1986. His anthology, *Calling the Wind: Twentieth-Century African-American Short Stories,* was selected as one of the *Publishers Weekly* Favorite Books of 1993.

Major published an earlier version of the slang dictionary in 1970. And immediately after it was published he started saving words and phrases for more than 20 years to include in this version.

And, of course, there is the language that he was raised with. He was born in Chicago to parents who had very "heavy Southern accents," he says. And mostly all he had to do was listen and write it down.

Major's dictionary has received nationwide acclaim in many major publications, including *People* magazine.

"I think this can be a great party book," he says. "But I did it mainly as a means of documenting an aspect of African American culture that has never been done to this extent. I want it to be used as a teaching device and to browse and enjoy. I'm trying to preserve a chronology of African American culture that seems to have been neglected." Major points out that recognizing the legitimacy of African American slang can be a useful tool in helping youngsters learn standard English.

He recalls a phone call from an elementary school teacher in Wisconsin, who had called a talk show to discuss his dictionary.

"He said, 'I used your book for many years while I was teaching in a ghetto school. I always started the class off with your book. And it got kids to talking. I reached them first. And then I would gradually bring them into an appreciation of standard English and using informal talks, as well. Once they became excited and interested in communication, the word is there and they never lose it. It was great."

Word. (interj. (1950–1990s) affirmation spoken in agreement; the truth.)

"What You Know Gets Expanded"

Nancy Bunge / 1995

It seems paradoxical that Clarence Major, author of 10 collections of poetry and 9 novels, claims he needs someone else's questions to provoke ideas about his writing, but this modest stance helps explain the depth and variety of his work. Clarence Major has not only produced poetry, fiction, and paintings, he has also compiled a dictionary of African-American slang, and has edited collections of African-American poetry and short stories. As his list of accomplishments grows, so does his interest and involvement in the rest of the world. He enjoyed putting together his anthologies because it gave him a chance to discover, assimilate and publicize fine work. He's delighted that the central characters in his recent novels differ so much from himself that they lead him into new territory.

Clarence Major offers a mundane reason for this intellectual and emotional vitality: he's moved a lot, so adjusting to new environments has made him flexible. Perhaps, but probably his hunger for new experiences, both internal and external, better explains the ever expanding range of his work.

Major's openness seems to rest on optimism. He says he's always had faith he'd make it as a writer. This interview reveals an equally deep confidence that fresh encounters will enrich his sensibility and his writing and that if he follows whatever attracts him, good work will emerge. These more specific tenets may well reflect his "sense of the ecology of things," for Clarence Major has been aware of the interdependency of all natural entities since childhood. This knowledge has as a necessary corollary the humbling insight that one moves towards fullness not by the impossible attempt to control the planet, but by resigning oneself to surrounding influences in the hope—often realized in Clarence Major's case—they will lead one into a dynamic interplay larger and more significant than anything one could dream up in isolation. So, Clarence Major welcomes someone else's questions.

CM: I never know what I think about my work 'til I start talking about it. (Laughter.) I'd prefer to follow your direction because maybe you can trigger thoughts. Otherwise, I don't have any. (Laughter.)

My perspective is clouded because it's so subjective and I've never reread any of my books. I've looked at parts, especially if I read a chapter at a public reading, but I haven't sat down and actually read any of them from beginning to end. I can't bring myself to do it. All I can remember is how I wrote the book. I can't remember the book.

NB: What do you remember about writing your first novel, *All-Night Visitors?*

CM: Well, *All-Night Visitors* was not written in any straightforward way. It was salvaged from four or five failed novels. The Vietnam section was originally a novel about Vietnam. I'd never been there, but I imagined this war story about soldiers in Vietnam and that didn't work. Then there was a novel about Chicago and there was this New York novel, a lower east side novel . . . So, bits and pieces pulled from here and there came together to make up that novel. As it turned out, only half of that book was published and since Olympia Press was interested in the sexy parts, they published a distorted version. My agent is now trying to get the full book published. It would be very different. It'll have that section in it, but that's the last part of the book and about 300 pages precede that portion that appeared as *All-Night Visitors.* I've always known that was not the true book and that the true book the way I wrote it should be published.

Maybe that was a learning process for me. I now plan it better and I don't risk as much as I used to. I don't have as much energy as I had when I was 20, when I could have the radio going, write a novel in two months, and write all day and then spend half the night out with friends, sitting around coffee shops; so I have to decide what I'm going to do and I have to think about it in terms of the amount of energy and time I have to do it. I don't just get excited and say, "I'm going to write a novel" (laughter) and then get 100 pages into it and say, "Oh, this is not working." I'm more skeptical about doing that now, but maybe that's not good.

Margaret Atwood was here recently and she visited my creative writing class. She said for every novel she's published, she's written at least four or five failed novels. I said, "You mean you write the whole thing out before you realize it's a failed novel? You have to do the whole five hundred pages?" She said, "Yes." I said, "You don't realize it a hundred or two hundred pages in?" "Nope," she says, "I have to do the whole thing and then I realize." I took comfort in hearing her say that she too has to put most of her work aside and not publish it and she finds herself salvaging parts of novels and using them elsewhere. I imagine a lot of writers do that: I wasn't aware that salvaging was so common. Over the years when I was doing it, I was doing it out of desperation, but . . .

NB: I thought your second novel, *NO,* came easily.

CM: I wrote NO on a long sheet of teletype paper. I got the idea from Jack Kerouac. It kept breaking because I had a (laughter) a manual typewriter and every time I'd go this way [hit the carriage return], the machine would go RRRRRR: it would tear and then I'd have to reinsert it. But I got a lot of momentum with that teletype paper. I finally learned to make it very loose. I'd go behind the typewriter and take a lot off the spool—part of a broom handle on a little rack—and then it just kept feeding it into the typewriter. And the momentum was really terrific; it worked. Of course, I was very, very young (laughter) and ambitious and courageous at the time. I guess that's part of being young. But that one came pretty easily.

That book I cannot bring myself to read. If I had to read any of my books again, that would be the last one I would . . . It should have been written another couple of times. It was close to being fully realized, but I didn't quite bring it to the point where it was fully articulated and focused and had a clear scenario. There's a very powerful story there, but it's submerged in the experimental surface of the book.

At least, I suspect that; I don't want to find out by rereading it. (Laughter.)

NB: It seems to me your work gets easier to understand. You're nodding as if that makes sense. Why does that make sense?

CM: Maybe because I'm more experienced at writing and I am more patient with giving a work time to fully develop and not rushing it into print. I rushed some things into print that I now regret, but, fortunately, I'm getting a second chance on *All-Night Visitors.* That can happen when you're young. I was eager to get going.

Also, I can think things through better. If I want to write a book, I don't want to know a great deal about it because that'll destroy the excitement, but I do want to have a sense of how it's going to look as a whole. In other words, I don't have to start from scratch, blindly feeling my way from day to day like I did with *NO* when I was in my 20's, writing whatever percentage of words and not seeing where I'm going, being lead by something in me I had no real control over. Now I can think in a more objective way and say, "Well, this is what I want to do." And yet I can still have the subjective experience and become emotionally carried away and lost in the creation of this character with one part of my mind and with [another] part of my mind being totally objective and controlling.

With *My Amputations,* I didn't know sequence by sequence what would happen, but I knew the shape of the book and I had the core idea in my mind: I knew that this would be a character on a quest. This would be a character who is looking ultimately to define himself as a figure in the western world and in relation to Africa as a distant legacy, but looking essentially for self-definition. I knew that much. I had no other clear idea about what would happen in terms of the sequence of events moment by moment.

But with *NO* I didn't have any clear sense of how that book was moving along. From day to day, I simply wrote whatever came to mind and the book sort of found itself. Well, normally, that's an ideal way to write a book, not to know what you're doing; but you have to rewrite it and rewrite it and rewrite it until you do know what you're doing. That's why I say it should have been rewritten again. I've often thought, well, maybe I'll rewrite that book. There's no rule against it. Lawrence wrote three versions of *Lady Chatterly;* I don't know that he did that because the first version wasn't clear, but all three versions are different.

NB: You talked about taking your dreams very seriously when you were young and you felt that prepared you for being a fiction writer and for letting things happen. Do you pay attention to your dreams now?

CM: Not as much, but I like to create dreams in fiction and I think that writing good fiction can be a way of constructing interesting dreams. I find it *really,* really remarkably easy to construct a fictional dream that makes sense as a dream and, in fact, that's what I tried to do with *Reflex and Bone Structure.* A lot of those episodes are based on what I like to think of as dream logic and I did that to some extent with *Emergency Exit*—those little episodes sort of stitched together with the logic of dreams.

NB: Do you ever have a visual shape in mind for your books?

CM: Very often. I'm a visual thinker. With *Reflex,* I knew that there would be a lot of space around each paragraph. And that's the way I wanted it to look on the page. That's all I knew about the shape of it: I wanted each paragraph to have a kind of presence, like a poem on the page—the space around it as important as the text itself. With *My Amputations,* I wanted what I was calling then verbal panels: panels like wall paintings or like Renaissance triptychs.

Such Was the Season, I deliberately wrote with straight, traditional chapters because I didn't want the physical appearance of the page to attract attention to itself. I wanted the story to take over in the reader's mind and I knew that the reader would be more willing to suspend disbelief if the reader didn't have to think about the page because that's what the average reader is accustomed to. They look at the page and they don't see it. In that case, the page is a pretext rather than a text.

NB: Do you paint while you're writing?

CM: I do. I do. I like to do that. It's a interesting break from one type of thinking to transfer to another type of thinking. And I can see some relationships between the two kinds of experiences: one, spatial and the other, temporal. But they are very close in every other respect. A painting is made up of paint, of things on a surface and a piece of text is made up of markings, of something on a surface.

NB: Do you paint the same way you write? If something interests you . . .

CM: Yes, I paint pretty much the same way I write. In other words, I discover what the painting is going to be as I work on it. That's very true. Although I may start with a fairly concrete idea in a formal sense, I start with a well-organized sense of the painting without knowing anything specifically about it. In that sense, it's exactly the same.

NB: You said that your painting had gotten better when you stopped worrying about being of your time.

CM: I used to worry a lot about that where the painting is concerned and I suppose with the writing too, but more with the painting because I had this notion that every good painter was of his or her time in some intrinsic way. All the great painters that I knew about were part of some period that was well-defined. Then I realized I couldn't box myself into that kind of frame. I didn't want to. It didn't make me happy. And why should I do it? The business of posterity is to take care of itself. I was not painting for posterity. I had to realize that was a rather phony and pompous position to hold. Although it may be true historically, it didn't give me any pleasure. What gave pleasure was doing whatever I wanted to do. In retrospect, I would say that there is no particular school dominant in our time in the arts, not since Picasso. Picasso worked in every possible modernist school and felt very free to do so from day to day: from realism to abstract expressionism and cubism and so on; but I just thought about that recently regarding Picasso. It's been very liberating to surrender all those notions.

There was a period when I thought I had to paint abstractly, or at least to do abstract expressionism. But it was never very satisfying.

NB: Did you have that feeling about writing, too?

CM: I always felt that my more so-called experimental writing was more fun to write but less fun to read (laughter).

NB: I can see how it would have been fun. In *Emergency Exit,* for instance, suddenly there's a picture of you with a bunch of cows and then there's a tennis match with words. Thinking up things like that would be fun.

CM: (Laughter.) Right, right.

NB: But wasn't it fun for you to write *Such Was the Season?*

CM: It was fun. Yes. It was fun to write. I had a lot of fun with that book; it was very driven. I was very energized and very excited about writing that book. It found its way very easily, very clearly from day to day.

NB: So your writing doesn't have to be wild to be interesting to do.

CM: No, it has to be a true experience. It has to be something that you're honest about. Something that's coming out of a true place in yourself, then you have a fairly good chance to get something going and to feel excitement about writing it. That's a lot of work to have to do in a state of boredom.

I think that even when I'm writing so-called non-autobiographical stuff like *Painted Turtle,* and Annie Eliza [*Such Was the Season*], there is some reference there that is a true reference. I'm not saying that you must write what you know. Shakespeare certainly didn't confine himself to autobiographical territory. A lot of good writers try to push beyond what they know and I don't have any problem with that. I think that's great. But what you know gets expanded. You come to know more than you knew and so it's still what you know; it's just that you enlarge yourself and you expand your horizon and you find yourself able to do things that you weren't able to do before. But that comes with some pushing and some preparation.

To break new ground, you have to push beyond what you know and if you make an emotional connection with it . . . with, say, the whole Zuni thing, I made an emotional connection there and cared about those characters *very* much. That's one of the essential keys to bringing a piece of fiction to life: if you care about the characters enough to make other people care about them—not just to like them, necessarily, but to *care* about them in the sense that they're going to be found interesting.

NB: Women are central to your work from the beginning.

CM: Right. My agent has always said that she loves the way I write about women most of the time, not all the time. And other people have mentioned especially Painted Turtle and Annie Eliza in *Such Was the Season.* Those two characters, Painted Turtle and Annie Eliza, tend to have a lot of appeal for women and they ask about them: how did I, a male, get into the characters, especially an older woman? How did I get into the character of such an older woman and make her come alive with so much conviction? My only answer is that I grew up in a house full of women. My mother was very much like this woman. I haven't told my mother that; she thinks that Annie Eliza is based on her sister, which is OK. In a way, she is based on her sister, but creating that character seemed very natural.

Like you learn to dance or you learn to ride a bike and then after a while you don't think about it; I know my mother fairly well, and I knew her better than I thought I did. When I started writing the book, I discovered how well I knew her. She came out as a convincing character because of that inarticulate experience. When I decided to do the book, I really didn't know that I could do it, but it was following a trip to Atlanta and I spent a few days with my aunt there and she and I would have coffee at the kitchen table very much the way the character and Annie Eliza have coffee and so on, but none of the other stuff really happened. It's not strictly autobiographical. I didn't spend a week there, I didn't go on a trip with her looking for my father's grave. . . . There was a big dinner party. That part was the first chapter I wrote to see if it would go anywhere. Then it looked like it could be a novel, so I kept playing with it and it did turn out to be a novel.

Painted Turtle is a different kind of experience. She evolved over a long period of time. My first attempt to write her story was as a first person narrative, and then I realized that the voice wasn't convincing. So, I rewrote it from her male lover's point of view; but even earlier than that, she was a black woman based on a movie star named Dorothy Dandridge.

Painted Turtle grew out a Dorothy Dandridge book which is why she's a musician. There's a chapter where's she's doing the limbo that was originally in the Dorothy Dandridge novel. Dorothy Dandridge actually did the limbo in Rio. I kept that because it was one of the better chapters in the Dorothy Dandridge book.

I find myself doing that, salvaging failed novels by using a chapter or two here and there and seeing if I can make them work somewhere else, or even as short stories.

NB: Are they better used later on as if they were part of something you hadn't figured out yet?

CM: I think that's very true. That's very true.

And I got interested in native American culture and spent a lot of time in the Southwest. We used to drive down there and go to some of the ceremonies. I got particularly interested in the Zuni culture because their history is unique: they have the only language that can't be traced back to any understandable linguistic family. Some people think it sounds closer to Chinese than it does to the other Native American languages in that area. Also, they early on encountered a giant Black man, Esteban, who came through there. I was interested in how they accommodated him and he became a leader in one of the clans. I had him in one of the earlier versions of the novel, but then I realized the more I learned about Zuni culture, the less interesting his presence became in the context of the novel, so eventually he disappeared altogether and my focus became much more centered on Painted Turtle.

NB: Did *Such Was the Season* evolve in a similar way?

CM: *Such Was the Season* was one of the nice experiences where the whole thing fell together early on and didn't change radically after I started working. Although it did, of course, go in directions I didn't anticipate. That always happens: that's the exciting part about writing.

There are certain works that come to you as a gift, ready-made. That happened with the short story of mine called "My Mother and Mitch." That came to me one morning. We were living outside of Philadelphia, I got up one morning and (snaps fingers) I wrote it in three hours at the computer, just wrote it and didn't change anything. It came out the way it is. I went thorough it and made a few penciled changes, but essentially there was no struggle. That's very rare for me. Usually it's a struggle and three or four drafts.

NB: When you write, each book is a new . . .

CM: discovery. Yeah. I'm trying to see what I think about a set of things or a situation or a character. With Annie Eliza [*Such Was the Season*], it was the voice and in *Painted Turtle,* I was interested in exploring Zuni culture through this persona and see what I could do with her at the same time.

NB: *Such Was the Season,* you focused on the voice. *Painted Turtle,* you started with something else. There's no pattern with you, is there?

CM: Well, a lot of these things were influenced by where I was at the time.

The sense of place is important. I lived in Colorado for twelve years and that's a very special place in terms of the landscape and the Native American culture all around you there. The book never would have been written had I not lived in Colorado, so it grew out of that experience.

NB: So, you think you find yourself in a certain place, you're fascinated by something, and you go with it.

CM: Right. Exactly.

NB: And probably part of what fascinates you is what you don't know about this.

CM: Right. And I discover places I want to know about how I'm relating to them, what it means to me, trying to bring some focus to it. I did a book-length poem called *Surfaces and Masks* that came out of the experience of living in Venice. I never would have thought, "Well, I'm going to write a long poem about Venice." Place for me is very essential and metaphoric. Unlike most writers, I don't have a particular place that I identify with like Faulkner or like Paule Marshall. We always moved a lot. I don't have the rootedness that some people have. I used to think that was a disadvantage, but now I think it's an asset because it gives me more flexibility and it gives me a chance to start over again in a fresh way with new ideas. I don't have to walk through the same river over and over and over and over and over. But it also, I suppose, in the market place has a disadvantage, because the way books are marketed has to do with what image a writer can establish and if each book is different, then publishers don't know what to do with you.

What has happened in my work is a little closer to the American experience now. Americans tend to have less rootedness than most people. They have a tendency to move from state to state, job to job, profession to profession. I read that most Americans nowadays will have two or three professions in the span of a lifetime which implies that they're going to be moving, buying houses, selling houses, leaving. . . . When we were living in France and in Italy, people were amazed that we had lived so many different places: "How could you have done that? That makes no sense to me. We have a family house here and we've always gone there every summer. We couldn't imagine ever going anywhere else." That's the way they live and think; it's very different from the way I've grown up and the way that most of the people I know have grown up.

NB: It seemed to me that when you wrote about Venice, you could have looked at Venice in terms of corrupt, capitalist, European . . . , but that wasn't interesting to you.

CM: I'm much more interested in people than I am in ideas. I'm interested in ideas from the point of view of being a fiction writer or a writer of poetry. I think of culture as the window dressing; all human beings are essentially the same. The writer has to trust most those factors universal in human nature. I'm interested in ideas to the extent to which they find expression in the actions of people or characters.

But with the Venice poem, John A. Williams wrote a review in which he talked about the political, social . . . There is a political subtext there. I wouldn't say that John was wrong in his reading of that poem. After I read his review, I thought back, "Well, there are all those literary references and political references and historical references set in a present day context, and a lot of references to western religion, Christianity and the relationship between the political history of Europe as represented in Venetian history to Christianity." But what I found interesting was trying to isolate a string of images that seemed dramatic to me . . . evocative, but interesting in themselves and that could be read the way you read a story or the way you read a good poem. I wasn't thinking about political implications.

It's the business of the subtext to take care of itself. I don't think that any kind of conscious effort on that level is legitimate and is going to serve anybody well because you run the risk of being too didactic. How can you consciously create a subtext? You can't do it. You just can't do it. It won't work. You're not writing sincerely if you do. I don't think you're writing anything anybody would care to read. (Laughter.) If there is a subtext, it has to find its own way. So if I am political, it's to that extent. But I think my primary conscious concern is with creating images and seeing if I can put them together in some fascinating way.

NB: You did that African-American fiction anthology and then you're redoing the African-American poetry anthology.

CM: I'm redoing everything I did when I was 24, 25. The anthology came out; I'm going to republish *All-Night Visitors;* I redid the dictionary [*Jube to Jive*] and the poetry anthology is coming out next year. I'm revisiting all of these things that happened at the beginning of my writing experience and trying to make them better. But it wasn't planned. I didn't plan to do the poetry anthology. It was suggested by an editor. Somebody asked me to do the dictionary and offered me an attractive advance; so I said, "Ok, I'll do it."

NB: You said you were having a wonderful time reading books that had been overlooked for your poetry anthology.

CM: That's true. That's true. They'd been in the vaults for years.

NB: Don't you get in trouble when you do that? Don't you irritate people because they have these notions of what you're supposed to include and then you add this other work . . .

CM: Right, right. Also, they want you to include the poems that have been documented and anthologized and critiqued, so that they can do them over and over and over and they don't have to think about anything new. I've made a slight compromise. Like, with Dunbar, I put in a couple of his poems that people know and then I add four or five poems that have never been published before a couple of years ago. People don't know them and they're *magnificent* works; they're *wonderful*. So, I've done that with some of the classic African-American poets. People will say, "Well, why didn't he use blah, blah, blah. Why did he use this . . .", but I'd like to break new ground because I don't want to just repeat the same things. I like people to see that there is a greater breadth and depth to the body of work that African-American poets did in this century than has been represented in anthologies. I'd like to think that this book is going to make a difference. It may take a few years for people to warm up to it, but who knows, maybe not. Actually, I think it'll be taught right away.

NB: Does all that reading take away from your own writing?

CM: Not really. It was a pleasure because you have to take a break from your own writing and from yourself. It was energizing and very refreshing to read a lot of good work. So, I'm very happy about it. I think it's a good book; it's a very good book.

NB: *Juba to Jive* looked like a huge amount of work.

CM: That was a killer. That was a lot of work. It's doing very well, actually. I've had writer friends call up and say they keep it right alongside the computer or the typewriter. That was just work. Some of the examples were fun to write; it was like writing fiction because I made 'em all up. (Laughter.)

NB: You said in an interview that you were pleased because you had gotten more and more out of yourself with your characters.

CM: That's true, that's very true. And that's even truer with the novel [*Dirty Bird Blues,* Mercury House 1996] that I'm working on now which is about a blues singer in the 40's and 50's who is as different from me as you can imagine. He's a cigar smoking, big, six foot, 250 pound black guy with a great booming laugh. He's jolly and he's full of life and he's charismatic. I've never worked with a character like this before. But I love him. He's just great. He's wonderful. I love this character. He's just beautiful. So, I can do that kind of thing now.

NB: Why do you think you can do it now when you couldn't do it before?

CM: I was so busy trying to articulate myself and trying to define myself. I don't think I need to do that anymore. I know who I am. It took a long time. (Laughter.) Fifty years, but I know now. It's done.

I can look at these other characters now and enjoy them and have a lot of fun creating them and following their thoughts and their feelings and seeing what they want to do, so that's very freeing.

Even when I was trying to write the Dorothy Dandridge novel, I was trying to move away from that self-centered approach, trying to move away from using myself as a model. And took a long time to get it right. I think it worked with Annie Eliza, it worked with Painted Turtle, and I hope it's working with this blues novel.

But it doesn't mean that I'm going to always write that way. I'd like to come back at some point and use myself again as a model, not myself in any kind of autobiographical sense, in a realistic sense, but to use my emotional life as a model for a character. In fact, I have in the back of my mind a novel I'd like to write about a boy and his mother and it's going to be in a sense based on my experience with my mother, but not in a strict sense since I didn't grow up with my mother alone. But I want to write a novel about a boy who has his mother to himself and the whole experience of that relationship. The idea is based on the short story that I wrote, "My Mother and Mitch." I like to play with that. I don't know if I'll write such a novel, but right now I think I will and I'd like to try.

My mother was much more authoritarian. She was not my friend in the sense that this boy's mother is his friend and they are at times like kids together. She was my caretaker, but she was not my buddy, and so I'd like to see if I can make that into a novel. I think that would be interesting.

NB: When you plan this novel about the boy and his mother, is that as specific as it gets?

CM: That's as specific as it gets. I don't know what's going to happen. I don't want to know. All I have is this idea about this relationship.

NB: So, it's just that something attracts you.

CM: Something attracts me. I'll tell you what it is: one summer, my older sister went away, I think she went to Atlanta to visit. And for some reason, I can't remember why, I didn't go. Although we had the habit of going together, this particular summer she went down there for about a month and my mother and I were alone together and *it felt so different. It felt so different.* It was a new experience; I'd never, never felt that way before, didn't feel that way after she returned and I had the kind of experience with my mother that maybe I preferred. I don't know. It was a wonderful experience and we were friends for about a month. It was great, it was great, it was great. And once my sister came back, everything fell back into place, into the old pattern; we all went back to our roles. (Laughter.) I found myself in a new relationship with my mother that was very appealing. Not that I want the book to be a happy, happy book. It probably will be a happy book, but not a silly book. I want it to be a serious book, but beyond that I don't know what it's going to be about except that I want it to be about that relationship. But in this book, he's going to be an only child; he won't have sisters.

It may be a book I won't write, but it's an interesting thing. I have a lot of ideas for novels that never get written. You'd be surprised at how many. I think about them for a month or two, sometimes a year, sometimes I might write 20–30 pages and realize this is not going anywhere.

I do have a rough draft of another novel that I haven't given up on. I have 260 pages, rough pages of the novel that I'm not really prepared to talk about; it's a novel about a young couple.

NB: Why don't you want to talk about it?

CM: It's more disturbing in that I don't know what I want to do with it. I don't know where it stands. And it's been problematic and it's annoying for me to think about it. (Laughter.) All I know is that every time I think about it, I feel slightly depressed because I can't quite figure out how to get the energy into it that I want. But I haven't given up on it.

NB: You mention that you've loved nature since you were small.

CM: I pity kids who grow up in these iron jungles like New York and Chicago, never see trees, never see flowers and plants and grass, never roll around on the grass. That's so essential for a small child to have that. When

I was a kid, we used to go exploring in the woods; the wonderment at nature was a very real part of my imagination and my early experience. I wouldn't trade that for anything. It fed my imagination.

It gives you a sense of how you connect with life. You can see all of the manifestations of life in that environment: you can see growing things, you can see reproduction, you can see the relationship between animals and plants: it's all there. Even if you can't articulate it, you can feel the presence and power of it. Although I probably would never be characterized as a nature writer, I feel the sense of that is in my work, and I like to think that I have a certain reverence for all of life, the whole earth, the ecology of things.

NB: Could you have ever been derailed?

CM: No, no. I had this romantic notion that somehow I was different (laughter). I always had a lot of self-confidence despite my inadequacies or my disadvantages. I know a lot of people who've been derailed, but I always think that they didn't have to write or they didn't have to paint. I have students come to me all the time asking, "Well, should I make writing a career?" And I always am tempted to say, "If you have to ask that question, the legitimate answer is No." You wouldn't ask that question if you felt a sense of calling, to put it in religious terms—not that I'm strictly religious. I like to think that I'm spiritual in some ways.

NB: Could you stop writing?

CM: No, no. I wouldn't stop writing. It's something I need to do; it's part of how I live and how I think. There might come a time when I feel I don't need to write, but I can't imagine that time. I can't imagine it. Right now, it feels like I still have a lot to articulate and it seems necessary. It's the hardest question in the world to try to answer. It's like saying, "Why do you breathe? Why do you have eyes or hands?" But it's also interesting because I wasn't born writing, but I was born breathing (laughter). So, the analogy isn't strictly legitimate. And, at the same time, maybe the impulse behind the writing is as intrinsic as breathing.

An Interview with Clarence Major

Rebecca Morrison / 1995

From *Poetry Now* (June 1, 1995), 7–8. Reprinted by the permission of
Poetry Now.

Clarence Major is the author of seven novels and nine books of poetry. His
three most recent novels, *My Amputations* (Western States Book Award,
1986), *Such Was The Season* (Literary Guild Selection, 1987/*The New York
Times Book Review* "Summer Reading" Citation, 1988), and *Painted Turtle:
Woman with Guitar (New York Times Book Review,* Notable Book of the Year
Citation, 1988), received wide critical attention. His story collection, *Fun &
Games* (1990) was nominated for a *Los Angeles Times* Book Critics Award.
His work generally has been the subject of many scholarly articles, disserta-
tions; two special issues of *African-American Review* (1979/1994) and trans-
lated into French, German, Italian and other languages. Author of *Juba to
Jive: A Dictionary of African-American Slang* (1994), Major has edited two
highly successful anthologies, *The New Black Poetry* (1969) and *Calling The
Wind: Twentieth Century African-American Short Stories* (Quality paperback
Book Club selection, 1993). He is recipient of many awards, among them, a
National Council on The Arts Award (1970), a Fulbright (1981–1983) and
two Pushcart prizes (1976/1990). He reviews for *The Washington Post Book
World* and has contributed to *The New York Times Book Review, The Los
Angeles Times Book World, The Baltimore Sun Magazine, The Providence
Sunday Journal, San Jose Mercury News, Denver Post, Essence, Ploughsh-
ares, The Kenyon Review, The American Review, The Review of Contemporary Fiction, The American Poetry Review, Michigan Quarterly Review,
Massachusetts Review* and more than a hundred other periodicals and anthologies in this country, Europe, South America and Africa. In 1991 he served
as fiction judge for The National Book Awards and has served twice on
National Endowment for the Arts panels. He has traveled extensively and
lived in various parts of the United States and for extended periods in France
and Italy. A graduate (Ph.D.) of the Union Institute and a professor for more
than 20 years, Major has lectured in dozens of US universities and in
England, France, Liberia, West Germany, Ghana and Italy.

Clarence Major is currently Professor of African-American Literature and

Creative Writing, University of California, Davis. The artwork accompanying this interview is reprinted with the permission of the artist, Clarence Major.

CM: So you want to know about poetry. What do you want to know about poetry? I suppose we could start with what William Carlos Williams said—that people turn to poetry for various things, and many people have perished for the lack of what can be found in poetry. In other words, you won't find the daily news in poetry, but you will find something that is life sustaining and something that is essential. I think poetry is really misrepresented a large part of the time in our culture because it's not understood to have this really essential correlation with life. In other words, the rhythms of poetry, for example, correlate with the very rhythms of our speech, the way we walk, the way we talk, the heartbeat, the rhythms of the ocean and everything. It's all so intrinsic to human life and by extension to all life because it has its basis in life, in natural rhythms of life. But I think what happens very often is that cultures don't exactly give up poetry but redefine how it's used and what it's called. For example, today, in a culture like ours which is this huge huge unmanageable, undefinable 3,000 miles of land, music or lyrics probably take the place of poetry.

RM: How long have you been writing poetry and how did you first get involved?

CM: I was a teenager before I really discovered that it was possible to write something good. I was reading a lot of things on my own. Not only just in school, but a lot of things that I was discovering on my own, and the first discovery that really mesmerized me was the discovery of the French poets, Rimbaud, Verlaine and Baudelaire—*Flowers of Evil, The Drunken Boat, Party, Illuminations*—those poets. And they were decadent. I didn't know what the word meant, but I knew I liked that imagination, and the color and the whole dislocation of the senses that was going on there that was just this beautiful kind of thing that I could visualize. And I thought, "This is something magical. This is something really incredible." And of course I never would have been allowed to read those poets in school because they weren't taught in school, not in the school I went to. I simply wandered into a bookstore one day and discovered a book, an anthology of the three of them, which became a kind of bible for me for a long time. And for a long time I tried to write poetry like that. So that's how I got started.

RM: You said earlier on the phone that you were teaching a class on "Poetic Theory."

CM: Yes, it helped me define my own theories about poetry. I mean, everybody knows that poetry is a kind of music made out of talk. I've known that for a long time, but I never got down to the very technical aspects of counting syllables or counting time. There are two schools of thought about this. A lot of poets believe you really should be able to count syllables. In other words, a certain number of syllables per line gives you a certain kind of measure, and a certain kind of control is established through careful manipulation of the number of syllables that lies in the falling of the human voice as it goes through those particular paces. But I discovered that maybe William Carlos Williams was right when he said, "Counting syllables is really silly." That's really not what it's about. Maybe what we need to do is count time the way you do in music. You count time, you talk about the beat in music, and counting time, and keeping time. I thought about that for a long time and struggled with that and I think there's a lot to be said for the terminology of music or the musical theoretical approach because poetry is a type of music. It's closer to music than it is to any of the other arts, in theory. In other words, what I'm trying to say is that in teaching a course like that, I was forced to make certain decisions that I probably would not have had occasion to make on my own. So I do feel that I learn things when I'm teaching courses like that.

RM: You say that poetry is a lot like music. What about painting? Your novel *Emergency Exit* contained some paintings of yours. Do you do a lot of visual art, and is there a relationship between that and your poetry and writing?

CM: Yes, not only in my work, but just generally, I think there's a strong relationship between modern poetry and painting. I know that's true in my work. In fact, I believe I've been more influenced by painters than I have by poets because I think of myself as a visual thinker. I see things in terms of pictures. I translate abstractions into visually accessible terms. I've listened to other poets talk about this, and in retrospect it seems to be a very common thing. I didn't realize it in the beginning, but e. e. cummings was a painter, William Carlos Williams was a painter, a lot of the modern poets painted. Derek Walcott is a painter. And maybe there is something complementary there. And the sensibility of the painting process, the way the imagination works for painting may be very very similar to the way it works for poetry. Poetry, I think, although it's close to music in terms of how it sounds, is certainly closer to painting than fiction is, in the sense that how it looks on the page is very essential, not just how it sounds, at least in terms of modern poetry. That's not necessarily true with fiction which just runs across the page and down the page. As long as fiction is clear and accessible, you don't worry about it too much. And it's not just a matter of color either, and lines, I think it has to do with the shape of things, the perceived shape of things. A word, an isolated word on the page, or a phrase that is set aside for emphasis, for example, can have an incredible amount of energy, the way a certain kind of perceived shape in a painting has. Although it's two dimensional, but the illusion of an object can take on a kind of presence I think that's close to the kind of thing I'm trying to describe in poetry, that can happen in poetry. Anyway . . . you've been reading my work. I'm really flattered.

RM: It seems like you work poetry into your fiction.
CM: Well, you do that too.

RM: Also, some of your characters seem to be seeking a truth. Like Mason in *My Amputations* who says, "The primary responsibility of literature involves creating truth." And I wonder if when you write, do you just want to tell a good story, or are you trying to discover some essential truth?
CM: I'm always searching for a new way to get at a stronger sense of what I'm trying to give expression to—whether it's truth, or reality, or whatever you want to call it. It becomes this thing in the world that has its own presence and it begins to represent a whole complex network of maybe ideas and feelings. Like a piece of sculpture might move you a certain way, and then another person another way, so it gets redefined by whoever is engaged with it. So yeah, I do try to blur the boundaries between the poetry and the fiction for that reason precisely. I am searching each time in an experimental way for a way to get at, to create that kind of presence. And I say it that way, because I want to deemphasize the idea of ideas a little bit. In other words, if I give expression to ideas, I want those ideas to be generated through the work rather than to be directly stated. In other words, through symbolism, through whatever. If it's fiction, through action of the characters. And if it's poetry, through the imagery, through the rhythms and whatever, but mainly through the imagery.

RM: Like William Carlos Williams said, "No ideas but in things."
CM: Right. Exactly. That's exactly it. It's the thingness that I'm after. And that thingness can represent a lot—thoughts, whole ways of life, who knows, in a young person.

RM: Someone told me you used to be a radical. What do you think they meant by that?

CM: I like to think that I was radical in a technical sense, radical in terms of esthetics. But I certainly had social ideas and I certainly was not conservative in the sixties. I cared about issues, but largely, I did my fighting in my work.

RM: How long have you been teaching, and have you seen students' attitudes change over the years? Are there more students interested in poetry now?

CM: It's hard to say. I think there's always been a large interest in poetry, relatively speaking. In a much larger context, there's been no interest at all in poetry in this country. But at the level of poetry workshops in universities, I don't think that the level of interest has diminished or increased very much over the years. I think there's been a consistent amount of interest on the part of a small coterie of people who have come along, one generation after another. I haven't seen much change in the last twenty to thirty years.

RM: What about the types of things that people are writing about? Do you see people writing about the "fin de siecle" madness?

CM: Well, I don't really think so. I'm on the committee that evaluates new incoming students, and I read a lot of the stuff that's coming in. And it doesn't look that different to me from what people were writing twenty years ago, really, in terms of subject matter. I really don't see very much doomsday poetry. Although I can't imagine why not with the way the world is going.

RM: I just wondered if you're working on any new books of poetry?

CM: I've been working on a lot of poetry lately. Not so much with a book in mind. Actually I've been writing animal poems, and maybe these poems will take shape and end up as a book with poems about animals, and insects and plants. I find it very very fascinating to try to see the whole universe in a moment in nature, or to see the whole expression, to see the whole drama of life, maybe through one moment of a lizard poised on a rock. Something like that. I'm very interested in exploring what's possible in that kind of moment. And I've played with a lot of those kinds of things lately, and published a few of them.

RM: Well, it looks like we're out of time. Thanks for taking time out of your busy schedule for this interview. I'll let you get back to your ringing phone and the people who keep knocking on the door. I'm looking forward to seeing some of those animal poems.

An Interview with Clarence Major

Charles H. Rowell / 1997

From *Callaloo* 20.3 (1998), 667–78. Reprinted by permission of Clarence Major.

The following interview was conducted by telephone between Charlottesville, Virginia, and Davis, California, on February 15, 1997.

Rowell: You began your career as a visual artist, not as a writer. You studied at the Chicago Institute between the late 1950s and early 1960s. Is there a relationship with your studying visual art and your writing career? When and how did your writing career surface as you went about the work of the visual artist?

Major: Well, that's a very good question. I started writing rather naively but seriously around the age of twelve. And of course I was painting and drawing much earlier. And the writing, I think, was always complementary to the painting and vice versa. It seems to me that when I started taking art lessons at the Art Institute, I was in high school. Chicago at that time had a program for talented students. They could get scholarships to places like the Art Institute. So that's how I got started there. And later on, I won a fellowship and continued there until I went into the Air Force. But, anyway, the writing was something that was much harder to master. And I continued with the painting and made whatever effort I could with the writing. It was so frustrating trying to write well. I can remember the frustration of writing novellas—writing them down in long hand and then reading them a month later and being very disgusted with the quality of the writing. But that was not true of the painting, and so I tended to gravitate toward the painting more, because satisfaction was almost immediate. So I found myself writing poetry more frequently than prose, because that too gave more immediate satisfaction and was somehow easier for me than trying to write those novels, which were really not novels, anyway. They were long stories and rather clumsily done, but still it was a useful apprenticeship. And, you know, we all need that.

We all need the apprenticeship, and, you know, there were times when I did have people I could turn to with the painting, but rarely with the writing.

I took private art lessons from Gus Nall, who was a well-known painter at that time in Chicago, and I learned a lot about what I needed to do with the surface of the canvas and so on. He built an easel for me and taught me how to stretch canvas and so on. But there were very few people I could turn to with the writing problems I had. My teachers were not always available. I mean there were a couple of teachers I can remember who were very encouraging, but it was just hit and miss all the time. There was an old man who ran a bookstore in my neighborhood who was also very encouraging. He had known Richard Wright. He talked about Wright a lot and got me started reading people like Wright and Chester Himes and so on. But he was one of the few, one of the few along the way early on who gave me a sense of direction and helped me.

Rowell: Do you know why the writing was more difficult—that is, the writing of prose fiction more difficult than the painting? And why poetry was easier and more satisfying than prose fiction?

Major: Well, it was more immediate. Because of the density and the way poetry tends to lend itself to a sense of play and music and so on. You know, I think we're all closer to poetry when we're younger than we are later on. But I think I was instinctively closer to poetry because of the rhythms and the patterns. We all grew up with a sense of poetry, in the nursery rhymes and so on.

Rowell: But we don't grow up with a sense of paint on the canvas. Why was that easier than writing? I realize that we don't grow up writing prose either, but we use the medium of prose from the beginnings of our lives. We talk.

Major: Well, who knows why anybody is drawn to a particular thing? I mean some kids just sort of gravitate toward music, sports or whatever. Who knows why we have a particular leaning toward one thing or another, which we generally call a talent? But you see kids everyday who just have a particular instinct for something.

Rowell: Does that translate also for writing? A particular instinct for writing and, therefore, the person becomes a writer? But doesn't one have to learn the craft and practice? It's no different, I would think, from learning to play the piano or learning to play basketball. They're all art when performed very well.

Major: I think that's true. In fact, I've always felt that to be, more or less.

I do believe that it is possible to have a talent for writing but not to have the need to write. In fact, one of my best friends in high school, for example, was a very gifted poet and prose writer, but he had no particular need to write, and of course he didn't become a writer. On the other hand, I think there are people who have no particular talent for writing but learn how to do it and make a career out of it because they do have the need. So I agree with you, but that's an exception, I think, to what you're saying. I think that there are people who have talent for writing. It's a harder thing to get a handle on than painting, which is what I was trying to say. Part of the problem has to do with materials. Painting has materials that are very accessible, very clearly defined, whereas, with the art of fiction or poetry, you are working with something that we normally use everyday almost unconsciously— speech. And that is something that is harder to get a handle on and something that is harder to see and less clearly defined, because of its nature. And there is the other factor, too, about it, because it's always changing, it's evolving a lot faster than the materials that one would use as a painter or a sculptor or a person who is working at any of the crafts. In that sense, maybe it's a little bit like music, but the material of music is even more difficult, I think, to get a handle on, for the same type of reason that speech is. Writing is linear. And I do want to make a distinction between writing and speech, but you can't make a sharp distinction. You can't separate writing too clearly from speech. Though you do have the text to deal with, and that's linear. Whereas painting tends to be . . . what's the word I want? Spatial! Painting is essentially spatial, while writing moves from left to right and down the page, and that's a temporal process. Yet, I think that there is a kind of innate relationship between the two forms because you can't really separate time from space.

Time and space are really intrinsic to each other. One could not exist without the other. So, in that really, really, core basic sense, I think that they [writing and painting] are grounded in the same place. I mean, I remember not long ago coming across a passage somewhere about this very subject. The point was that writing is just scratches on the page, you know, just little marks, usually in black ink on the page. And how is that so different ultimately from what drawing and painting are really basically about? In the Chinese or Japanese language you can see the relationship clearer. This is also true of some of the more primitive languages and earlier languages. We have pictures that are clearly bridging that space between the symbol and the image and what later becomes the more abstracted form of the picture, which is what we have with the letters of the alphabet and so on. But they are just abstracted forms, symbols, of what were pictures essentially. So, I think, in the basic sense what I'm trying to say is that there is a very, very intrinsic concept of a picture or an image or a symbol at the root of both painting and writing. In that sense they both try to do the same thing essentially. Although in art, and to some degree in post-modern literature, you have these efforts to get away from representation to some extent.

There is a much longer history to that effort in painting. You can find it starting out right around the turn of the century then in Western writing in poetry and so on. Remember the whole idea of making it new and making the language so concrete that it represents less? It attempts to stand for itself more than it has for a long, long time. Not that these efforts hadn't happened before in the history of painting and writing. The Egyptians were exploring what could happen beyond representation. And certainly tribal people in the earlier periods were automatically doing less representation—letting the image somehow speak about itself and so on, speak at least as much about its own presence in the world as about, say, an animal that was worshipped for it was a means of survival. I would say that throughout the while history of art and writing that there has been a kind of see-saw effect. The Renaissance moved more and more toward representation with the advent of perspective coming in and the whole elevation of the notion of perspective and so on which is what turned everything around. But then of course we eliminated that and started sabotaging perspective and doing interesting new things in the modernist period which I mentioned earlier. And then it was totally eliminated by the time the New York School developed Abstract Expressionism, which led to Abstract Art, and so on. So perspective was no longer necessary to at least a good percentage of artists who were being taken seriously. So I think since the mid 1950s, 1960s, we've had both. We've had a much more democratic arena for both writing and painting, because you've got people doing everything you can imagine and using every conceivable approach you can imagine and much of it is good or at least interesting.

Rowell: Do you ever consciously draw upon what you learned from painting when you're writing your fiction?
Major: I do. I do.

Rowell: Will you demonstrate that with the text?
Major: Well, I'm a visual thinker. I imagine the thing before or as I am developing it on the page, and I can see it. I can see it as clearly as I can see actors on a stage. And if I don't see it clearly, I keep working at it until it

becomes clear. The colors, the sounds, the smells, everything that gives it its particular life. But in writing and in painting, you don't put everything in. Even if you're a Nature painter, for example, you go to Nature for inspiration, and you change it. Nature is not perfect. It's never really been a matter of translating Nature to the canvas. It's a matter of selecting and rearranging Nature, which is what you do when you write a scene. You select the elements that are going to make that scene come alive. And anyway you could not possibly put everything in. So I think you have to have a kind of ear and an eye for those elements that add just the right touch. Just as a painter has the right touch that brings a landscape to life. Not everything is necessary. I mean sometimes a tree is in the wrong place, and you eliminate it. So it's the same thing with writing a scene. You wouldn't want everything that was said necessarily in that particular scenario. You want the key elements of a piece of dialogue. You want the key elements that are going to render that scene and bring it to life. You may have to work at it. It may not happen the first time you try it. Over time I think you develop a sense of what's good. You know when it's not good, and you know when it's not working, and you keep at it till you get it right. In other words, what I've learned about form in painting is that composition is really, really essential to the organization of the painting. And the same thing is true about writing—writing a particular scene, a sequence of scenes called a novel. Organization. Selecting the right elements, eliminating elements that don't work. So it's a very similar process. The notion of perspective corresponds very nicely with point of view, which I believe to be the controlling factor in any good piece of fiction, for example. Point of view controls everything else that goes into the fiction. And point of view is essentially the same thing as perspective.

Rowell: From your experience as well as from a theoretical position, what would you recommend to a new writer to do in order to develop what you were talking about: a sense of knowing when a scene or moment is well-developed or knowing what to eliminate from the scene?

Major: How would I tell a new writer how to do that?

Rowell: Yes.

Major: Keep working at it until you understand what needs to be done.

Rowell: How will that new writer find out what needs to be done?

Major: The new writer finds out by writing—the practice of writing itself is the best teacher.

Rowell: Do you do it by reading too? And I keep asking the question because people need excellent models early on if they're going to develop the kind of aesthetic sensibility which will help them discern good work.

Major: Yes, you do it by reading. Reading as much as you can. Reading the great writers and watching how they did it. In another sense, just as if you were an apprentice painter, you'd go to the great museums and look at the paintings. It's the same thing. That's essentially what you do. There's only so much you can tell a new writer; the rest has to be learned through practice, which is what apprenticeship is all about. You have to write in order to learn how to write.

Rowell: We have this new component in the academy called creative writing programs. What are they about? What has been their impact on writing in the United States? We are one of the few countries with such programs or departments. In fact, you were once director of the program at the University of California, Davis.

Major: Well, yes, and I think they're good. I think it's a good thing. I would have developed a lot faster had I had the advantage, had I had the chance to take creative writing when I was younger. I think I would have made much faster progress than I did. The thing that's advantageous in the workshop is that you have immediate responses to your work. Intelligent response from a group of like-minded people who are sensitive to what you're doing. That's valuable. And these workshops don't always turn out great writers or good writers, but they turn out, at the very least, good readers—people who are able to go back to the practice of reading and read with greater sensitivity. But I think that that's the best that a workshop can hope to do. It gives the potential writer a set of responses to his or her work so that she can move along a little faster than, say, I did, for example. I look at the things my students are writing, and they are so much more sophisticated than what I was doing when I was their age. There weren't any workshops when I came along—except the Iowa Writers' Workshop.

Rowell: What are some of the implications of technology for the creative writer? Of course, I think immediately of television and film and the tape recorder, as well as the computer in all of its manifestations.

Major: Well, you know, I started off writing, as I said, writing these crude little novels in school notebooks when I was a kid. And then I graduated to the manual typewriter. And then in the late 1960s I got my first electric typewriter. And here I am now using a computer and a modem and all of these things and sending e-mail messages. Is this Progress? It's change, certainly. One has to sacrifice some things in order to gain others. It's easier to write a novel on a computer because you can move things around and make easy changes, but a certain amount of tactile control is lost. But I still use long-hand and occasionally a typewriter. I always do some handwriting right alongside the computer while working at the computer. I have a legal pad on which I write out some things before I even write them on the computer. But the computer is very convenient. Although it tends to be very wasteful, too. It used to be such a heartache and such a headache to have to white-out and type over the white-out. Trying to get a final, clean draft was so awful back in the old days. And now you don't have to worry about that. You can just keep switching things around and moving things around, and you can do your final draft; you can do all the changes right up to the last minute on the computer. So that's the big advantage, for me. Then the printer spits out a finished copy for you.

Rowell: You knew the Black Arts Movement first hand. You were a participant in that movement in some way or other, because I remember seeing your books of fiction and poetry, and your many publications in periodicals. I also remember your anthology of "new black poetry." You created a dictionary of black speech. You did a lot of things back in the late 1960s and early 1970s. A lot of us—and I am one—have begun to make a lot of negative statements about the Black Arts Movement. We must be careful not to misrepresent it. After all, there was much good to come from that movement, too. As a contemporary of the architects of that movement witnessing the national scene, did you learn anything from them in terms of writing fiction? We all probably learned something about the politics of art and the politics of the production of art.

Major: Well, you know, Charles, I was not really a part of that movement. Not really. Although I did that anthology, *The New Black Poetry,* I really wasn't considered part of the movement. And I really didn't want to be, although I published in a lot of the same magazines. I published widely in magazines but they were mainly little poetry magazines and not necessarily black, although I did publish in all the available black magazines. In 1965, when the black aesthetic talk started, I hadn't published a book. By the time I did the anthology, *The New Black Poetry,* three years later, I was already moving firmly away from any notion that art needed to be a conscious instrument of social or political change. I believed that it *could* be but that it did not *need* to be. My aesthetic position can be seen clearly in my anthology selection. It seemed to me that to think of art as—and, when I say art, I'm talking about writing as well—merely a cultural extension of a political or social objective was a bad idea. Look at Soviet art and writing under Stalin. It's pretty awful stuff. Look at any totalitarian regime, and you can see how bad the art was in any given period where there was an overriding political concern or objective, and everyone had to goose-step to whatever policy and political notion was in the air. So that's what I objected to. I didn't want to goose-step. I felt that art could be useful to people on its own terms. Now, I'm also aware that DuBois said that all art is propaganda, but that not all propaganda is art. And that's true. But I thought that it was very difficult to make good propagandistic art. In painting done under the sway of religion, say, during the Italian Renaissance, good art succeeded a good deal of the time. But it was always a struggle. Michelangelo had to fight the Pope for artistic freedom every step of the way. But in my case, it seemed to me that everywhere I turned I saw nothing but bad poetry and a lot of trite fiction. And it just really bothered me. By 1967, I didn't want anything to do with it. So I declared myself clearly not a part of that movement and separated myself from it over the next several years as much as possible, although I had been identified with it in some kind of murky unclear way, because I hadn't really thought about it until I was forced to think about it. It just seemed to me that whatever political statement I could make had to be made on the terms of the art itself. I felt that more lives had been changed for the better by real art than by propaganda. Perhaps it was the Black Arts Movement that forced me to realize what my position was. Because in a sense I was reacting to it in the formation of a position.

Rowell: You are one of the most innovative fiction writers in this country. One wonders how to describe your fiction. Experimental? But I am afraid that is inadequate if for no other reason than the fact that the term "experimental," when applied to a literary text today, has little meaning. How do you want us to describe your innovative fiction? Will you talk about what it is that you've been doing, especially that which sets you apart from other fiction writers?

Major: That's a good question. Well, I think that back in the 1970s when I was writing novels like *Reflex and Bone Structure* and *Emergency Exit,* I was trying to find my way with language and with the art of fiction. And it seemed to me that those were experiments in that sense. I would say that by the end of the 1970s and the beginning of the 1980s, I was beginning to realize that I couldn't go on doing that. I couldn't go on just imitating myself or doing the same thing over and over. It seems to me that I needed to take what I had learned from those experiments and try to gravitate to some more formal notion of fiction. I wrote *Reflex and Bone Structure* to try to see if I could just do anything I wanted to do and still create a thing that had form— that still had its own compositional integrity. After that, the essential thing that I wanted to do then was to move on. By the time I did *Such Was the Season,* which some people call an old fashioned novel, I was doing another kind of experiment. It seems to me that I had learned what I had learned from the earlier stuff. Mysterious things going on in that novel that are not immediately accessible or available to the person who's simply reading for pleasure. And then by the time I got around to doing *Painted Turtle,* I was trying to extend beyond *Such Was the Season.* And there are some surrealistic moments in *Turtle* that I enjoyed playing with. So what I'm trying to say is that there was continuity and a kind of progression to a more formal stance, but at the same time I had not come to any kind of acceptance of realism. I don't believe even today that I am writing straight realism. Even *Dirty Bird Blues*—another kind of experiment, this time with the language of the Blues—I think of as a novel that is in no important way realistic. If they choose to do so, readers should be able to read a novel on many different levels. Or, some people should be able to read a novel for pleasure and not have to think about what's going on with the language or subtextual matters.

Rowell: You use the term realism. What are you talking about? Of course, we all learned something about that in school, but what are you talking about when you speak of realism here in 1997? In relationship to what you just said, you said, "I was trying to find my way with language and the art of fiction." How is that related to the subject of realism and fiction?

Major: By realism I meant the old social realism and naturalism. I don't have any interest in repeating social realism, although something new might be learned from an exploration of it if one could find a way to extend its terms.

Rowell: Who are you when you write? Is there a difference in who you are from novel to novel? Do you want us to know where the writer is in your novels.

Major: Well, you know, I lend myself to different characters. I lend parts of myself to different characters. I think that's what any writer does. You never really represent yourself in writing. I don't think that's possible. I find that a character is more interesting if you are free to let that character evolve on his or her own terms. And what I find myself doing is—if I have a character who is in some way based on myself, I will try to keep that character as flexible and free of me as possible, so that I can give the character a few things that might be useful to the character as himself—this is an effort to not tie the character down to me. I don't want to stagnate the character or pamper the character's development, if you understand what I mean. I basically have tried to write autobiographical fiction and learned the hard way that you can't do it well. You know, you can write bad autobiographies. You can write bad autobiographical fiction, but you can't write good fiction and stay close to your models, if you have any. I have created characters that don't have clear models and usually what I do is combine several different models. If I'm using a person, I usually end up using five of six different people or maybe three people as the basis for a character. And it helps me keep the shape of the character in mind better if I have a particular real person back there somewhere, I mean, two or three persons. I don't think it works with just one real. Because you get too trapped in that one person as model. But it's a danger and I'm always pointing this out to my students. I think the truth of fiction lies not in the representation. The truth of fiction lies in discovering the reality of the fiction itself and letting that reality come to life on its own terms. I don't know if that makes any sense, but I can't say it more directly. It's like I said earlier—in painting you may go to Nature but you don't go to Nature to copy it. You go there for inspiration and you try to paint your response to Nature. And I think that's what a novelist does. What I try to do is create my response to life in experience and ideas, emotions and so on, in the sense of history and the sense of culture, and how all of that interplays in the life of a character.

Rowell: Will you comment, then, on the writer and his or her ability or need to become an other than actual self, to become another voice that is another gender, another race, another cultural figure, etc.? How did you do this, for example, in *Painted Turtle?*

Major: That's interesting, because I think when you get beneath the cultural trappings, we're all pretty much the same, you know. So, I was interested in exploring Zuni culture, learning about it. I used to live in Colorado. For twelve years I lived out there. And I got very interested in Native American culture and spent a lot of time down on the reservations—particularly on and around the Zuni reservation—and got to know the history and culture. And actually it was a black man who came through there with an expedition at some point and decided to stay, and the Zunis had never seen a black man before, so they immediately made him a god, and he took on something like twelve wives and ended up with, I don't know, one hundred children. That story always fascinated me, and I started looking more into the Zunis. So when I started writing that novel, *Painted Turtle,* he was somehow going to be in the novel as some kind of looming mythic figure in the history of these people. But the more I worked at the novel, the more I saw how unworkable his presence was. So I eventually wrote him out of the novel and realized that I wanted the novel to be focused on Painted Turtle, the woman. And I wanted to write a novel about that culture, using her as my vehicle, But also another avenue led to that novel that I don't usually mention, and that is that I had originally planned to write a novel about the black actress, Dorothy Dandridge, and it was going to be a historical novel. And I did a draft of that, and it didn't work. So I used some parts of that failed novel as the starting ground for *Painted Turtle,* and I started working my way towards this Native American Culture, keeping the notion of Dorothy Dandridge in mind, but totally giving her up by the time I had created the character Painted Turtle itself. But I said that just to show you how convoluted and complex the creation of a novel can be, for me at least. Inspired by two very different African Americans, in the finished product there wasn't a single African American in the novel. I just have a lot of curiosity about cultures. I'm working on a novel now about a Chinese-American woman—an ABC. I like to think that my interest is expanding. And I always feel that I need to do new things. I don't like to walk through the same river twice.

Rowell: Shifting just a bit here, let me ask you about the role of memory. There's a type of past which is represented through memory. How does one talk about how memory plays in the writing process? How does one use autobiography or one's own experience in the writing of fiction? "Of course!" we could all say. And furthermore we would all argue that all creative texts probably begin with authors' lives, what they do or what they witness or what they know. It seems that the artist always has to remain the self and the other simultaneously. Will you just comment on how one uses autobiography in the writing of fiction? Will you use your own experience about the process in your own texts?

Major: Well, that's always an interesting dilemma, because I think you use memory of your own experience, of course, and your experience is not just something that happened to you, it's your mind, it's your feelings and so on. I think the thing that the writer has to do is to always keep in mind that life is one thing. Life doesn't need to have compositional integrity. But a piece of literature does, and that's the difference. When the experience seems too attractive, or becomes too much of a guiding force in the writing, then it gets in the way. You have to tame it; you have to limit it; you have to tell it where to get off. You have to basically use only that part of it that goes to serve your compositional end. And it's very much like, you know, research. If you research a subject for a historical novel or a historical poem, for example, and you have all of that research on your index cards, and there it is stacked up there on your desk, and you're writing—the temptation is to use as much of it as you can, but of course you know from experience that you can't use it all. You cannot get it in because it's going to get in the way, and nobody's going to care, and it's not going to be interesting to anybody. So it's the compositional integrity, the compositional aims of the work itself that matter. So to that extent, life has limited uses. It's useful only up to a point. In other words, if you get into this notion that everything that has happened to you is interesting, then you're in trouble. Not everything that has happened to you is—and the problem with it, of course, is that it has no shape. And you cannot use it to give shape to art. Art has to find its own shape.

Rowell: Yes, sure, I follow you. But I think you will give the new writer a special gift if you demonstrate how you have used an autobiographical moment in your own fiction.

Major: Well, take the most realistic novel I've written, and that was *Such Was the Season.* That was based on a trip I made to Atlanta—actually to Albany, Georgia, but I stopped in Atlanta for a few days to visit relatives— and that novel grew out of that experience, although nothing like anything that happens in this novel actually happened to me in real life, even though the trip became the framework for the novel. You know, a young man coming down from the North, going back to visit relatives he hasn't seen in many years. I chose to tell the story from the point of view of another character— his aunt—not from that of the young man, Juneboy, who is remotely based on myself. I did that deliberately because of the possible ironic effect that I could get from that. Also it is never wise to write directly out of or about yourself in the first person. Juneboy is ultimately a metaphor for the exploration of that particular time in the lives of his family. So I guess what I'm trying to say is that I made very limited use of the actual experience. I did not describe my trip to Albany, Georgia, to Albany College where I met with students for several days. I didn't write about any of the things that I *actually* did—the trip to Martin Luther King's tomb or anything like that. Instead I have Juneboy go with his aunt to visit his father's grave, which is something I did not do. Maybe I should have, but I didn't. You know, so basically I was trying to let the fiction lead the way. That's what I think the writer has to do, and that's the relationship, I think, of fiction to experience. Experience has to be kept under control and used sparingly, has to be used only to the extent to which it's useful.

Rowell: Is audience, as an external construct, important to you as a writer? Does it play a part in your creative process?

Major: You know, that's something I don't think about. Unless I'm writing an essay or a book review, I really don't think about audience. I hope for the best and I try to write something that *I* would be interested in reading.

Rowell: You write in different genres—poetry, prose fiction, and nonfiction prose of various kinds. *Surfaces and Masks,* your long poem, is my favorite. Can you explain why that experience took the form of a poem as opposed to a novel? Will you talk about the genesis of *Surfaces and Masks* as opposed to the genesis of your novel, *My Amputations?*

Major: Well, *Surfaces and Masks,* you know, was written in Venice. I wrote it mostly as a project of note keeping and journal entries. I was trying to keep a kind of on-going intellectual and cultural response to the place in which I was living. I was on sabbatical. My wife and I were living there in an apartment right on one of the canals for close to a year. And I was doing a lot of reading about the history of the city and about all of the great historical visitors to the city and so on; and reading about all of the conflict that had plagued that city for centuries, I began to realize that it was the first great sea trading city. It had this glorious ancient history, and it was Marco Polo's city; some of the things he brought back from his voyages were right there in the great church. The city had had links with just about all of the known world— especially with Africa—and that was reflected in the people and the culture. And then I remembered that Shakespeare set his Othello drama in Venice. And that there were all of these African figures turning up in the paintings, very often, and not all of them as servants, but many of them as military people—like Othello. Well, you know, Venice was a very powerful military presence in the world—the East, the Middle East, Africa, all of Europe—so what I wanted to do was to try to take a look at the vast complexity of what

all of that meant, because it really seemed to represent everything that had
shaped my life. In a sense Venice was the summation—at least it had been
the summation of the Western Experience. And, you know, with its use of
cultures from many other parts of the world, it seemed to me the right subject
as a metaphor, but I also wanted to write about it for itself and to try to see
if I could render some of my responses to my own particular moment there.
And it seems to me that there was the decline and decay of the city, and I
was interested in trying to say something about that, too, in relation to its
glorious past and to look at that decay in relation to the whole Western Experience. Venice was a crossroads for so much that could be said about the
world. I was a foreigner, a stranger looking at all of this with hopefully fresh
eyes. And that's the same thing that I was trying to do, in some ways, at least
on some level, with *My Amputations.* But there again, I was interested in the
so-called complex network of social, historical and political forces that had
come to shape the character who was a kind of trickster figure. And many of
those forces were of course Western. By Western, you know what I mean. So
he finds himself going into the museums looking for connections. He's a kind
of detective, really, who's trying to put together the fragmented pieces of
history that would give a sense of wholeness to who he is, and he's looking
everywhere, and of course by the end of the novel he ends up in Africa in a
hut out in the bush with a wise man who makes a literary allusion to Ralph
Ellison, which is as far from realism as you can get—but anyway, that's what
I was trying to do. There are direct correlations between those: the poem
(Surfaces and Masks) and the novel *(My Amputations)* in their origin, in their
impetus, at their crux. Both were written outside of this country. I wrote the
one, as I said, in Venice and the other one was written in Nice. I wrote both
books on the same portable manual typewriter. I like to think that maybe that
had something to do with the similarities that are there, in terms of their
concerns and so on. But that's just magical thinking, I'm sure.

Clarence Major on Poetry, Meaning and Inspiration

Barbara DeMarco Barrett / 1998

From "Writers on Writing," February 3, 1998, KUCI, 88.9 FM, Orange County, California. Printed by permission of Barbara DeMarco Barrett.

BB: In an interview with *Poets & Writers* back in 1991, you said, "As William Carlos Williams said, there is no such thing as free verse. There is really no such thing as a free novel. It's not like life. Life is kind of formless and pointless at times, but a novel really can't be that way just as a poem can't be that way." Will you elaborate on that idea?

CM: (*Loud laughter.*)

BB: And do you still believe that? (*Laughter.*)

CM: I still believe that. I still believe that. Well, life . . . I'm not going to be much of an expert on life, but I can tell you that I still believe that the only form or structure life has is that which we impose upon it. I do think it's necessary in human activity to have order. That's why we have ritual. In a similar way, we try impose a sense of order on the poem or at least discover where that order is coming out of the work in some organic way. Usually that's what I find happens. I don't so much impose an order consciously. . . . Let's say it's a poem, for example, I might begin with a couple of words or a phrase, or a feeling or just any little thing that triggers the sequence that becomes the poem and I don't know what the final form will be. What I try to do is to follow the direction that seems to be established by itself. I do believe that there is something in each of us as we write that knows more than we know. I hope that doesn't sound mystical, but I don't think that you can be extremely objective about a piece of creative work while you're in the process of interacting with it.

Gertrude Stein was trying to make that point in the book called *Lectures in America,* when she was talking about composition. It's like riding a bicycle or skating. You may remember when you were a kid and you first learned how to ride a bicycle or to skate . . . if you look at your feet and get conscious of what you're doing, you lose the whole rhythm of it.

BB: Right, or if you start thinking about words, you start forgetting what
they mean.

CM: Yeah, that's exactly what I mean. I can't think of any better way to
put it.

For example, when I was in France on a Fulbright, I visited Cézanne's
house. We went to his studio in the south of France, and there was the garden
and everything as I had seen it for years in the paintings and so on, very
different in a way, but the house essentially the same. And I came away from
that experience with no intention of writing a poem necessarily, but I ended
up writing a poem, one of the poems that's in the book [*Configurations*],
actually; it's on page 78, "Atelier Cézanne." Do you want me to read it?

BB: Yes, I'd love it.

CM: Blue chair.
    We whisper.
    Blue chest. We whisper here.
    Dresser.
    Here's the green apple.
    A woman with braided chestnut hair
    enters carrying green apples.
    Here's a red one.
    The candle.
    Old jar.
    Your top hat.
    Your stained suit.
    Your frozen garden.
    It's like Van Gogh's girl
    Against a wheat field: the wheat
    is more important than the girl.
    Things don't grow and express
    themselves at the same time.
    The bottle with the peppermint
    I accept in its stillness, the rum too.
    My eyes may swell red
    and my fingers may grow thick.
    I will die as you have died.
    I will choose, at the last moment,
    to see death in everything—in corn,

in flowers, in birds, and bats.
Your frozen garden is close
to the skyline that we call
the edge. We do not plan
To eat things from it.
It on the other hand eats at you
and me—and Vincent, too.

BB: Hmmm.

CM: Hmmm. Well, you know, I noticed for the first time a sentence there that really complements what we were talking about: "Things don't grow and express/ themselves at the same time." Interesting. A kind of commentary on the creative process in a way, if you think about it.

It's hard to know when you first start out where you're going and what you're doing even. Once I've found myself pretty far along in the process of what ever it is, let's say a second or third draft, I can tell whether or not I have something. And sometimes I don't. Very often at that point I find myself getting rid of a manuscript or giving up on an idea, especially if it was an ill-conceived idea.

The hardest chapter is always the first one—the first and the last chapter are always the hardest. And those very often have to get moved around or even eliminated. Very often I find myself telling my students, "Get rid of this first chapter." Or, if it happens to be a short story, "Get rid of the first paragraph." Sometimes even the whole first page or the first two pages might be superficial and that's very, very common, so I find myself advising them to find the true beginning of the work. When you start writing, you're really just warming up to the subject; you're trying to discover your direction. It really pays to step back and take a good clear look at what you have there. When you do that with some objectivity, you will find yourself getting rid of any parts that are not contributing to the forward movement and to the vigor of the work. The movement really holds things.

BB: You have a lot of birds in your poems.

CM: (*Loud Laughter.*) I was not aware of how many birds are in my poems until this book [*Configurations*] was finally put together. Then it just occurred to me. You notice the cover is a picture of birds. I didn't select the cover, although it's one of my paintings. All I did was send the publisher a bunch of slides and they selected that. Apparently they were very much aware of how many birds are in there, throughout the whole book.

BB: It's interesting. Are birds symbolic of something?

CM: I really don't know what's going on with me and birds. (*Laughter.*)

BB: Would you read the poem "Waiter in a California"?

CM: Yeah, it's very interesting how that poem came about. I used to go to this restaurant at lunchtime here in Davis and there was a waiter who seemed so awkward all the time and I got to know him a little bit and realized why he was so unhappy. Anyway, the poem came out of a very real experience. This is "Waiter in a California Vietnamese Restaurant."

> With the smell of firebombing
> still in his nose,
> he brings our plates to the table
> pausing for a vertiginous instant,
> holding them as though they are two stones.
> When he tries to smile his face
>   turns purple like sky above
> that Red River delta.
> He once stood against a tree
> with both arms above his head,
> like somebody about to dance
> flamenco, but he wasn't, it was
> the time of the Spring Offensive,
> and he was looking into the barrel
> of a rifle held by a boy
> whose trigger finger
>   Had turned to stone.

BB: Tell me about this. You said that there was a waiter in a restaurant. . . .

CM: Well, I discovered that he had just recently come to the United States as other members of his family had been living here for a long time and he was brought over. He had been a soldier in the war and had obviously experienced trauma and he just never really seemed like a waiter. He didn't seem to know how to walk . . . he seemed so awkward and it struck me that here was a very unhappy man who could well have been in a state of shock, still, all these many years later—this is a poem written in 1989. But, of course, a lot of it is made up: I don't know the details of his experience of the war; I just know that he was in the war and I had to imagine the rest of it.

BB: How do you judge whether a poem succeeds? Are there many poems you get rid of or do they succeed because you've created them? (*Laughter.*)

CM: (*Laughter.*) No such luck. (*Laughter.*) Oh, man, well, it takes time, Barbara, for me, anyway. Sometimes when I first finish a poem, it looks great. I have to put things away and look at them later before I have any sense of how good or how bad they are. So, I keep folders with half-finished poems and it takes sometimes years to know whether or not a poem is going to really hold up. In putting this book together, *Configurations,* I agonized over the nine previous books and the selection process, going through them meticulously, . . . not so much with the idea of selecting the best ones, although I was attempting to do that, but I also left out a lot of poems that I still believe in because they didn't somehow fit this particular construction. I wanted this book to have a certain kind of sequence. And I also wanted it to stand for the other nine books because most of those books are out of print and this is the one that people will probably have access to for at least the next few years or so.

BB: When you're writing, at any stage of the process, do you have your readers in mind at all, or do you just keep them at bay until you're done?

CM: Well, I like to think that I myself might be an ideal reader, so I try to please myself and, hopefully, I will please other readers . . . No, I can't say that I have in mind an abstract reader or an ideal reader when I'm working on a novel or short story or poem. I don't think I ever have. (*Laughter.*) Maybe I should have a reader in mind. Actually, I do have at times a kind of tendency to pull back and not do certain things because—not because so much of a feeling that the reader won't respond to this or won't like this, but because it offends me. I was just listening to what's the guy's name—Ellis— the new hot shot—

BB: Oh, Brett Easton Ellis?

CM: Yeah. On Bravo. He was talking about writing, what was it *American Psycho*?

BB: Ah, huh.

CM: And going into how painful that was: people sent threatening letters and so on, and he talked about, "But they don't know: I love women and I grew up in a house full of women and my mother is a woman and I have sisters and I don't hate women—I got all these threatening letters." He said, "It was also very painful to write that vicious, violent stuff." And I thought, "Wow! He obviously believes that he had a larger goal to achieve by putting himself through the torture of writing that"; I don't think I could write something that offends my own sensibilities. Maybe that's a flaw; but if I find myself offended by something that I'm writing, I find myself pulling back. So maybe in a sense, just to answer your question in a roundabout way, maybe that is a way of self-censorship or a way of shaping the way the work will be received by listening to my own responses. Taste is certainly a factor.

I don't think of myself as a prude, by any means. I have written things that would offend some people. *All-Night Visitors,* the book that was just republished, has some very difficult scenes in it because it really is a book about the sixties and we all know that those were very difficult times in America with a lot of violence and the sexual revolution and so on. And that book tries to capture some of that feeling of intensity and the world coming apart: it deals with Viet Nam, it deals with a lot of sexual excess and violence and also racial conflict; but, there again, it was written in the sixties in the context of those times and it didn't feel offensive to me at the time. Today, I'm not offended by it, but I have a somewhat different reaction to it. I had to reread it recently in preparing it for publication in its new form. It had been published originally in a very altered form.

BB: That was actually my next question: *All-Night Visitors* was originally published in 1969 in an abridged form?

CM: Right.

BB: Why was that?

CM: Well, the publisher had a line of hardback books that he wanted to bring out at a certain price and, you know, pricing of books corresponds roughly to the physical size of a book. I had this huge manuscript and he said, "Well, we'll publish it, if you will agree to cut out about half of the book." (*Laughter.*) I was so desperate. I was young and very eager to have a book published . . .

BB: So, this was your first book?

CM: My first book. But, you know, it was a traumatic experience to have to butcher my book that way.

I was not happy with the publication of the book, although it was praised and people liked it. It had a certain life, for many years, as a kind of underground classic. I just never felt vindicated until the book was published, republished just recently, this past December.

BB: And how did that come about?

CM: They wrote to me and asked if I would consider bringing it out and I said, "Well, look, I'll do it, but I want to restore the book. I'll let you publish it, but I want the book restored to the way I originally wrote it." They wanted to just bring it out the way it had been published in '69. I said, "No, I won't do it."

BB: You said, "No, not again."

CM: "No, not again. I want to restore the book to its original form." And then, it happened and I felt very good about it. There is some balance there now.

BB: You've been published by a range of publishers and I'm curious whether you prefer large presses or small presses or how is the experience different?

CM: Well, it depends. I've been published by HarperCollins and Viking, two books from HarperCollins and one from Viking, one from Putnam and a lot of literary publishers. It seems to me that small presses can do certain things better than big presses. Copper Canyon is an excellent publisher of poetry which is why I let them do this book [*Configurations*]. I could have had the book published by 3 or 4 different other publishers, but they know how to sell poetry and they do a good job with the design and I'm very pleased with the book. In fact, they know better how to sell poetry than HarperCollins does; HarperCollins would put out a book of poems, but it's like dropping it in the ocean. I'm not saying that's true with every book of poems they do, but it's not something that they're going to nurture and take care of and find a market for. I may get criticized for saying that, but I don't care.

Certain manuscripts are better off with smaller publishers, and other manuscripts are better off with larger publishers. There are certain things that I would go to Viking and HarperCollins with because it's the best thing to do. I'm going to write a memoir of my mother's life and that book no doubt will be published commercially because it has commercial potential; but nobody expects to make a fortune off poetry, so what's the point in going to a big commercial publisher? A lot of distinguished poets are published now by smaller presses, I suspect for the same reasons and out of the same logic that I'm talking about which is why you can find many of them at Copper Canyon as well as Ecco Press, Sun and Moon and so on.

BB: I wanted to ask you if you read all of your reviews and what you do with what you read?

CM: I read the reviews. Fortunately, most of them have been pretty good. I've been lucky in that. I've gotten a lot of critical attention. I'm not a super commercial writer; the sales have not been enormous except with the books I did for HarperCollins and Viking. Those two anthologies I did were expected to sell. I don't know if you ever saw those.

BB: I have one of them, of African-American short stories?

CM: Right. Those books sell by the thousands. They're everywhere.

BB: I can see why—wonderful writers: Dorothy West and Ralph Ellison.

CM: Yeah, yeah. But, anyway, if I start reading a review and it really seems to be personal and vindictive, I'll just stop reading it. I write reviews, too, for various newspapers and magazines and I just won't waste my time tearing to pieces a book; I'd rather not review it if it's going to be entirely negative.

BB: In that same *Poets & Writers* interview that I mentioned earlier, you also said, "Very few of us come to a piece of writing with the intention of giving it a chance to talk to us. We would rather talk to it" which I found a very interesting thought.

CM: (*Laughter.*) I might have been angry at one of my critics that day. You read reviews and then you realize, "This person hasn't read the book that I wrote" And you say, "Oh God, what book is he talking about?"

Very often people will read a text and they will go to a text almost always with preconceived ideas. We tend to impose on the text whatever critique we already have in our mind. I very often get very frustrated over the realization that most of us—and I'm no exception—most of us want what we already know confirmed rather than wanting to open our minds and hearts and emotions—open ourselves to a new experience or to new information. I'd be the first to say that I'm exactly that way, but I'm frustrated with being that way. In my best moments, in anybody's best moments, we manage to put that tendency aside and be more open to fresh experience and new information.

BB: A couple of weeks ago I had Douglas Messerli, who's the editor and publisher of Sun and Moon Press on the show and he said that he wants literature to shake things up.

CM: Disturb the peace.

BB: Yeah.

CM: Well, that's always been the function of art, is to disturb the peace.

It should reaffirm our best and larger sense of life and not necessarily our immediate and most selfish and petty sense of things. So, I agree with Douglas 100 per cent. The best art is always a disturber of the peace.

BB: Do you think it's important for poets to know the traditional poetic forms—what a sonnet is, how to write a haiku—before they do free verse?

CM: Oh yes, yes, I think it's important to know meter, to know the rules before you start breaking them. It can't hurt as long as you're not stifled by those rules. There's always something new to be gathered from the practice of traditional meter. It doesn't have to be simply repeated in the way that it was done like say in the eighteenth and nineteenth centuries. I've seen things recently that rely very heavily on the eighteenth or nineteenth centuries that manage to be entirely new without imitating the structure of—just taking, say, the sonnet, as you mentioned, and doing something entirely original with it. The possibilities are still endless in terms of what can be done in a new and fresh way. I teach a literature course in modern poetry and I always encourage my students to write their own poetry, usually near the end of the quarter, and encourage them to play around with some of the forms that we've been discussing and also to experiment with those forms. They get a big kick out of that.

BB: As a teacher of writing, do you believe writing can be taught? And how important is natural talent?

CM: I think writing can be taught in the sense that you can help someone with talent to learn to become his or her own best critic and try to help them learn how to see their own manuscripts with a certain degree of objectivity and to learn how to detect structural problems and problems in characterization, problems in focus—all those kinds of things can be taught. You can point these things out and over time, the writer can begin to get a handle on how to do it herself or himself.

BB: Well, what about talent?

CM: I think talent is essential, but not absolutely essential. A lot of people can learn to be competent writers without any particular talent. You do need a kind of love for language, I think, because writing is agonizing over draft after draft. It may be painful, but there has to be some pleasure in it as well. If you don't love doing that, then it's probably something you shouldn't bother with.

BB: Well, we're at the end of our time and I wonder if you have any parting words or any . . .

CM: Parting words of wisdom. *Laughter.*

BB: Parting words of wisdom for all of the writers listening.

CM: Well, to the writers who may be listening I would say if it bores you that's a pretty good sign (*Laughter*) that maybe you should stop working on that particular piece and start something else.

BB: (*Laughter.*) Ah, huh.
CM: Yeah.

BB: Well, I must say that for all of your success, you're one of the most humble writers I know and that's a valuable commodity in these days of out-of-control egos.

CM: Well, I appreciate that, Barbara.

An Interview with Clarence Major

Leigh Morgan and Wendy Sheanin / 1998

From *Spark* (Online Magazine) June, 1999. Reprinted by permission of Leigh Morgan and Wendy Sheanin.

Perhaps most widely recognized for his best-selling, 1997 novel, *Dirty Bird Blues,* Clarence Major has published numerous volumes of fiction and poetry, and edited such critically-acclaimed anthologies as *The Garden Thrives* and *Calling the Wind.* He has been called "an avant-garde novelist, short story writer, and poet known for his bold experiments with language and style." In a review of *Dirty Bird Blues, Booklist* said Major "thrills us with some of the wittiest, most melodious inner dialog ever written, and moves us with dramatic confrontations between loved ones that are remarkable for their sensitivity, authenticity, and significance."

Major's most recent book, *Configurations: New and Selected Poems, 1958–1998* (Copper Canyon Press) includes selections from eight previous volumes spanning four decades. *The Kirkus Review* has noted that Major's poetry is often characterized by "an improvisational, jazz-like quality." Major, a professor of literature and creative writing at UC Davis since 1988, is also a visual artist. He created the oil painting showcased on the cover of his latest book as well as the three pieces featured in this interview.

Spark: Is it exciting to have a new book out—or does it become less so when you've published so many?

CM: I think the main thing that we all really have to remember as writers is that the reward is in the process of writing. That's the real reward, that's the real pleasure for me. The thing that matters is the struggle with the sentence. The struggle to get it right, the struggle to articulate what you feel and think. So I think the finished product is nice but it's not the real source of pleasure, because you are always pushing on to the next thing.

About *Configurations,* it's nice to know that it's there, that I went through it and it represents the best of my poetry. But I'm more interested in what I'm writing now—the poetry that I want to write and the fiction that I want to write.

Spark: What are you working on now?

CM: I just finished two short stories after struggling with them for something like four years. I mean I had drafts, drafts, of those two stories that long ago. Suddenly both of them made sense. What I had to do was so clear and so easy to fix. They were problem stories. They had just been sitting in my computer dormant because they didn't work. I wasn't about to send them anywhere. Then I woke up—I don't know, it's just that something comes. There are moments like that, both of them needed a similar fix. I was able to finish them rather quickly and send them both out. I happened to have on hand a request for stories. In the last couple of years I haven't been able to send out stories in response to requests because I didn't have anything ready. So I was happy to have that solution.

Spark: It sounds like letting a piece of work sit for a while creates a space where a solution can come to you.

CM: It takes me a very long time, sometimes, to see a problem. Sometimes I'll finish a painting or think I've finished a painting and hang it on the wall. And then I may walk by that painting for a whole year, you know, back and forth, without thinking about it consciously. In the back of my mind I'm worried about something that has to do with that painting and I don't know what the hell it is. But something about it bothers me. Eventually, whatever that is begins to surface, comes to consciousness, and I realize exactly what's wrong with it. But it may take a year for me to realize what's wrong with it. Just like those short stories that didn't work.

On the other hand, sometimes, things come out right the first time. And I know it right away, with a painting or with a poem. Maybe three or four drafts and then it's done, and I know that it's not going to look shabby a year later.

Spark: Maybe it takes a year or more sometimes to find out what's right about something.

CM: Yeah, I think that's absolutely right. That's the way I work. In that sense, I work pretty slowly. I work fast and slow. You know, I may be able to put down a draft very quickly, but it's far from finished.

Spark: Can you describe your writing process in terms of where your work begins? Do you know, when you begin a piece of writing, what form it's going to take?

CM: Do I know when an idea needs to be a story or a poem or a novel?

Well, with a novel, obviously, you need to think about it a long time. It needs to grow as a very complex network of ideas, feelings and emotions that won't go away. I mean, you should try to make it go away if you can. If it refuses to go away, it probably needs to be a book. But in order for it to be an interesting book, it has to come out of a deep place, I think, in the writer. It has to be not a singular kind of response but a very complex response.

I think there's a feeling when something needs to be narrative or linear. I think of poetry as something that needs to be more circular or less linear. Something that requires a kind of compression. I guess that's the best way to put it. Something that isn't really begging for a narrative line. Although, clearly, there is plenty of narrative poetry around, but I'm just thinking of my own impulses and my own particular approach. So I would say when the idea or feeling is round, I tend to want to make it into a poem. And when it's linear, I tend to want to make it into a story.

Spark: Round versus linear shapes.

CM: I guess the word I want is sequence. When there seems to be a need for sequence, connecting not just one image to another, but stitching together a sequence of scenes that are going to be the best way to render the particular idea. That idea doesn't have to be preachy, it doesn't have to be didactic, it could be just a feeling. It doesn't have to be clear in my mind. It could be an emotional response to something I have experienced or something I have been close to in some kind of way. My worse fiction is the fiction that comes too much out of ideas. And I know it, I know it, but sometimes I find myself so passionate about the idea that I forget that it's going to be bad fiction. Fortunately I haven't published much of that.

In fiction, you have to be, I think, very careful of letting your ideas drive your work too much. Better not to know very much about what a particular piece of fiction wants to be, especially at the beginning. In other words, let it be an act of discovery. If I'm writing something that's based on my own experience, I get better results when I haven't consciously explained it to myself, or I haven't thought about it a lot. I might just look back and think, "What was that all about?" That's the sort of moment that works best as a basis for a piece of fiction. Something I haven't really articulated for myself very much. The worse kind of thinking is, as I've said, to start with some preconceived abstract idea.

Spark: Do you ever worry about losing the germ of an idea during that time when you're not free to write?

CM: Oh yes. And I have had the experience of not writing down something that I wish I had. Because it's gone forever and I keep thinking, 'Well, maybe it will come back,' but it very often doesn't. I try to jot down things when they appear. Usually good ideas will hit early in the morning before I get up. You know, when I'm lying there thinking about the ordeal of getting up (laughs). I'll have a good idea and I keep a pencil and pad by the bed, and for years I developed a habit of working in the dark. Especially if I'm working on a book and obsessed with the book, I'll wake up all times of the night and jot down things in the dark. Don't even need to turn the light on, just write very large. It's just for me, so I can remember that I need to deal with a particular thing when I go back to the computer.

Spark: It's like the mind is always working on everything that's going on.

CM: Right. Which is why, once you start a book it takes possession of you. And that's why I'm so reluctant to start a book when I have a lot of distractions. It becomes enormously frustrating. But if I can get a draft done, even if I have to put it away for a year—or an academic year. I've done that many times: Get a draft done, put it away, and go back to teaching. It's always back there in my mind, but it isn't as frustrating or worrisome as it would be if I had only done a chapter or so. I like to be able to think of the work as a whole thing. Even with a very, very rough draft, it just feels better to me to have a sense of wholeness there to go back to.

Spark: Do you find it difficult to switch gears between writing and other demands in life?

CM: Not very difficult, no. To switch gears, sometimes it takes a few days. Like, let's say, once the academic year ends and I'm going to pick up the book that I started, the memoir, it'll probably take me a week to warm up to that book. I haven't looked at it in such a long time, but I've been thinking about it and I know what I need to do—precisely what I need to do. But in a sense, it's cold. It's something that I need to get back into in a way that feels fluid. So I know that it'll take a while.

Spark: You've mentioned the memoir you're writing about your mother. How much do your parents play a part in your work?

CM: I've used my parents as the basis of characters before. So, that's one way. But I think we all do probably, one way or another. I don't know that I want to get very far into that topic of the memoir I'm working on because it's a bit premature. But I wrote a novel called *Such Was the Season,* based on my mother's sister. She was the model for that book, and to some extent, my mother was too. It's written in a first person narrative from a woman's point of view. An elderly woman, a middle-class woman, mother of a minister . . . I'm getting real life mixed up with fiction, so I have to sort it out here. In real life, he's really a lawyer (laughs). But you know it's kind of interesting how we use people around us, our family and so on, as models.

Spark: Do you find transferring real life into art happens differently in poetry?

CM: I like that word 'transferring,' but I think also what really happens, in the best sense, is that there's a transformation. No experience we have can be transferred into art. I think it has to be transformed into art. The terms of art are very different from the terms of life. Forms can be imposed on both, but they are very different forms. We know what kinds of forms we're talking about when we're talking about the sonnet and the novel, with chapters and sequence and so on. Life can have order, but very often that order is hard to detect. That's why we have ritual and patterns, and so on, that we rely on. Using experience as a basis for art is, of course, primarily what we have to work with, but it's never a matter of looking at that experience in terms of factual information. But looking at experience in terms of a kind of larger truth about it that has to be reshaped. I had enough failures in my own attempts to know that it has to be done in a certain way before it works.

Spark: Do you think about your readers when you're writing, and how do you imagine them to be?

CM: Well, I think of myself as an ideal reader. You too?

Spark: No, I hadn't thought about that. But of course I'm the ideal reader. (*Laughter.*)

CM: I ask myself, 'Now, is this a book that I would like to read? Is this a short story that I would like to read? Is this a poem that I would like to read?' And if the answer is no, I know I'm barking up the wrong tree. I'm working against my own better judgment. So, I try to keep that in mind.

Spark: Are you in a writing group or workshop?

CM: I get my feedback from editors, or my agent, who tends to love everything a little bit too much. And my wife. My wife doesn't love everything. But, you know, when she does, well it's something I can trust to be a success. She's been right about ninety-nine percent of the time. The two short stories that I just finished, she thought they were great. So, I said wow, you know. That's it, that's it. She doesn't lie to me at all. She doesn't try to flatter me or polish my ego in any way (laughs). It's miserable at times, but she's a very, very tough critic.

Spark: Do you ever write to music?

CM: I do, I do. In fact I wrote that whole book (*Dirty Bird Blues*) while listening to the blues.

Spark: Which artists?

CM: I played everything. A lot of them were early blues because I was trying to get the flavor of the blues in the forties, since the book is set in the late forties, early fifties. Charlie Patton, Robert Johnson, Jimmy Witherspoon, Lightning Hopkins, Mississippi Fred McDowell.

Spark: A lot of blues have narratives, they're storytelling.

CM: Exactly. Right. And I noticed that someone like Lightning Hopkins will never sing the same song twice in the same way. It's always different. I have different versions of him singing the same song and it's just like a total reinvention of that particular scenario. I have albums on which he is actually making up songs right on the spot, you know. Straight out of his life. Songs with no titles. I mean just pure, sheer invention, just creative energy going. And it's something he can never sing again (laughs).

Spark: Do you play an instrument?

CM: No, but I wish I could. I play around a little bit. I'm not good at making music.

Spark: Though poetry is a little bit like making music.

CM: Well it certainly is. That's the kind of music I make.

Imagining a Life

Margaret Eldred / 1999

From *Writing on the Edge* 9 (Spring/Summer, 1998), 99–112. Reprinted by permission of *Writing on the Edge.*

Poet, novelist, artist, and fan of the blues, Clarence Major started writing poetry in grade school and fiction in high school, but he had to wait to adulthood to publish his first novel, *All-Night Visitors*; his first book of poetry, *Swallow the Lake,* followed soon after. Since then he has published seven novels, eight books of poetry, and a short story collection, *Fun & Games,* which was nominated for a *Los Angeles Times* Book Critics Award. His most recent work, *Configurations: New and Selected Poems 1958–1998,* has just been published by Copper Canyon Press.

Two things struck me as I was preparing for the interview. First was Major's concern for what it means to be human in late twentieth-century America. His characters are musicians, writers, thinkers, people trying to make sense of their lives. The protagonist of his most recent novel, *Dirty Bird Blues,* is named Man and is Everyman in his search for love, friendship, and self-respect. Second, his works have resonance—days after finishing them, I am still thinking, pondering over his characters, his poems, and his life.

Major has received several awards for his writing, including a National Council of Arts Award for *Swallow the Lake,* a Western States Book Award for *My Amputations,* a Fulbright, and two Pushcart Prizes. He has read from his works at the Guggenheim Museum, and the Library of Congress, and has served as fiction judge for The National Book Awards. Major currently teaches creative writing and literature at the University of California at Davis.

Woe: In reading your novels from *All-Night Visitors* on, I immediately felt your sheer delight in playing with language. You do things with words that are fun. When did you first discover the pleasures of playing with words?

Major: It came very early—I was about three or four. My mother wrote a poem for me and I had to read it in church. So I realized early that people actually wrote things. Many kids grow up with the notion that things in books, especially the Bible, have nothing to do with real living human beings.

Print seems totally removed from the activity of daily life. When my mother asked me to read the poem, I got the sense that it was possible to write and use language in a musical way, poetry being what it is. So I grew up with the sense of rhythmic language as a possible way of communicating. I wrote poetry long before I wrote fiction. It came naturally, like learning to roller skate or to ride a bike.

Woe: You knew early on that writing was something you wanted to do?

Major: I knew that writing was something I loved; I loved the opportunity to invent images for the same reason I liked creating images with paint. Drawing and painting came first; they were much more accessible. I don't know when I knew I first consciously wanted to write as a way of life, but I wrote my first novel when I was fifteen. It was awful.

Woe: How did you learn how to write?

Major: I am still working at it. Despite the pleasure in the process, every time I attempt to write something, it's a struggle—a good struggle, though. It's like I've never learned anything from what I've done before, like I'm starting from scratch each time. It feels so painful—yet fresh, like being just on the verge of some great breakthrough. I don't know why it's that way, but it keeps all kinds of possibilities alive. I struggle to get that first draft down, then the second becomes an even more interesting challenge, but different, because by then I know more about where I am going. I've talked to many people who have the same experience, although I've heard there are people who can get it right in the first draft. Joyce Carol Oates, for example, has never rewritten anything and she writes three or four books a year. Kurt Vonnegut does not rewrite at all; he cannot go back through a manuscript and revise the whole manuscript—he'll revise page by page but not go back.

Woe: How many drafts do you write?

Major: It depends on the particular manuscript. Sometimes there are as many as eight or ten; but most often I need to go through three or four drafts before it looks close to finished. My process is to get it all down on paper in any kind of form that looks like the concept in my mind. Once I get it on paper, I can begin to see what the piece may want to be. I don't worry about structure until later stages—it looks pretty messy for the first several drafts. I write in a frenzy when I am working on a book and it surprises me sometimes to go back and see what I've actually put on the page. Some of it breaks my heart and yet among the rubble there are at times little miracles. My job is to take the miracles and try to develop them, to stretch them out into the thing that is taking shape.

Woe: Did you have a teacher who inspired you, people who were supportive?

Major: I had quite a few early on and all through. I don't think any writer can survive without that kind of support. I was influenced early on by painters. I was very much impressed with the French Impressionist painters. I was also influenced by American and French modernist poets and discovered William Carlos Williams when I was very young. I was impressed by what the modernist poets were doing with images. The things that had the most lasting impression on me were things I discovered outside of school, such as Williams' poetry and Van Gogh's paintings, which impressed me enormously—and still impress me.

I grew up in Chicago on the South Side and won a scholarship to the Art Institute of Chicago when I was still in high school. I started taking classes there—they have a great French Impressionist collection, so maybe that collection had a more profound effect on my writing than the things I read at that period. As a teenager, I found the whole visual experience extremely exciting. I was totally caught up in the energy that was set in motion by the life these painters generated on canvas. Painting and writing are different in the way we process them. Yet painting has some correlations with writing. Both usually take place on a two-dimensional surface. But in the final analysis painting is spatial and writing is temporal. One takes place in space and we experience it visually and the other takes place in time. But they still have this enormous amount of interconnection. I guess maybe that's what I was trying to do—bring to the writing what I was learning in the painting.

Woe: What can you do in your art that you can't do in words?

Major: I paint only the things I can't write about and vice versa: I write about things I can't paint. There are many things I can't paint well—I can't paint a certain network of emotions as well as I can present that same network of emotions through the interactions of characters generated through prose and sometimes through poetry. In painting I am much more interested in painting what I feel about what I see rather than in painting what I see or can see. You know the Cubists painted what they knew, not what they saw. Although I don't care much for Cubism, I understand the usefulness of such an approach. What one feels or what one knows is much more interesting than trying to represent the natural or the unnatural world in paint—especially since it can't be done anyway. Even super-realistic painters like

Richard Estes don't paint what is actually there. He moves buildings around, the way Italian Renaissance painters did with Venice, to make the composition more functional and coherent. So in writing I find myself gravitating toward subjects that cannot be painted. But sometimes I find myself stepping away from the writing of that particular book, story, or poem and doing a painterly version of the same thing. As I was writing *Dirty Bird Blues* I did several blues paintings as well.

Woe: What's a blues painting?

Major: I have to show you [indicates the dust jacket of *Dirty Bird Blues*]. This was intended to be a blues painting. Suggesting music visually was a challenge. You can see it is just a dance floor with people moving around apparently to music, and because of who the people are, how they look culturally, and the colors too, hopefully we get a sense of the type of music they are responding to. If they were in formal dress and long gowns, and in a great hall moving slowly, we'd get the sense of another type of music.

Woe: Most of your energy now seems to be directed toward writing. Why did you decide eventually to focus on writing instead of painting?

Major: That's a hard question; I don't know how to answer it. Over the years I tried to follow my instincts, and my strongest impulse kept me primarily doing writing. Actually, I find painting very frustrating; I don't tolerate the frustration of painting as much as I tolerate the frustration of writing. The pleasures are different too. When the painting has gone well it gives you a relatively quick sense of final satisfaction. Writing fiction and even poetry usually requires the postponement of that final satisfaction. Which is not to lose sight of the fact that the important gratification for both is in the process. But in terms of dealing with the frustrations when things don't go well, the two activities can be a challenge. It's true, you can walk away from the painting or paint over it and start again. And in its own way, you can do that with writing, too. So, I guess I can't really answer your question. I really don't know why. For whatever network of unconscious reasons, I have given more time to writing than to painting.

Woe: How do you get your ideas?

Major: That's another hard question. Good ideas come at every conceivable moment—sometimes during sleep, sometimes early in the morning when you wake up. If you don't jot it down, it's gone. An idea for a book or a novel has to percolate for a long time. A book idea has to simmer for a certain amount of time before it really has a presence, something that you can begin to live with as creative activity. I've occasionally tried to start writing a novel before I should have. I get twenty or thirty pages into the book, then I realize it's going nowhere and have to put it aside. The preconceived notion was insufficient—it hadn't reached the stage where I could develop a novel from that idea. A novel has to be a combination of feeling and thought; it has to have a level of emotion before it can be genuine. It needs to come from a deep place in you before readers can respond to it. If it is too intellectual, too mental, it's not going to cause that feeling. With fiction or poetry people want to feel something as well as think about something.

These issues are so subjective and difficult to articulate that I always feel like I'm just making up my answers. It may not be true, but, after all, a novelist does make things up. I guess it is an occupational hazard.

Woe: You've just had a new book of poetry published—*Configurations: New and Selected Poems 1958–1998* and "Configurations" is the name of the picture on the front cover as well as the title of the book. What is its significance? What were you trying to convey?

Major: Relationships. I'm interested in the relative nature of things. I'm interested in the compositional questions inherent in the way objects or characters interact. And I am interested in the relative disposition of the parts within an object or those within a character, such as inner conflict. Closely related, the American sensibility is rich territory for cultural exchange and conflict, and for what we in literature call double-consciousness. I'm interested in the possibilities of paradox inherent in form and design.

Woe: You are in the prime of your writing career. Why did you decide in *Configurations* to publish what is at least partially a retrospective?

Major: It's a myth that a poet has to be dead or close to death before she or he puts out a new and selected. If you look at the historical record you'd see that Whitman did it from an early age and kept it up throughout his life. He kept publishing updated, new versions of *Leaves of Grass* right up till he died. William Carlos Williams started early too with the new and selected volumes. This was more characteristic than unusual. In other words, almost all modern poets started releasing such volumes early in their careers. And certainly contemporary poets—like Simic, Komunyakaa, and Kinnell, for example—do it all the time. I'm actually very late in bringing out a new and selected. My friend Al Young, who is younger than I am, brought out his first

new and selected twenty years ago, and—like most of our contemporaries—
he's published several new and selecteds since then.

Woe: One critic says that your early poems follow in the tradition of the
Harlem Renaissance. Are you consciously trying to follow this tradition? If
not, how do you see your poems as differing from this tradition?

Major: I wasn't much influenced by the Harlem Renaissance writers,
although it sounds good to say that I was. I mentioned some of my early
influences a little while ago. The Harlem Renaissance was a period that corre-
lated with the rise of modernism. Some of the writers, such as Toomer and
Hurston, seem to me to be especially linked aesthetically to the imagistic
ideals of modernism. One of the central thematic shortcomings of the Harlem
Renaissance was its tendency to buy into the white idea of primitivism and
the notion of the Noble Savage as morally superior and exotic. The truth is
that most black people arriving in the cities, like most white people, were
simply country folk—or call them peasants. But they were not primitive nor
were they any more savage or noble than anybody else. So I said all of that
to simply say that that was then and my work takes place in a different social
and historical context. It necessarily has all the problems and benefits of my
own time—which is not to say that some sharp critic can't make a convincing
argument linking my work back to the Harlem Renaissance. But it is not
something that I would do.

Woe: The newer poems in *Configurations* seem to shift in focus, broadly
away from the urban themes of the earlier poems to the natural world—of
crickets, the apple-maggot fly, September in Mendocino. What brought you
to make this shift?

Major: I have always had an interest in responding to natural objects and
the natural world in general—in poetry, fiction, and painting. I think of the
early things I wrote in novels like *NO,* for example, which is set in a rural
area of the South, and how that novel concentrates on the natural world, and
I think of early poems like "Keeping Just the Real," which looks at natural
objects and the idea of death or decay that might be inherent in them. So the
interest has always been there but I may be doing more of it lately because
it's been many years now since I have felt emotionally caught up in urban
life.

Woe: Do you use your own experience at all? Are any of your novels
autobiographical?

Major: My novels aren't autobiographical in a literal sense but in the sense that I'm emotionally involved in whatever the issue is, whatever the theme is. I'm interested in giving life to that complex network of feelings and thoughts. Often I will use something I have experienced or something that someone else experienced as the basis for scenes or sequence of scenes, but I have to be emotionally involved in order to animate the work with life. The sequence of scenes about Vietnam in *All-Night Visitors* came out of the whole preoccupation with Vietnam we all remember from the 1960s.

Woe: Were you in Vietnam?

Major: No, but it was an emotional issue and I imagined myself there. I tried to visualize the whole sense of what was going on there. Rather than writing about Vietnam in the way I was reading about it in the newspaper, I tried to imagine what it was like in just a couple of instances—the soldier stranded on the mountainside, for example, just that one moment. I projected myself into *All-Night Visitors*—I never grew up in an orphanage. I had enough experience with people who had had some kind of institutional experience to get a sense of what it might have been like. I tried to connect with whatever it was on an emotional level. That's essentially what I think is necessary to bring a scene to life. At the same time it is very difficult to use your own experience. You can't do it with any kind of conviction. No one is going to believe it.

Woe: What do you mean?

Major: I mean that your own experience is inaccessible; it has to be transformed, it has to be changed in some kind of way. You can use it as the basis for making literature; it can never serve in a direct way. Even if you are writing an autobiography, you can't use it. If you are writing an autobiography and want someone to read it, you are going to have to transform it and give it the kind of shape you give fiction. Art demands its own forms. Life has whatever kinds of forms we impose on it—religious, social, mythic, whatever—but they are not the same as those we use for art.

Woe: In *Some Observations of a Stranger at Zuni in the Latter Part of the Century,* one poem says

> She put on a mask—comedian mask: it
> was like entering . . . entering
> A different point of view

In one sense, "entering a different point of view" is the work of all novelists. In fact, most of your novels seem to have a double point of view. *Such*

Was the Season was written from the point of view of the family matriarch, but as I read it I kept thinking of the point of view of Juneboy, which is very different. And in *Reflex and Bone Structure,* the first-person narrator is both a character and a creator / manipulator of the text. Did you intend this double perspective?

Major: Yes, but I am not able to tell you why I've always been interested in exploring various personas. I remember one of the early novels I wrote as a teenager. It was composed of multiple points of view. It was a rather interesting novel—it also had tapes and letters and everything. This novel was never published, but I have always been interested in getting into the point of view that challenges my own perception of so-called reality. Most often I write from what is presumably my own point of view, whatever that is, but I also create personas. In a sense, these are still projections of myself, perhaps a little more removed from what I imagine to be myself; they are like satellite personas, not quite as private. But I believe it's healthy to look at a situation from a point of view that's not your own. I think that's really one of the most valuable imaginative activities we command. Usually it serves us well in dealing with other people.

Woe: The narrator of *Such Was the Season* is a woman and the narrator of *Painted Turtle* is a Navajo. Do people ever say, "You can't do that? You don't have that experience"?

Major: Oh, yes. I hear that a lot. I was reading a section from *Painted Turtle* at the Library of Congress last June, and when I finished, a cranky lawyer in the audience asked, "How can you write about the Native Americans? You are an African American." I responded by saying that I am interested in the human condition. Culture is only the surface. And that shut him up. I gave the old Shakespeare example. How can Shakespeare write about Italians? He never went to Italy. Nor to Denmark, for that matter. Those were cultures beyond his immediate sensibility and experience. At least I had first-hand experience of Zuni culture. Also remember that a man wrote *Moll Flanders,* and it is a really convincing novel about a woman from a woman's point of view. This type of imaginative exercise and projection is something that has been going on for centuries, and I think it is a near-sighted presumption, very myopic, to say that one, in the first place, should assume that such limitations exist because of gender or culture or even sexual orientation. I just don't buy any of that kind of political garbage.

Where *Such Was the Season* is concerned, I grew up hearing voices like that—my aunts, my mother. I didn't see gender as an obstacle. I feel a tremendous amount of authority in creating that female voice; I know that voice as well as I know myself. I don't have any, any trouble at all, believing in my right to create that voice. It is a voice in me. And I feel the same way about Painted Turtle—and not because I have Native American ancestry, but because I understand how Zuni culture works, because I have a feeling for the behavior of the characters, and the conflicts between the tribes, and the conflicts within the tribes, between the clans and the families. Feeling as I do about this, why shouldn't I create such characters as Painted Turtle and Baldy? I always feel silly making this argument. It's so absurd—absurd that it has to be made.

Woe: So you have the Navajo male telling the story of the Zuni woman.

Major: A lot of people read the novel as a first-person narrative from the woman's point of view, and at first I actually wrote it that way. Then I changed it to second person, to Baldy's point of view because it did not work the other way.

Woe: Of course, he's there mostly in the beginning and the end, and in the middle he's not really in it a whole lot except as a character.

Major: That's right. I lived in Colorado for many years and became really interested in Native American culture. I spent a lot of time on the reservations and did a lot of research. As I suggested a moment ago, as far as I am concerned culture is something you can learn about a group of people. Human behavior is pretty much the same everywhere. To be a good fiction writer what you need to understand is human behavior. Culture is the easy part. It's only the trappings. And so I figure *Painted Turtle* was the story I wanted to tell. But at first my interest was sparked by the fact that there was a black man who had lived among the Zunis in the eighteenth century. He had started out with one of the expeditions going west, and he stopped and stayed rather than continue west. I forget his name, but he became a very important leader among the Zuni. I set out then to read everything I could about the Zunis. And I started going to the reservation and going to ceremonies and became really interested in their culture, but as I wrote the book he disappeared. He was in there as a kind of ancestor figure, a type of god—as he is among the Zunis now. But I realized the way the novel was taking shape, he had no place in it, even as an ancestor figure. Eventually I wrote him out of the book entirely. The other thing I wanted to do was to write a book about a woman who was a performer, a singer. I tried to do this with another form that didn't work, so I wrote a novel instead.

Woe: A couple of other novels seem to have this same interplay between history and culture. When I read *Dirty Bird Blues,* I kept being reminded of newspaper accounts of poor local communities, often black, but not necessarily. This external perspective, or double vision, has a very powerful effect. It creates a sense of impending tragedy because the newspapers talk about crime and drugs and all the disastrous things that happen in these communities. I was relieved when the book ended with a kind of cautious optimism. Did you expect people to read with this kind of foreboding vision of what they see in the newspaper?

Major: No. It's true that throughout the novel there's the feeling of impending danger. But I didn't think consciously about it. I was trying to imagine what the life of a young, uneducated black man (who is gifted as an musician) might have been like in the late forties right after the war. It was a big period for the blues. The blues had been coming up from the South for four or five decades. It had started coming up with the great migration of blacks from the South and arriving at places like Chicago. The Delta blues, the Louisiana blues, the Texas blues all converged in Chicago and New York. But Chicago became the mecca for a particular type of blues, which is one of the reasons I chose Chicago as the setting. Besides, I knew Chicago well enough to use it as the basis for the story. I wanted to use my character's life as a way of looking at that particular period. But most of all I meant the novel to be a celebration of the blues as an art form. And also I was interested in exploring the sense of place and time when my parents were young adults and just beginning to make their way in the world.

Woe: In your novels and poetry, the settings seem particularly important; you vividly describe a wide range of places from the South Side of Chicago, to New York's Lower East Side, Atlanta, Zuni areas of the Southwest, Venice, Cap Ferrat, and Paris. What's the relationship between the settings and the emotion you're trying to convey?

Major: The sense of place interests me tremendously. I'm especially interested in its role in shaping character and sensibility. Gertrude Stein talked about something she called the American space in relation to the shape of personality. Space or place can operate as metaphor in fascinating ways. You see this in Willa Cather and in Sherwood Anderson and of course in Faulkner. Anyway, Stein also makes the point that the English people, for example, being an island people, are different in personality from Europeans on the mainland, and her point has everything to do with the impact of place-as-island in making this difference.

Woe: You often write about music—in the novels *Dirty Bird Blues* and *Painted Turtle,* and two books of poetry, *The Syncopated Cake Walk* and *The Cotton Club.* Where did your interest in music come from?

Major: I think maybe because music is so intrinsic to our African American culture. The blues is one of the big contributions African Americans have made to this country. It is native to America; it is intrinsic to American art forms. It was just something that I thought was part of the culture, that I gravitated toward.

Woe: Do you play the saxophone like Man in *Dirty Bird Blues?*
Major: No. (*laughter*) I wish I could. I am not gifted that way.

Woe: How are music and literature related for you?
Major: With poetry that relation is obvious. We are all basically interested in rhythm; we all respond to it from the earliest age. There is cadence in speech—and by extension, writing too—that shares with music a basic beat or rhythm or meter. In novels there's a kind of pacing that we are instinctively pulled into.

Woe: On the back cover of your Zuni poems, the publisher says the poems are "integrally related" to *Painted Turtle.* I noticed something similar taking place in the other novels. For example, as I read *All-Night Visitors,* I kept being reminded of some of the things in the title poem of *Swallow the Lake.* In particular, I'm thinking of the passage

> Gave me loneliness.
> Feelings I could not put into words
> into people. Blank monkeys of the hierarchy!
> More deaths! Stupidity and death

The novel and poem seem to me the two halves of one thing. Is that pairing, that discussion of common themes, deliberate?

Major: They came out of the same experience in Chicago. I was young then and very angry, poor and unhappy most of the time. All young men are angry, it's true. Some more than others. We are all promised more than the world can deliver. My anger had a cultural, social, and economic basis. But I had enormous confidence in myself. It just at times seemed that the world was too indifferent to what I believed I had to offer. And I saw all around me young men like myself giving up at an early age because they too felt the same way about the world. But I was still very optimistic. At times foolishly so. In any case, I knew I had to change my life. "Swallow the Lake" and *All-Night Visitors* represent that period in my life. The novel is patched together out of the best parts of three failed novels. One was a Vietnam novel, one was a novel set entirely in Chicago, and the other was a novel set in New York. I took the best parts of the three novels and made one novel, which is why it is so fragmented and episodic. All the same, I think it has a kind of 1960s emotional content. The spirit of the sixties permeates the book—the sexual revolution brought on by the pill, the violence in the streets, the whole atmosphere, the civil rights movement, the anti-war movement, everything that was going on. It was a time of great upheaval. And there is no way to write anything that is not going to reflect who and what and where you are at any given moment.

Woe: How do your artistic and musical interests affect your teaching of creative writing?

Major: They feed into each other very nicely. I learn things in the classroom that I am able to take to my own writing experience. I like the balance of being able to work at a piece of writing. They complement each other.

Woe: Do you bring your own writing to show students?

Major: Not often. I workshopped one of my stories—"My Mother and Mitch"—once. The students were very good; they really were not shy about commenting on it. It's not the sort of thing I would do often because the classroom time belongs to the students and their work, although I think most of them thought of it as a valuable exercise.

Woe: Do you teach fiction the same way you teach poetry writing or do you do things differently?

Major: There are some basic issues that can be approached in the same way, such as the technical side of things, but the spirit of a piece of fiction is significantly different from the spirit of a poem. Poems are often discontinuous while the poet depends on a continuous compression and refinement of language and works often, in terms of subject matter, in a nonlinear pattern. The fiction writer, on the other hand, often casts a wide net and moves out from a center of gravity, attempting to create a large narrative network while depending on linear sequence.

Woe: How do you get your students to play around with language the way you do?

Major: Very often they come already made that way and when they don't, I'm not sure it can be accomplished in a quarter. Anyway, by the time they come to me they are pretty set on what they want to write and how they want to write. They are primarily looking for good criticism to help them get to that objective they already have in mind—whether it's plain or richly imagistic prose. I know many students who have been influenced by what I told them but none that has been influenced by my own writing. I know people who've been influenced by my writing but they were never students of mine. And maybe that's a good thing.

Woe: What do you like best about teaching?

Major: Just the intellectual excitement, the possibility of learning. I like to know that I am going to learn something when I teach a course. I like to be involved in that process. I don't like the idea of teaching what I already know, although of course I need to know it to some extent. I like to be able to extend what I know about the subject—that's where I find teaching exciting.

Woe: Can you give me an example?

Major: Well, I keep learning things about subjects I've taught for a long time. Right now I'm teaching a course on African American literature from the Harlem Renaissance to the present—a course I've taught many times before. And the more I read about the period the more I find myself reshaping my own thinking about that movement called the Harlem Renaissance and its concerns, say, with primitivism, with the idea of the picaro as male model, with rural life as an ideal, with the disillusionment over and fascination with urban life, with folk culture generally.

Woe: What are you working on now?

Major: I'm working on a memoir of my mother (it's really fiction), and I'm trying to hammer it into shape because it started off too long, too much like a biography. So I have to give up a whole lot of things that I thought valuable—her childhood, for example. I have to focus and exaggerate some areas of her life (which were those fictional techniques I talked about before). I want it to read like a novel. I've got to make it more like fiction if I expect anyone to read it. I need to emphasize certain more dramatic moments of her life and play down the less dramatic ones, because all of it seems interesting to me. I've already eliminated about forty percent of what she told me and I still have more to cut.

Woe: Did she like to tell you stories about her life?

Major: No. I set out deliberately to interview her over a period of almost two years and tape her, just what you are doing here; it has been a long-term project. I hope to have it done by the end of this summer. I've gone through at least four or five drafts already. It is just a matter focusing, of cutting and reshaping. I hope she hangs around until I get this book published, so she can see it. My plan is to have a picture of her as a young woman on the cover. She's standing barefoot in the back yard, looking very gorgeous. She was a striking, beautiful woman—she looked something like Lena Horne. She is standing in the back yard in a long skirt looking extremely self-confident, and she has this smile.

Woe: That sounds like a real change in direction for you.

Major: A memoir depends on truth—not facts—just like fiction does, actually the same kind of truth, a truth built on a certain consensus about reality and the history of human behavior. You have to get beyond the trap of facts to write a good memoir. So the more I realize how it has to be, it's not really a change in terms of the technical approach. It's not all that different from fiction in terms of how the book needs to be written and in terms of its final effect.

The Vision of a Single Person: Clarence Major and His Art

Mary Zeppa / 2000

From *Perihelion* (Online Magazine), Volume II, Number 2 (2001). Reprinted by permission of *Perihelion*.

Clarence Major is well and widely-known as a poet, novelist, essayist, editor and teacher. His first novel, *All-Night Visitors,* came out in 1969; a year later, his first poetry collection, *Swallow the Lake,* won the National Council on the Arts Award. Major continues to publish steadily in both these genres. He is also the editor of two poetry anthologies, a collection of short stories and two volumes of *African-American Slang. Configurations, New & Selected Poems, 1958–98,* was a 1999 National Book Award finalist. He recently completed both *Inez,* a memoir of his mother, and a book of essays, *Necessary Distance.* A long-term teacher of poetry and creative writing, he has been on the full-time faculty of the University of California at Davis since 1989.

Less well-known is that, for more than 40 years, Clarence Major has also been a serious painter. The first entry on the creative chronology I made in preparing for this interview was: *1950 Oil painting entry in exhibition, Carnegie Institute, Pittsburgh.* At the time of that exhibition, Major was 14 years old. He has been both a working, exhibiting artist and a working, publishing writer for most of his adult life. A collection of essays on his work, *Clarence Major and His Art: Portraits of An African-American Post-Modernist,* edited by Bernard Bell, is due out from the University of North Carolina Press in January 2001.

On August 1, I drove to Davis where, after a tour of Clarence Major's art-filled and artful house, we had a wonderful two-hour conversation. What follows is some of what we said.

Mary Zeppa: Most of your life you've been both painting and writing. I've read about some of the things that contributed to your early awareness of the power and beauty of language: the poetry of the Bible, your Mom reading to you and your sisters, the books in your personal library that you read over and over again. But I don't remember reading anything about your early visual experience.

Clarence Major: That hasn't gotten as much attention as the writing and it's something that I've done from the very beginning. The painting started *before* the writing.

I won a scholarship, very early, to the Art Institute of Chicago and continued on there over a number of years. And also took private art lessons during that time and later. Now, some attention is beginning to be focused on the paintings—a book is coming out that has a good representation of the paintings over a 30 year period.

MZ: And there are essays about your work.

CM: Essays on the paintings, on the poetry, on the fiction and color reproductions of paintings.

MZ: Can you talk a little about your early memories of visual, well, how you . . .

CM: How I learned to see?

MZ: Thank you! That's *exactly* what I mean! (shared laughter)

CM: I can't say where that impulse comes from but it was *there*. I had the need to try to represent what I saw and what I *felt* about what I saw, which is more important, as early on as I can remember.

One of the earliest memories I have is doing a crayon drawing of a big red apple and bringing it home to my mother and she was very proud of me. So, maybe, who knows, maybe that was the beginning of it, that she was so proud of this red apple she showed it to everybody in the neighborhood. (laughter)

MZ: So you were a little guy, 5, 6, 7 . . .

CM: This was before school. Had to be nursery school.

And one of the *big* influences, early on—in the '50s when I was in my mid-teens—was seeing a show of Van Gogh's paintings at the Art Institute of Chicago. It was a huge, landmark exhibition. The biggest that had ever been outside of Europe. I went *every day.*

And was just *mesmerized* by the intensity, the power, the colors, the attention to people in all kinds of moods, poor people, peasants. I'd never seen anything like that before in my life. It was absolutely mesmerizing and moving to see in sequence, room after room after room, the vision of a single person. I was very deeply touched by it all.

MZ: It was 1950 you had that first piece in a show at the Carnegie Institute.

CM: That's right, that's right. For high school kids.

MZ: So, you had already started when you saw this exhibition.

CM: Right, right. One of the nice things that came out of that experience was that my stepfather bought me a very, very expensive exhibition catalogue which cost an enormous amount—for us. My parents owned their own business but we were not rich. We couldn't afford, very often, things like that.

It was very touching. One of the nicest things he ever did. I didn't have a good relationship with him, generally.

MZ: So it's especially nice that you have such an important thing to remember.

I was talking with a friend who's both a poet and a painter. I wanted, since I'm not a visual artist myself, to pick her brain. We talked about other people who did both. Blake, Van Gogh. . . .

CM: Van Gogh was one of the most literate painters in modern times. Most painters didn't read. Van Gogh read a book *every night*. He'd finish a painting and he'd go home and read a book. He was a *reader*. Very literate and very interested in literature.

MZ: My friend characterized visual art, for her, as "visceral and psychic and feeling." I thought that connected pretty directly to what you said in the interview with Elisabeth Sherwin about *Configurations*. You said it again, today: I try to paint what I *feel about* what I see rather than what I *see*.

CM: That's true but more and more, I find myself consciously aware of what I'm really doing. For years and years and years, I did paintings without a lot of conscious thought about what I was after. I'm sure I was after something very interesting all the time but I didn't think about it.

In retrospect, I can see that I've always been trying to solve problems of composition. Looking at compositional possibilities and trying to see what kinds of solutions I could come up with that would be most interesting and dramatic. Drama is a term Van Gogh used a lot: how to find the most dramatic representation of a composition.

There are only a few kinds of constructs that are interesting: triangles, squares, rectangles, circles. We don't have a lot. You can look at almost any great painting and find those kinds of constructs, those dramatic interactions between forms within a composition. Such as a circle adjacent to say, a triangle. Almost any good painting could be abstracted to those kinds of levels.

The other thing I've become more and more conscious of is that for years and years I was working with what the Impressionists had taught me: That you had two primary things: light and shadow. That was how you illuminated things, that was how you created form: light and shadow, light and shadow, light and shadow.

But, over time, I came to realize that what I was most interested in, and this is something that has grown recently, over the last 7 or 8 years, is how a thing is illuminated *from within itself.* I've found that the hardest kind of painting to do is to find the terms on which an object can come to life *without* that process of light and shadow: with its own illuminosity, with its own inner integrity that gives it a position without a composition.

It's very difficult. I was trained to create objects in terms of contrast. And of course color. What I learned from Cezanne was that you could do it with color, layers and layers of color, warm colors and cooler colors, warmer colors in the foreground, cooler colors in the background. But that was not the same thing as finding the terms on which an object can come to life on its own.

MZ: Before I began reading *Configurations (New and Selected Poems, 1958–1998),* I looked up the word configuration in the *American Heritage Dictionary of the English Language.* It has a number of meanings: The arrangement of the parts or elements of something. The form of a figure as determined by the arrangement of its parts. And then, in psychology, of course, it's a gestalt.

Now, the cover art for that book is your painting with the same title. So, I'm wondering whether that painting, either the images themselves or the title, had any impact on the choices you made when you were putting the book together.

CM: Yes. Absolutely. The word, I thought, really represented what I was trying to do with poetry. It also represents pretty well what I'm trying to do with the paintings. With both, in some ways, I'm looking for ways to create an interesting composition.

Poetry, whatever else it's about, is always about itself. It may be about anything but it's *always, always* about itself. Unlike prose, it's a very intense investigation of its own process and, in that sense it's always been very self-conscious, self-apparent.

MZ: You're painting with the materials—canvas and paints, to be literal—but also with colors and shapes. And there's a sort of parallel for a writer: you've got your pen and paper or your keyboard. But it seems to me that the words are both more fixed (because there's a definite spelling, number of letters, and so forth) and slipperier because the meanings, especially in conjunction, can spill out from here to eternity.

And, at first, I was thinking that colors and shapes are more *elastic* because the meanings are implied rather than stated. But the nuances are still there, they still open out after your initial reaction to the primary image or definition. So you're still working with the implications of "blue" whether it's four letters on a page or a hue on a canvas.

CM: That's a very interesting dilemma. The way I see it is: painting is visual. Actually, both are visual. I mean words are little things on paper. Writing is little scratches on paper and of course, painting and drawing also take place on a two-dimensional surface.

Writing is primarily *temporal,* takes place in time. And painting is primarily *spatial,* takes place in space. These are the two things we have that we can never define: time and space. They may be the same thing, for all we know.

But the points you made about the similarities are also real which is what makes it so difficult to talk about. The word "blue" is not the color. The word "blue" is possibly much more about its own linguistic history than it is about the color that it represents. In *any* language. It may have more to do with its own etymology.

That's one of the problems with representation in writing. A writer creates a series of illusions through artificial means; a painter creates a sequence of illusions through artificial means. The results are different. The processes, in some ways, are similar. Now, when I say artificial means, I come back to the relative ability of words to represent what we call reality or experience. There are limitations on what words can represent. "Couch" is really not this thing I'm sitting on. It's a word.

Contemporary art has gone through an enormous sequence of changes over the last 50 years. Artists are trying to put mud on canvas, real hair. Trying to deal with just the question of representation. Rather than painting a shirt, take a shirt and glue it on the canvas. The issue is always there.

I don't have any inner agony over representation. I went through that 20 years ago. I was never happy with abstract art, with so-called non-representational art. And I spent a number of years in that encampment doing nothing but, you know, *expressing myself.* (shared laughter)

And I went back, with a great deal of relief to representation. But slowly, through a series of more expressionistic kinds of things. I think I've been back for the last 10 years.

MZ: Do you paint and write at the same time? If you're writing a book . . .

CM: I can, I can. But I don't (chuckle) jump up from the computer and run over and paint a little bit! Although, I've done that.

MZ: They feed each other, though, don't they?

CM: They do! Very often.

MZ: I was fascinated to read about (the painting) "Country Boogie" coming out of the novel *Dirty Bird Blues*. A kid of overspilling, a need to express something in a different way. Is that a common experience for you?

CM: Sure! That happens often. Actually, I find myself writing poems about things I can't paint and I paint things that I can't write about.

MZ: Do you ever struggle with something and discover you've been trying the wrong medium, or . . .

CM: Sure, sure, sure, yeah. False starts.

MZ: And it's nice to have another medium to go to. Do you think of yourself as a painter who writes or a writer who paints? Or do you feel those things are equal for you in both your passion and your skill?

CM: Well, obviously, I'm better known as a poet, a writer but what I feel is. . . . How can I put this? There is no hierarchy of commitment. Both are so subjective as experiences. I've never thought about ranking them. *That's* the word I want. I've never ranked what I love and what I do and the kinds of accesses to expression. They're just *different means* of expression for me.

I don't think anyone has ever asked me that question before. It's a very good question. It makes me think about it and I can honestly say I've never ranked them. I'm certainly aware of the fact that I'm not as well known as a painter. And, in all honesty, I'd have to say that may affect my self-perception. Make me a little less secure as a painter. Although I think my sense of security as a painter has been growing.

MZ: My poet/painter friend tells me she thinks painting is more fun. Do you feel that way, too?

CM: It used to be *agony* for me at times because of the problem solving. But I've gotten better so it's more fun than it used to be. I set certain problems for myself and they were harder to solve 20 years ago than they are now. And I *think* more about what I'm doing. *Ahead of time.*

Also, I know more about technique and I know more about materials. And how to control them which was a *source* of my agony 20, 30 years ago.

(laughter) What do I do with this? It's not acting right. It's the same with writing a poem. There are agonies in writing a poem. And then there's great satisfaction when you get it right.

MZ: You've talked a lot in interviews about process. How, for you, the pleasure's in the process. So, do you ever have one of those poems that's just (snaps fingers) there?

CM: Yes, yes. That's a great pleasure. That's a gift. Everything falls into place just beautifully. But sometimes, with poetry, I have to see the shape of it on the page. *Over and over and over,* before I find the poem that's in there somewhere, somehow, trying to emerge. I do a lot of drafts.

MZ: How do you feel about the difference between the way a poem is on the page and the way it might be at a reading? The trade-off between someone alone, silently reading one of your poems, able to take her time and think about it in different ways or that same someone hearing you read it, hearing the rhythms and the intonations as you intended them.

CM: Most of my poetry lends itself to the voice and is meant for the ear. I hate to think of the page as solely a blueprint. I think a lot of visually interesting things are going on on the page. But reading the poem to an audience is a different experience. *Poetry is a verbal art.* It's music made with words.

And those words have a certain shape and relationship to each other. A certain kind of cadence and a certain kind of sequence, the rising and falling of the voice, the line.

I teach poetry. I teach a very large class (about 125) called "Close Reading of Poetry." I try to get the students to understand these issues and to enjoy the poetry first, because if you go at 'em right away with "You gotta learn all these technical terms," you lose 99% of the class. I've had some successes, I think, with students, because I take just the opposite approach. I think the difference is that a person who writes poetry understands poetry in a different way than an academic, a scholar.

MZ: How does teaching interact with your work? Do you find that it feeds your work, too?

CM: Yes, yes. I *learn.* I'm not happy with teaching unless I'm learning. I like to learn and I like to learn through the process of teaching. I try to teach things that I want to know more about. If I'm teaching 5 or 6 books, they're usually books that I've recently read and want to understand on a deeper level.

MZ: And then the interchange with students . . .

CM: . . . and with the *poetry, too.* If I teach the same poems over and over, I'm understanding them on a deeper level all the time. I've taught Elizabeth Bishop for 10 years now and every time I discover something new and different in the same poems. Because they're so complex and rich. And I find myself saying things that I've never said before about the same poems so that each group of students hears something different.

Teaching is a great balance to the loneliness of writing, the isolation. To write, you have to be alone. You with the blank sheet of paper.

MZ: Can you write and paint during the school year?

CM: Not as much as I'd like. No. Because I'm usually (chuckle) grading papers. It consumes me. But I try to keep the summers free so that I can catch up.

MZ: When I was preparing for this interview, I made up a creative chronology. And I am amazed by how prolific you are in all the different media. When you were in your teens and twenties, your focus was on painting. And then, in 1969, your first novel, *All-Night Visitors*; the next year, your first book of poems, *Swallow the Lake.* And almost every year since then, you've had a book of poems or a novel or a collection of other people's work that you've edited come out. Some of those years, you've also had exhibitions of your paintings or some of your visual art has been reproduced in books or anthologies.

And we're not even talkin' about the two volumes of *African-American Slang* that you edited. So, now obviously, you must be a very high-energy person. But it's *still* quite an astonishingly high output!

CM: Everyone says that. And I guess it's true but you have to realize that I've been writing and painting for a long time. 30 years or more. But you know it feels to me like I don't have *enough* time. I don't write every day like most writers. I wish I could but I don't.

MZ: You must have, then, periods of time when a great flood of things comes out.

CM: Right, right. I do write *very intensely* when I'm working on a book. I try to work every day. And I try not to start a long book during the school-year because I get too frustrated not being able to work on it. I've had to put manuscripts aside for *a whole academic year.* And it's *agony,* it's *frustration.* I wake up with ideas and I have to jot 'em down, put 'em in a folder and then I have to go on and do something else. And I can't do anything about it.

That's how I wrote *Inez*. It just happened to start during the teaching, the academic year. And I had to put that aside for a whole academic year. All I could do was just scribble a few notes and throw them into a folder. And then, one summer, I just poured myself into it. And then, I had to put it aside again for *another whole academic year*. That's how it got done. Getting a final draft took several years. Hopefully, it will be out either late next year or early 2002.

MZ: And will she be around to read it?

CM: I *hope* so. She's not in good health. She has emphysema but she's genetically programmed to live *forever!* (shared laughter)

Her mind is absolutely superb. She'll be 82 this year and she's sharp as a whip. Memory better than mine. Her recall ability is just like (snaps fingers) that. And not just with things years and years ago like most people up in their 80s.

MZ: Good genes to come from. I look forward to reading it.

I recently finished your novel *Painted Turtle: Woman With Guitar* and a couple of things intrigued me. One was the likely connection with your collection of poems, *Some Observations of a Stranger at Zuni*. That seemed like an overspilling of one medium to another. Am I right about that?

CM: They came out of the same time and place. The poems in *Some Observations* were written at the very same time that the novel was written: side by side. There were things I felt I needed to say about that culture that felt better in poetry, in verse form. So I found myself with two different typewriters in a sense.

I was working, interestingly enough, on a manual typewriter on that book. And I have this feeling that the kind of materials you use actually has a subtle relationship to the final product. I can at least feel a kind of difference in the pacing. It's the way the keys on a manual typewriter kind of clang and the feeling of the lines in the poems and the shape of each sentence in the novel.

But also, the novel was meant to be very lyrical. So it's not all that far in spirit from poetry because that's the kind of novel I was writing. I try for a lyrical quality in all my novels. Lyricism of one type or another. *Dirty Bird Blues* certainly draws on the blues tradition.

MZ: I read about how you did the research for that by listening to all your blues records. Boy, that's *my* kind of research! (shared chuckle)

CM: Yeah, that's literally what I did. Listen to blues records. Not when I was doing the first draft but when I was working on the revisions. During the revisions, I listened to blues constantly. Kind of in the background, so it sort of fed the spirit of the book.

MZ: To go back to *Painted Turtle* for a moment: maybe it's because I'm a singer, too, but I wanted the music for her songs so badly. Did you imagine the music for those songs?

CM: Well, they don't really look like real songs on the page. They're more like poems than songs.

MZ: That's true. I wondered if they had precedents or models . . .

CM: . . . in the culture. Yeah, they do. In terms of subject matter, they were very carefully selected to represent certain aspects of Zuni culture, certain concerns and obsessions of Zuni culture that keep recurring throughout the history of the people, and their mythology and their social life. So, I called them songs, but they are really poems in a sense.

You have real songs in *Dirty Bird Blues*. Songs that could be put to music because they follow the blues pattern, because it's about a blues singer and I wrote the songs for him.

MZ: You said in one of your interviews that you like to try new things and that the most challenging thing about writing fiction is selecting the right voice and developing and understanding that voice.

You also assume personas in a few of the poems in *Configurations*—in the long poem "The Slave Trade" and in the Zuni poems, as well. Was this because both of these were so far out of your direct experience?

CM: I tend to write poetry in the first person.

MZ: That was my observation and that's why I noticed the difference.

CM: But you know it's a different experience from writing fiction.

MZ: Can you talk about that at all? Say *how* it's different?

CM: Umm . . . *it's so hard.* (laughter)

MZ: I know. I've come to you as *an expert.* (shared laughter)

CM: It's really hard. In poetry, we try to say what cannot be said. We are after things that speak to us on a much deeper level. That represent something so innate, we know it but we can't really say what it means. We know it when we see it.

And that's never been the objective of fiction. Fiction has always had more of a relationship with history. By that I mean: it represents, through the device of historical consensus, the truth of collective human experience. People go to Dickens, say, because he gives us a picture that validates that consensus.

Poetry is about this other inexpressible thing.

MZ: I think you did very well articulating that. (shared laughter)

I know you've spent long, productive stretches of time in Europe. In Paris and in Nice and that incredibly productive year in Venice. You talked in the 1996 *NY Times* article about the artistic nourishment and the energy that Paris gave you. How satisfying it was to live there with the streets named after artists and writers—your kind of city. But you came back! And I'm wondering whether language was a part of that.

CM: Language, yes, yes. And it's only *one* of the elements that pose a problem. There's also finding a means to live abroad, to sustain one's self. We've made peace with spending long periods of time in countries we like. We love Italy.

The other thing I, as a person, as a human being, have come to realize is that I'm not completely at home, *there or anywhere.* I've made peace with that. And I see it now as an *advantage,* as a positive thing because it gives me a kind of really intense, conscious edge on my experience and my participation in any circumstance or community in which I find myself.

See, I came from a broken family and my sense of home was interrupted very early. There are social issues, too—race is part of it—there are all kinds of things we could talk about. But just on a personal level, I come from a place that I think gave me a toughness about community or a sense of . . . *not belonging.* And I felt that early, very early.

I saw it as a disadvantage for many, many years and I *worried* about it. It was one of the things that drove me to other countries. And in Europe, my identity was clear to me for the first time: I was *profoundly* an American. But I didn't know that since I hadn't felt all that comfortable as an American in my own country.

I want to emphasize that not all of that was social. A lot of it came out of my own personal roots, out of that sense of dislocation early in life. Coupled with the social problems of racism and so on. I began to see that the sense of dislocation became an advantage: there were certain avenues to objectivity that I would not have had otherwise. And I was able to make a certain kind of peace with dislocation, with being an outsider.

MZ: I feel a little bit of that myself. And it also ties into an idea that I've had for a long time: that our weaknesses are our strengths. If we know what to do with them.

CM: Right. Right! *Exactly!* You said it very well. That's it.

MZ: Thank you. (laughter) I've thought about it a lot. And I think it *is* an advantage for us if we know what to do with it.

CM: Sure. But it takes a long time to learn . . .

MZ: . . . that you've been fighting something all these years only to find out it could *help* you. (shared laughter)

CM: That it's something you could *use.*

MZ: What do you think is the purpose of writing? Why do we do it? What's it for? I was preparing to interview another poet years ago and this phrase came full blown into my head: "Literature is enriching and life-enhancing like any *other* natural resource. Like the Rockies or the Redwoods. It's the human voice." And her response was: "It adds energy to the universe."

CM: I like that answer. But I would be a little less spiritual and say that it adds another cornerstone to civilization, to culture, that helps to make us more humane and more human and, hopefully, more civil. And it gives us a greater intellectual, artistic and aesthetic sense of who we are as the human race. That's a very secular response but I think it's valid. It intensifies what we already call our culture and civilization. Builds on, I guess is a better way to put it.

MZ: Well, it does *both,* I think. It's a lens.

CM: A lens. Right. I think that's a very good way of saying it. Now, what personal satisfaction could one get out of that? Well, I think it's an interesting way to participate in one's community, in the life of one's culture. And to be a productive member of society.

MZ: And, for people like you and me, it's pretty important. And I don't mean just in terms of our own work. But in terms of what's already been produced, to which we have access.

CM: I always remember something Einstein said in an interview. Someone asked, "Well, how do you account for all the great things you've done?" And he said, "What little I've accomplished was because I was standing on the shoulders of giants." But that's all *any* of us are doing. We have a history, a cultural history, that we are working out of and sometimes against. At best, what we do is to add a little bit *to* that history before we go on.

Major's League

Greg Tate / 2001

From *The Village Voice Literary Supplement* (May 2001). Copyright © V. V. Publishing Corporation. Reprinted by permission of *The Village Voice*.

There is such a thing as an exemplary literary life. Clarence Major, groundbreaking novelist, poet, professor, and peripatetic, has already lived it to workmanlike excess. Among his more than 20 books are novels, nine volumes of poetry, two fiction anthologies, and a dictionary of African American slang. His novels, particularly *All-Night Visitors, NO, Reflex and Bone Structure, Emergency Exit,* and *My Amputations,* have made him the premier purveyor of experimental writing in the African American novelists camp, mostly because he plays fast and loose with the verities of the trade—memory, identity, lush language, acidic wit, conversational non sequiturs—like ain't nobody's biz if he do. Thulani Davis, Jessica Hagedorn, and Ntozake Shange would all cop to taking cops; Ishmael Reed just might be his only long-running peer.

A painter as well as a National Book Award-nominated poet, Major brings his plasticity and pictorial sensitivity into his narratives. In *Reflex,* where sex, revolution, and pop culture converse and convulse in a surreal post-'70s haze, he makes grand, sometimes grotesque imagistic leaps, fracturing the identity of his characters. In *NO,* Major adroitly collapses sexual awakening and cosmological consciousness in the psyche of a young boy growing up in the Crayola-tinged South. In *My Amputations,* he turns the paranoid spy thriller on its head.

His new book, *Necessary Distance: Essays and Criticism,* is a collection of essays, criticism, and lectures, less mind-bending than his fiction, but valuable for the insights it provides into his working-class Chicago upbringing and his love affair with the worlds of ideas and painting. The anecdotes drawn from his stumbling, naive steps toward literary community and comprehension are acutely moving. The reviews portion of the collection offers appreciations of writers as diverse as Donald Barthelme, Claude McKay, Carlos Fuentes, Joyce Carol Oates, and John O'Hara. Criticism is not among Major's strongest suits, but his travel writing on trips to Paris and Yugoslavia gives him ample room to put his astute novelist's powers of observation to winsome use.

When I spoke with Major by phone he sounded as warm and encouraging as he had a quarter century ago when I attended his creative writing class at Howard University. Now a professor of English at the University of California at Davis, Major offers that African American fiction has a strong experimental bent which precedes him by several decades.

"You can go back to people like Charles Chestnutt and Jean Toomer and find things that are formally adventurous," he bantered from his house on a quiet Sunday. "LeRoi Jones—not Amiri Baraka—was doing groundbreaking things with his first novel. There are also the plays of Adrienne Kennedy to consider. Even Ellison, if you think about the moment when *Invisible Man* appeared, that really is a very experimental novel and I think he thought of it that way. Paule Marshall's first collection of short stories in the '50s was very experimental too. Actually, the word I'd prefer to use would be 'innovative' rather than 'experimental.' Experimental somehow sounds like it's unfinished."

Self-interrogation is the über-theme of the African American novel, just as self-invention is in its white American counterpart. Major's prose and poetry—particularly *My Amputations* and *Surfaces and Masks*—revel in the expansion of self possible for black Americans once they leave the country. In "A Paris Fantasy Transformed," one of the new collection's deft, detailed autobiographical essays, Major writes "paradoxically, Paris gave me my national identity, although I hadn't gone looking for that part of myself."

He explained, "I first came across that thought in Jimmy Baldwin long before I went to Paris, but I didn't know what it meant on a gut level until I was there and saw how I was received and perceived by the French."

In the essay, Major notes that though there was undeniably racism in Paris it was not directed at him but Algerians. "As soon as the French discovered I was not an African or Arab from one of their former colonies, I was treated well. This was an ironic and ambiguous position to be in. All my life, in my own country, I had seen Americans treat Africans and Arabs—people they had no historical ties to—with the same kind of dubious respect. The point is, in Paris—as pathetic as it sounds—I felt American for the first time."

Like their author, Major's characters often take the road less traveled into the black subconscious. Major's tendency to subject black figures to surrealist treatment was not always by design.

"In my own writing the emphasis on self-consciousness was a gradual thing that I learned by writing my first novels. The notion that identity is a fluid thing is, I think, the great American theme. It started in the 19th century with people like Melville. You can even see that in American writers who may not seem so conscious of it, like Hemingway. Toni Morrison looked at that very closely in *Playing in the Dark.*"

Carnal knowledge spills from every other page of Major's early work, which still reads as bolder and more unblinking than anything of recent vintage by African Americans. Major's recombinations of metaphysics and sex were interpreted as bearing a strong Henry Miller influence when they were first published. He doesn't contradict this view, but advises we recognize which Miller was influential on him. "I didn't read his erotic novels until much later because they weren't available when I was growing up. The books by Miller that I read were the nonfiction ones like *The Cosmological Eye, Colossus of Maroussi,* and *The Air-Conditioned Nightmare.* Miller was a writer who was not a part of the establishment and really talked about America as it was without, as Bob Dylan would say, pussyfooting around. He was an outsider taking a hard look at America without being mean-spirited."

Because he's a writer whose work seems to have found as much of an embrace outside of the African American community of readers as within, Major seemed a good person to ask whether writing by African Americans was still perceived as black first and writing second.

"That whole focus on sociology and pathology I thought was finished. That was certainly something Jimmy Baldwin was trying to put to rest in the '50s with his essay "Everybody's Protest Novel." There are all kinds of books that show that the African American experience is not monolithic—the schlocky romance stuff and the detective novels are not all bad. What has gone on in the last 20 years is far more astonishing, rich, and diverse than anything that happened in the Harlem Renaissance. I'm not knocking it, but it doesn't compare at all in terms of subject matter, voice, and style." To underscore this, we need only refer to the range reflected by such luminaries as Thulani Davis, Danzy Senna, Colson Whitehead, Walter Mosley, Octavia Butler, Gayl Jones, Jeffery Renard Allen, Samuel Delany, Suzan-Lori Parks, August Wilson, Edwidge Danticat, Omar Tyree, and E. Lynn Harris.

Reflex and Bone Structure is my favorite among Major's novels for its adroit blend of hard-boiled sentences and schizophrenic, artsy-militant characters who are like me and my peeps. "I was living in New York when I wrote that book and I consider it to have a New York nervous system," Major said of its genesis. "I would get up every morning and try to write these little episodes, and things that were going on out the window or the radio all fed into the nervous system of that novel. But I want you to know that I never reread any of my novels and I'm leery of looking back on something I was doing then and imposing on it something that isn't true. I'm not quite sure I'm telling you the truth, I just want you to know."

Never expect a straight answer from a dealer in metafiction. Don't sleep on this Major dude either, no matter how much you may have to spend online to acquire the out-of-print *NO, Emergency Exit,* and *My Amputations.*

Index

Abish, Walter, 29
African-American Review, 123
Air Force, 49, 70, 128
Albany College, 140
Albany, Ga., 139, 140
Allen, Jeffrey Renard, 186
American Book Review, xxii, 70
American Booksellers Association, 48
American Communist Party, 8
American Poetry Review, xxii, 70, 123
American Review, 123
Anderson, Sherwood, 167
Angell, Roger, 51
Art Institute of Chicago, 20, 49, 72, 84, 128, 160, 173
Artaud, Antonin, 72
Atlanta, Ga., 49, 56, 77, 93, 115, 139, 167
Atwood, Margaret, 110

Baldwin, James, x, 7, 9, 29, 53, 95, 100, 185; "Everybody's Protest Novel," 186; *Giovanni's Room*, 100
Baltimore Sun Magazine, 123
Banks, Russell, xii, 29
Bantu, 105, 106
Baraka, Amiri (LeRoi Jones), 8, 70, 185
Barrett, Barbara DeMarco, xvi, xviii
Barretto, Ray, 8; "Live and Mess Around," 8–9
Barth, John, 29, 32
Barthelme, Donald, 29, 32, 38, 86, 184; *Dead Father, The*, 38
Baudelaire, Charles, 29, 56, 124; *Flowers of Evil*, 124
Baudrillard, Jean, 80
Baumbach, Jonathan, 29
Beckett, Samuel, 29
Bell, Bernard, 172; *Clarence Major and His Art: Portraits of an African-American Post-Modernist*, 172
Bellow, Saul, 53
Black Arts Movement, 134–35
Blake, William, 174
Blues, 83–84, 157, 158, 167, 168, 180–81
Bolling, Doug, x, xiii
Booklist, 152
Borges, Jorge Luis, 29

Boulder, Colo., 50, 51
Brautigan, Richard, 29, 34
Brooklyn College, 93
Brown, Cecil, x, 12
Brown, Rosellen, 29, 101
Brown, William Wells, 29; *Clotelle*, 29
Bullins, Ed, 70
Bunge, Nancy, *Finding the Words*, 87
Burroughs, William, 29, 72
Butler, Octavia, 186
Byron, Lord George, 101

California, University of: at Davis, xxiii, 93, 105, 124, 152, 158, 172, 185; at San Diego, 79
Calloway, Cab, 52; *Hipster's Jive Talk*, 52
Calvino, Italio, 29
Cap Ferrat, France, 167
Carnegie Institute, 173
Carver, Raymond, 61, 103
Cather, Willa, 167
Cazenovia College, 3, 4
Cézanne, Paul, xii, 56, 84, 143, 175
Chambers, George, 29
Chaplin, Charlie, 38, 86; *Modern Times*, 38
Chesnutt, Charles, x, 64, 185
Cheyenne, Wyo., 49
Chicago, Ill., 48, 50, 52, 56, 83, 93, 107, 110, 128, 129, 160, 167, 184
Chicago State University, Literary Hall of Fame, xxiv
Cleaver, Eldridge, 7
Coleman, Ornette, 84
Colescott, Robert, xxiii
Colorado, University of, at Boulder, xxii, xxiii, 48, 52, 58, 79, 93
Conrad, Joseph, xii, 49, 56; *Heart of Darkness*, 49; *Secret Sharer, The*, 49
Contemporary Authors, 78
Cooper, James Fenimore, 28
Coover, Robert, 29, 83
Copper Canyon Press, 148, 158
Coyote, 79
Creeley, Robert, 70
cummings, e. e., 125

Dandridge, Dorothy, xiv, 37, 115, 120, 138
Danticat, Edwidge, 186

Darwin, Charles, 15
Davis, Calif., 73, 172
Davis, George, 52
Davis, Thulani, x, 184, 186
Defoe, Daniel, 100; *Moll Flanders*, 100, 165
Delany, Samuel, 186
Demby, William, x, 12
Denver Post, 51, 123
Dickens, Charles, 43
Disneyland, 80
Dolphy, Eric, 71
Don Quixote, 4
DuBois, W. E. B., 135
Dunbar, Paul Laurence, 119
Dylan, Bob (Robert Zimmerman), 186

Ecco Press, 148
Einstein, Albert, 183
Eldred, Margaret, xi, xii, xiv, xvii
Ellis, Brett Easton, 146–47; *American Psycho*, 146–47
Ellison, Ralph, 35, 64, 96, 100, 141, 149, 185; *Invisible Man*, 30, 100, 185
Essence, 123
Estes, Richard, 161

Fair, Ron, x, 12
Faulkner, William, xiii, 19, 30, 52, 117, 167
Federman, Raymond, 29, 72, 83
Fenton, James, 101
Fiction Collective, xxii, 48, 72
Fitzgerald, F. Scott, 42
French Impressionists, xii, 160, 174–75
French Symbolists, xii
Freud, Sigmund, 14–15, 90
Fuentes, Carlos, 29, 184
Fulbright award, xxiii, 75, 123, 143, 158

Gaines, Ernest J., 29
García Márquez, Gabriel, 29
Gayle, Addison, 9, 33
Genet, Jean, xii, 84
Gibson, Bill, 80
Gilman, Richard, 33
Ginsberg, Allen, 70
Girodias, Maurice, 25, 70, 90
Goya, 71
Gregory, Sinda, 73
Guggenheim Museum, 158

Hagedorn, Jessica, 184
Handke, Peter, xii, 29
Harlem Renaissance, 163, 170, 186
Harper, Michael, 15
HarperCollins Publishers, 148, 149

Harris, E. Lynn, x, 186
Harvard University, 8
Hawthorne, Nathaniel, xii, 28, 49, 56
Hemingway, Ernest, 18, 42–43, 54, 64, 96, 186; *The Sun Also Rises*, 64
Hendrix, Jimi, 71, 84
High Plains Literary Review, xxiii
Himes, Chester, 74, 129
Holloway, Joseph, 106; *African Heritage of American English, The*, 106
Hollywood, Calif., 56
Hopkins, Lightning, 157
Howard University, xxii, 93, 185
Hurston, Zora Neale, 163

Iowa Writers' Workshop, 102, 133

Jazz, 72, 83–84
Johnson, Robert, 157
Johnson, Weldon, 74
Jones, Gayl, 186
Journal of Black Poetry, 70
Joyce, James, 32, 60; Stephen Dedalus, 11; Molly Bloom, 100; *Ulysses*, 100

Kafka, Paul, xvi
Katz, Alan, xiii
Katz, Steve, 29, 72
Keaton, Buster, 38, 86
Kennedy, Adrienne, 185
Kenyon Review, 123
Kerouac, Jack, 72, 83
Kilmer, Joyce, 56
King, Coretta, 77
King, Martin Luther, Jr., 77, 140
Kinnell, Galway, 162
Kirkus Review, 152
Klinkowitz, Jerry, 75, 81
Komunyakaa, Yusef, 162
Kosinski, Jerzy, 29
Kresge Art Museum, xxiv
Kutnik, Jerzy, xvi

Lawrence, D. H., xii, 32, 84, 112; *Lady Chatterly's Lover*, 112
Lawrence, Jacob, 34
Le Clezio, J. M. G., 29
Lerman, Rhoda, 29
Levi-Strauss, Claude, 45
Library of Congress, 158, 165
Literary Guild Selection, 58, 93, 123
London, England, 60
Los Angeles Times, xxiii, 123, 158

Mailer, Norman, 53
Major, Clarence: African-American artists and writers, x, xv, 29, 50, 53, 63–64, 95, 118, 119, 149, 168, 185; African-American slang, 83, 105–08, 172, 179; black aesthetic, x, xvi, 3–4, 5, 7, 11–12, 24–25, 32–34, 50, 53, 59, 64, 70, 73–75, 100, 134–35, 186; character names, 17, 19; criticism, 32, 33; dreams, 55, 112; fiction, 8, 9, 12, 14, 18, 20, 28, 29–30, 38–39, 86, 94, 96, 126, 135–36, 137–40, 153, 154, 161–62, 169, 185; language and literature, 10, 14, 18, 20, 22, 23, 37–38, 45, 46–47, 61, 68, 72, 81, 85, 87, 88, 101, 135, 158–59, 169–70, 176; on music in his literature, 157, 168, 178, 181; nature, 55, 109, 121–22, 127, 132, 163; nonfiction, 26–27; painting and writing, relationship between, xiii, 56, 72, 84–85, 88, 89, 113–14, 125, 129–32, 159, 160–61, 175–76, 177; personal experience in literature, 23, 24, 39, 48, 76–78, 98, 114, 137, 138–40, 142, 154, 163–64, 168–69, 170–71; on place, 109, 116–17, 167; poetry, 20, 26, 124–27, 145, 150, 157, 168, 169, 175, 178; realism, 11, 14, 18, 20, 29–31, 37–38, 63–64, 71, 72, 75, 81, 82, 113, 141, 160–61; religion, 5, 15, 67, 118; teaching, xvii, 25, 39–42, 46–47, 65–66, 87, 93, 94, 97, 98, 99–100, 101, 102–04, 144, 150, 169–70, 172, 178–79, 185; titles, 89; women and female characters, views of , 44–46, 59, 66, 78, 115; writing and learning, 55, 61, 114; writing and self-discovery, xiii, xiv, 21, 35–37, 52, 71–72, 76–77, 90–92, 120, 136–37, 186; writing process, 19, 20, 25, 26, 35–37, 49–50, 85, 120–21, 140–41, 144, 146, 153–56, 159–62, 178, 179–81; writing programs, 42, 102, 133; writing prose and poetry, relationship between, xiii, xvi-xvii, 20, 60, 65, 68, 85, 86, 126, 153–54, 159, 169, 181–82
Works: *Africa Speaks to New York*, xxii; *All-Night Visitors*, xiii, xxii, 5, 7, 10, 11, 12, 13, 15–17, 20–21, 25, 28, 35, 36, 52, 70, 71, 76, 89–90, 110, 111, 118, 147–48, 158, 164, 168–69, 172, 179, 184; "Atelier Cézanne," 143; "Black Criterion, A," 11; *Calling the Wind: Twentieth-Century African-American Short Stories*, xxiii, 75, 83, 93, 107, 123, 152; *Coercion Review, The*, xii, xxi, 70; *Configurations: New and Selected Poems, 1958–1998*, xv, xxiv, 143, 146, 148, 158, 162, 163, 172, 174, 175, 181; *Cotton Club, The*, xxii, 71, 168; *Dark and Feeling: Black American Writers and Their Work, The*, x, xii, 70; *Dictionary of Afro-American Slang*, xxii, 52, 82, 172, 179; *Dirty Bird Blues*, xiii, xiv, xxiv, 120, 136, 152, 157, 158, 161, 167, 168, 180, 181; *Emergency Exit*, xiii, xxii, 28, 30, 36, 45, 52, 61, 64, 71, 72, 112, 114, 125, 135, 184, 187; "Father Unauthorized," 58–59; *Fires that Burn in Heaven, The*, xxi, 70; *Fun & Games*, xxiii, 63, 65, 67–68, 69, 123, 158; *Garden Thrives, The*, 152; *Human Juices*, xxi; *Inside Diameter: The France Poems*, xxiii; *Juba to Jive: A Dictionary of African-American Slang*, xv, xxiii, 105–08, 118, 119, 123, 172, 179; *Love Poems of a Black Man*, xxi; *Man Is Like a Child*, xxii, 70; *My Amputations*, xiii, xiv, xxiii, 48, 51, 58, 60, 61, 72, 76, 88–89, 93, 107, 112, 123, 126, 140–41, 158, 184, 185, 187; "My Mother and Mitch," 116, 120, 169; *Necessary Distance: Essays and Criticism*, xxiv, 172, 184; *New Black Poetry, The*, xxii, 3, 43, 70, 123, 134; *NO*, xiii, xxii, 10, 11, 12, 17, 18–19, 25–26, 28, 35–36, 52, 71, 76, 89, 111, 112, 184, 187; *Painted Turtle: Woman with Guitar*, xi, xiii, xiv, xxiii, 52, 58, 59–60, 61, 66–67, 69, 71, 77, 78, 79, 93, 99, 114, 115, 116, 120, 123, 136, 137–38, 165–66, 168, 180, 181; "Paris Fantasy Transformed, A," 185; *Parking Lots*, xxiii; *Private Line*, xxii, 70; *Reflex and Bone Structure*, xiii, xiv, xxii, xxiii, 26, 28, 30, 36, 52, 61, 71, 72, 76, 112, 135, 136, 165, 184, 186–87; "Slave Trade, The," 181; *Some Observations of a Stranger at Zuni in the Latter Part of the Century*, xxiii, 164, 180; *Such Was the Season*, xi, xiii, xiv, xxiii, 55, 58, 61, 71, 75, 76, 77, 78, 80, 82, 93, 112, 114, 115, 116, 120, 123, 136, 139, 155, 164–66; *Surfaces and Masks*, xiv, xxiii, 60, 69, 85, 117, 140–41, 185; *Swallow the Lake*, xxii, 70, 158, 168–69, 172, 179; "Swallow the Lake," 169; *Symptoms and Madness*, xii, 71; *Syncopated Cakewalk, The*, xii, 20, 168; "Waiter in a California Vietnamese Restaurant," 145; *Writers Workshop Anthology*, xxi, 70
Major, Inez (Inez Huff), 20, 48, 55, 56, 115, 120–21, 158–59, 170–71, 172, 180
Major, Pamela (Pamela Jane Ritter), ix, xxii, 43, 50, 73, 89, 91, 156–57
Malamud, Bernard, 53
Marshall, Paule, 117, 185
Maryland, University of, xxiii
Massachusetts Review, 123
Massachusetts, University of, 50
McCaffery, Larry, 73
McCullers, Carson, 20
McDowell, Mississippi Fred, 157
McKay, Claude, 74, 184; *Home to Harlem*, 74

McPherson, James Alan, 50
Melville, Herman, xii, 28, 29, 49; *Moby Dick*, 30
Mendocino, Calif., 163
Messerli, Douglas, 149
Metcalf, Paul, 29
Michelangelo, xii, xvi, 135
Michigan Quarterly Review, 123
Miller, Henry, xii, 84, 186; *Air-Conditioned Nightmare, The*, 186; *Colossus of Maroussi*, 186; *Cosmological Eye, The*, 186
Millet, Jean François, xii, 43
Modigliani, Amedeo, xii, 44
Morgan, Leigh, xiii
Morrison, Rebecca, ix, xviii
Morrison, Toni, 64, 71, 96, 101, 186; *Playing in the Dark*, 186
Mosley, Walter, 186
Motley, Archibald, xxi
Motley, William, 53, 64; *Knock on Any Door*, 53

Nall, Gus, xxi, 129
National Book Award, xxiv, 86, 158, 172, 184
National Council on the Arts Award, 123, 158, 172
Natsoulas Gallery, xxiii
Negro Digest, 4
Neubauer, Alexander, xi
New Lincoln School, New York, xxi
New School for Social Research, xxii
New York Board of Education ACE Program, xxii
New York, N.Y., 39, 44, 51, 58, 110, 167, 186–87
New York School of Painting, 131
New York, State University of: at Albany, 49, 93; at Binghamton, xxiii
New York Times, The, xi, xxiii, 27, 52, 55, 58, 93, 182
New Yorker, The, 51
Nice, France, xiii, xxiii, 49, 52, 89, 141, 182
Nickel Review, 3, 17
Nin, Anaïs, 29
Nixon, Richard, 101

O'Brien, John, x, xvii
O'Connor, Flannery, xii, 68
O'Hara, John, 184
O'Henry (William Sidney Porter), 56
O'Neal, Mary L., xxiii
Oates, Joyce Carol, 159, 184
Olympia Press, 70, 110
Orlovitz, Gil, 29
Overstreet, Joe, xxiii

Palmieri, Eddie, 8
Paris, France, xxiii, 49, 58, 167, 182, 184, 185
Parker, Charlie, 84
Parks, Suzan-Lori, 186
Patchen, Kenneth, 29
Patton, Charlie, 157
People magazine, 107
Perlman, Jim, 69
Picasso, Pablo, 113
Pierson, William, 106; *Black Legacy: America's Hidden Heritage*, 106
Pinget, Robert, xii, 29
Ploughshares, 123
Poets & Writers magazine, 142, 149
Porter-Troupe Gallery, xxiv
Pound, Ezra, 54, 87
Powell, Bud, 84
Price, Richard, 100; *Clockers*, 100
Prince, 84
Providence Sunday Journal, 123
Publishers Weekly, 107
Pushcart Prize, xxii, xxiii, 55, 123, 158
Putnam Publishing Group, 148
Pynchon, Thomas, 3

Quality Paperback Book Club, 123
Queens College, xxii

Radiquet, Raymond, 84
Random House, 69
Rap, 83
Reed, Ishmael, 8, 15, 29, 31, 34, 50, 52, 53, 70, 71, 184; *Mumbo Jumbo*, 31
Review of Contemporary Fiction, 123
Rhode Island, University of, 7
Rimbaud, Arthur, 72, 84, 124; *Drunken Boat, The*, 124; *Illuminations*, 124
Rosenblatt, Roger, 33
Roth, Phillip, 53
Rowell, Charles H., xv, xvi
Rubens, Paul, xii, 44

San Diego, Calif., 79
San Jose Mercury News, 123
Sarah Lawrence College, xxii, 51, 93
Saturday Review, 42
Saunders, Raymond, xxiii
Scharper, Alice, xi, xvi
Schuyler, George, 29, 34
Seek Program, Brooklyn College, xxii
Selzer, Linda Ferguson, xv
Senna, Danzy, x, 186
Shakespeare, William, 47, 114, 140, 165; *Othello*, 140
Shange, Ntozake, 29, 50, 184

Sheanin, Wendy, xiii
Sherwin, Elizabeth, 174
Sherwin, Judith Johnson, 29
Simic, Charles, 162
Simulmatics Corporation, xxi
Sinclair, Upton, 74
Soviet art, xvi
Sparrow, Joyce, xxi
Stanford University, 102
Stegner, Wallace, 102
Stein, Gertrude, xii, 29, 31, 42–43, 49, 54, 84,
    142, 167; *Lectures in America*, 142
Stephens, Michael, 29
Stern, Lawrence, xii, 29
Sukenick, Ron, 29, 72, 83
Sun and Moon Press, 148, 149

Tate, Greg, x, xviii
Toomer, Jean, x, 29, 84, 89, 163, 185; *Cane*, 7;
    "Such Was the Season," 89
Trilling, Lionel, 32
Twain, Mark (Samuel Clemens), xii; *Huckle-
    berry Finn*, 82; Huck Finn, 83
Tyree, Omar, x, 186

Union Institute, xxii, 49, 93, 123

Van Gogh, Vincent, xii, 56, 71, 84, 160, 173,
    174
Venice, Italy, xiv, xxiii, 60, 69, 117, 118, 140–
    41, 167, 182
Verlaine, Paul, 124
Vietnam, 25, 110, 147, 164
Viking, 148, 149

Vizenor, Gerald, 79
Vonnegut, Kurt, 29, 34, 159

Walcott, Derek, 125
Walker, Alice, 64, 71, 95
Washington Post Book World, 123
Washington, University of, at Seattle, xxii, 93
Waters, Muddy, 83
Welburn, Ron, 17
West, Dorothy, 149
West, Nathaniel, 40
Western States Book Award, 48, 58, 93, 107,
    123, 158
Whitehead, Colson, x, 186
Whitman, Walt, 162; *Leaves of Grass*, 162
Wideman, John, 50
Williams, John A., 118
Williams, William Carlos, 44, 65, 70, 124, 125,
    126, 142, 160, 162
Wilson, August, 186
Witherspoon, Jimmy, 157
Wolf, Douglas, 29
Wolfe, Thomas, 74
Wright, Charles, x, 12, 29, 50, 53; *Messenger,
    The*, 53; *Wig, The*, 53
Wright, Richard, 7, 53, 74, 84, 95, 100, 129;
    Savage Holiday, 100

Yerby, Frank, 64
Young, Al, x, 12, 50, 162

Zeppa, Mary, x, xii, xvi-xvii, xviii
Zuni culture, xiv, 52, 59, 61, 66, 71, 78, 79, 80,
    99, 114, 116, 137–38, 165–66, 167, 181